DIVERSE VOICES

PROFILES IN LEADERSHIP

Foreword by
Harold Burson

Edited by
Shelley & Barry Spector

PRSA
FOUNDATION

Diverse Voices: Profiles in Leadership

Foreword by Harold Burson

©2018 PRMuseum Press, LLC
All rights reserved. Printed in the U.S.A.
First edition, 2018
10 9 8 7 6 5 4 3 2 1
Library of Congress Control Number: 2018910266
ISBN 978-0-9990245-4-6

PUBLISHED BY PRMUSEUM PRESS, LLC, NEW YORK, NEW YORK

Contents

Foreword

DIVERSITY ON THE MARCH
By Harold Burson, founder, Burson-Marsteller

For most of the 75-plus years I have been engaged in
the practice of public relations, diversity has had high
priority as a goal of substantial importance. After World
War II, returning soldiers and their fellow Americans
nurtured high hopes they were entering a more equitable
and peaceful world. Women had proved their skills on
thousands of assembly lines that turned out once
unimaginable numbers of airplanes, shiploads of guns and
ammunition, even delivering thousands of airplanes to their
wartime bases. Black Americans constituted one of the
stellar units of the U.S. Army Air Corps and an all-Japanese-
American fighting unit was one of the most decorated in
World War II. The highly secret Oak Ridge facility in
Tennessee, producer of the first atomic bomb, employed
more women than men.

For more than a century, women around the world have strived to seek equality of opportunity, in recent years claiming that women had earned their place in almost all fields of economic endeavor. After a slow start, females began to fill the ranks of public relations practitioners. In the early '70s, I made a speech supporting the hiring of women because it would substantially increase the talent pool of potential hires. Today, approximately two-thirds of our company's professional staff are women. Our CEO is a woman, as are half our regional and country managers. Numerous other public relations firms and corporate and private sector institutions are on the same track.

The other prime area in the quest for diversity in public relations staffing deals with race and ethnicity. Well before the end of this century, people of color will outnumber the Caucasian population as they more fully benefit from the equal rights promised in the opening statement of our Declaration of Independence like all Americans. Just as with women, they will add to our talent pool and enhance our knowledge of the contributions African-Americans, Hispanics, Asians and other communities have made to American history and culture.

To further the inclusion of these groups in the ranks of public relations, a dedicated group of counselors affiliated with the Museum of Public Relations and PRSA Foundation has published this book, "Diverse Voices: Profiles in Leadership," where each chapter recounts the personal experiences of more than forty communication leaders from diverse backgrounds.

The purpose of the book is to provide inspiration and guidance to minority students and early- to mid-level career professionals to join and remain in the field. It also is designed to guide employers on ways they can support diverse professionals as they move up the career ladder.

All proceeds from the book will go to the PRSA Foundation, which will make grants and provide scholarships to help multicultural students commit to a career in public relations. The book project is being supported by Page, PRSA, The Public Relations Council, The Institute for Public Relations, The LAGRANT Foundation, The Conference Board, and others.

You should know why this is a top-of-mind issue for me. The college I attended was Ole Miss, an institution to which I am closely attached and deeply indebted despite past episodes in its race relations record. It was the last public university to be integrated — in 1963 — and it took 10,000 U.S. soldiers and 100 U.S. marshals to get it done. The governor of Mississippi was actually at the door of the administration building to keep the one student applicant from matriculating. President Kennedy and his brother, Robert, the U.S. attorney general, pleaded with the governor to be reasonable. Though that was not to be, James Meredith was admitted as a student and spent a productive year on campus, accompanied by 300 U.S. Army soldiers to protect him. Since then, the university has apologized to him and a statue of him has been erected in a prominent place on campus. And the school's acceptance of minority students is now equal to or better than other state universities.

More recently, in 1997, University of Mississippi Chancellor Robert Khayat sought my help in ridding the campus of Rebel flags, a task I thought near impossible. I spent a few days on campus trying to identify the magic that would peacefully enable disposing of the flags. The reason for removing the flags, other than moral, was that one of the chancellor's goals was to elevate the Ole Miss status to that of "a great public university." Ole Miss had no Phi Beta Kappa chapter and he was informed that a Phi Beta Kappa chapter would not be forthcoming as long as the Confederate flags were displayed on campus.

The key to success came in my final interview with the football coach, Tom Tuberville. My first question was, "Are the Confederate flags affecting the football program?" The Ole Miss team had suffered several losing seasons. Tom's response: "They are killing us!" I asked for elaboration. He said the most sought-after recruits included a large percentage of African-Americans. "... When our recruiters first meet with the athlete and his parents, they are delighted their son would be able to attend Ole Miss." In the state of Mississippi, Ole Miss represents an amalgam of Harvard, Yale, Princeton, Oxford and Cambridge. But when the Ole Miss recruiter later returned to sign up the athlete officially, the family had changed its mind.

Coach explained: The other college recruiters' first question to the athletes and their families was, "Do you have a DVD player or a VCR?" Almost all had one or the other. The recruiters would then play a recording of a recent football game at the Ole Miss campus showing Rebel flags flying and the Ole Miss Band playing "Dixie." The opponent recruiters then asked the candidate's family, "Do you want your son to go to a college with that kind of environment?" When the family made their choice, nine times out of 10 it was not Ole Miss. The coach followed up with, "As long as the Confederate flags are on campus, Ole Miss will not have a winning football team."

My counter to the coach was, "Did it ever occur to you that those rabid Ole Miss football fans would rather have a winning team than all the memorabilia of a war that was lost more than a century ago?" He asked what I wanted him to do and I told him, "Go public with the information you just gave me." His response was to the effect that, "You don't know how stubborn the team's supporters are on the race issue and I am not going to touch this with a 10-foot pole."

I reported to the chancellor that the coach was the only person who could get the flags out of the stadium because Ole Miss fans and supporters — most of them alumni — would rather have a winning team than the Rebel flags. I suggested he use his persuasive powers with the coach, along with the observation that, "With a decent season, I believe the coach would be prone to do a press conference that would deliver the message that the price of a winning team was getting rid of the Rebel flags."

With two weeks remaining in the season, the coach called to tell me he was ready to follow my plan for a press conference to make clear that Rebel flags on campus were a barrier to a winning football (and basketball) team. Believing the coach would eventually support my proposal for a press conference, early on we sought and received support from the student body president, the campus newspaper and a group of student leaders. Despite death threats to him and his family, Chancellor Khayat was stalwart in pursuing our goal. We were ready to do a press conference in 48 hours and we achieved the result we hoped for. News coverage was highly favorable. At the first game after the press conference, flag reduction was about 80 percent. At the last game, against archrival Mississippi State, flags were almost totally missing and no one can remember whether the band played "Dixie." Within a week or so the coach resigned to go to another Southeastern Conference university, one that had rid itself of Confederate flags early on and that had a winning football team.

The key is to identify rewards of diversity and the high price organizations pay for not having it.

Introduction

The PRSA Foundation is proud to partner with the Museum of Public Relations to publish "Diverse Voices: Profiles in Leadership," a groundbreaking collection of candid interviews detailing the career journeys of more than 40 leading diverse public relations professionals.

Public relations is an exciting, fast-moving industry comprised of thousands of people who work hard every day to shape corporate reputations, create long-term value for global brands, and engage meaningfully with a rapidly changing array of stakeholders.

We spend untold financial and intellectual resources searching for more effective ways to drive impact and interact with customers and influencers around the world. This has ignited a breakneck evolution in the way we work.

The one critical sphere in which change has been uncharacteristically and counterproductively slow is diversity, equity and inclusion. As communicators, we are charged with engaging with a world of stakeholders whose demographics are changing at blinding speed. Forty-three percent of millennials are people of color, the highest percentage of any generation. Forty-seven percent of millennials consider diversity and inclusion to be determining factors in where they work.

Despite this, our business remains stubbornly homogeneous: In 2017, roughly 81 percent of PR industry employees were Caucasian.

We cannot wait for this situation to correct itself someday. The industry may have created it unconsciously, but we need to be fiercely intentional in order to change it.

"Diverse Voices" is a manifestation of that intention. In addition to describing their career paths and how they overcame the challenges that can come with being different, the interviewees offer advice to organizations about how to increase workforce diversity and create inclusive environments in which people from all backgrounds can thrive, along with practical tips, encouragement and inspiration to aspiring diverse PR practitioners who would follow in their footsteps.

As James Baldwin wrote, "There is never a time in the future when we will work out our salvation. The challenge is in the moment. The time is always now. Those who say it can't be done are usually interrupted by others doing it."

We can and must be those others.

Acknowledgements

This book was a labor of love for everyone involved. The PRSA Foundation is deeply grateful to each of the corporate and agency leaders who took the time to generously share their stories, perspectives, observations and counsel.

Boundless thanks to Shelley Spector and Barry Spector at the Museum of Public Relations, without whom this book would not exist. The herculean effort they and their team put into every stage of this project, from conducting the interviews to editing, designing and publishing the book, is a testament to their unsurpassed work ethic and unwavering commitment to the Foundation's mission of advancing diversity and inclusion in public relations.

The Foundation is eternally grateful to Jennifer Prosek, Josette Robinson and the team at Prosek Partners for enthusiastically providing pro bono public relations support far beyond our expectations. We are equally indebted to Ann Melinger and her team at Brilliant Ink for providing, on a pro bono basis, outstanding marketing materials and content development for this book. The generosity of these wonderful partners is an amazing gift that will keep on giving well after the launch of this book. We are also very appreciative of Doug Simon and D.S. Simon for providing

multimedia support, Jocelyn Jackson and Nicole Moreo of
Ketchum, and Todd Grossman of Talkwalker for volunteer
support including pro bono measurement.

The Foundation also would like to thank Hilary Fussell
Sisco, Ph.D., associate professor of strategic
communications at Quinnipiac University, for creating the
lesson plans that will enable the academic community to
share the book with their students and facilitate thoughtful
discussions about the content.

We are honored by Harold Burson's immediate and
wholehearted agreement to participate in this book, and
greatly appreciate the experience and wisdom he shares in
the foreword.

We are also deeply grateful to our director of programs
and operations, Beth-Ellen Keyes, for her unstinting efforts
to coordinate the ever-growing number of moving parts
necessary to ensure timely completion of the book. Her
tireless work was instrumental in advancing "Diverse
Voices" from concept to fruition.

Our gratitude extends to the PRSA Foundation Board
for their support of this project, and their commitment to
advancing the cause. A special thank you is owed to
Foundation Trustees Renee Wilson, Craig Rothenberg,
Nyree Wright and Yanique Woodall for their support of the
project.

We are also deeply appreciative of PRSA National
Chair Anthony D'Angelo, CEO Joe Truncale, and CFO Phil
Bonaventura (who serves double duty as our Foundation's

CFO) for the great partnership we share between our organizations.

Reflecting the message of inclusion that carries through on every page of this work, "Diverse Voices" is a project that brought together the industry in a unified effort. We are so thankful for the support that we received from Page, PR Council, Institute for Public Relations, The LAGRANT Foundation, International Association for Measurement and Evaluation of Communication, The Plank Center for Leadership in Public Relations, National Black Public Relations Society, Hispanic Public Relations Association, ICCO, and The Society for New Communications Research of The Conference Board, among so many others.

And last but in no way least, my greatest thanks to PRSA Foundation President-Elect Joe Cohen, without whom this book would not have been possible. His relentless focus, marshalling of resources and unflagging faith in the importance and potential of "Diverse Voices" have been invaluable, as is his partnership.

JUDITH HARRISON
President, PRSA Foundation
New York, New York
October 2018

Diverse Voices

Mr. Kim L. Hunter

Mr. Kim L. Hunter is founder and chairman & CEO of The LAGRANT Foundation (TLF), a nonprofit organization that provides undergraduate and graduate scholarships to minority students pursuing careers in advertising, marketing and public relations. He is also the chief executive officer of LAGRANT COMMUNICATIONS, an integrated marketing communications firm, and managing partner of KLH & Associates, an executive search firm specializing in placing mid-to-senior level ethnically diverse candidates among the Fortune 500 and top 20 advertising and public relations firms. Mr. Hunter received a Bachelor of Arts in business administration, concentration in marketing, and a minor in anthropology, from the University of Washington, and a Master of Arts in international management, with a focus in Latin America, at the University of St. Thomas in St. Paul, Minnesota.

People always ask me, "Where does the 'LAGRANT' come from?" Actually, it's my middle name. I'm named after my great-great-grandfather. I use "LAGRANT" because it's the name I'm the most proud of. Growing up in the inner city, I didn't like my first name. People thought it was a girl's name.

I run three separate diversity and inclusion organizations: LAGRANT COMMUNICATIONS, the integrated marketing firm I started 28 years ago; The LAGRANT Foundation (TLF), which began 20 years ago; and the third, KLH & Associates, an executive search firm founded six years ago, primarily for diverse candidates.

These organizations are like my three children. I am one proud papa!

It is my life's work to help the new generations of diverse talent to succeed. TLF exists to help those kids that have drive, are resourceful and want to advance. Many people don't know that TLF has four components to it: scholarships, internships/fellowships/apprenticeships/entry level jobs, career development and professional developments (CDPWs), and mentorship programs. Over the past 20 years, we've provided more than 500 diverse students with scholarships. We've also placed more than 350 young people into internships, fellowships, apprenticeships and entry-level jobs. On top of that, we produce more than 25 CDPWs every year.

More than 80 percent of TLF scholarship recipients are still in the business, and many of them are in the pipeline to eventually become CMOs or CCOs. I'm proud to say that some have already risen to very high spots including one young woman who today is director of strategic communications for Blue Shield of California. Another alum has been with Google's marketing team for the past 11 years, and another one is running a very successful integrated marketing firm in Wisconsin with more than 20 employees.

When I was growing up, there were no organizations like TLF. There were no organizations to help a poor black kid like me, growing up in a broken home in Philadelphia's inner city. We were on welfare and food stamps. I was the ninth of 11 children. Our parents — both high school dropouts — were separated, leaving us kids to essentially fend for ourselves.

I was the only one of my siblings to go to college. In fact, many of my brothers and sisters never graduated from high school. Even though I was one of the youngest kids, I didn't have anybody to depend on besides myself. I became so self-sufficient and responsible that I was called the "reliable one." I was the one who had to pick up the welfare checks, to take the clothes to the laundromat, to go food shopping. Look, I had no choice but to take responsibility for all this because my siblings weren't doing it.

I remember thinking at 5 years old — 5 years old! — that as soon as I turn 18, I'm going to leave Philadelphia, and never come back.

Look, I didn't make the decision to live in the inner city. My parents made it. I made the decision to get out. It was not a popular decision in my house, but it was something that was important to me.

But I did see a path out of there: Central High School, the No. 1 public high school in Philadelphia. The only problem was that it was 45 minutes by public transportation each way. I could've gone to the local school where my siblings went, but I was urged by my middle school counselor to go to Central. It was an all-boys school, mostly Jewish. Central High was a change agent. It set the course for the rest of my life.

To support myself, I worked as a cashier after school. I also sold chocolate candy bars to raise money for school. I worked every day, even during school vacations. On weekends I stayed home to study.

I read every Shakespeare book in high school I could get my hands on. We were required to read 15 books per academic year. Despite the rigor of the program, I graduated among the top 50 students out of 534. To this very day, my high school education was far superior to both undergraduate and graduate school. My high school degree says: Bachelor of Arts, not high school diploma.

In my senior year, I applied to eight colleges including the University of Pennsylvania, Cornell, Purdue, Texas A&M and Penn State, among others, and won scholarships to all. But I chose the school that was the farthest away from Philadelphia: the University of Washington.

You may be surprised to hear this, but my goal was never to become a marketing, public relations or communications professional. I applied to all of those eight colleges and universities with the intent of becoming a veterinarian. So I entered the University of Washington as a zoology major. I was very much engaged with the STEM program in high school, which identified a number of kids to go into the sciences. So while STEM is big today, STEM was really big when I was growing up.

In my first year at UW, I changed majors three times. I went from zoology to political science — with the intent of going to law school — and by the end of freshman year, to business. And then I stayed a business major.

American Hospital Supply Corporation, which later became known as Baxter International, came to the UW campus and recruited me, so I went directly from college into the workforce. It was the early '80s, and I stayed at Baxter for seven years.

After that, I went to work for a small minority-owned advertising agency in Los Angeles. During the year I was there, I helped build out other components of the agency such as public relations and public affairs.

One day I had an epiphany that it really didn't matter whether I was working for a Fortune 200 or a small boutique firm. I needed to go out on my own.

So in 1990, I did just that, and founded LAGRANT COMMUNICATIONS. From day one we were an integrated marketing communications firm.

Along the way, I got my master's degree in international management at the University of St. Thomas in Minnesota. I knew that the world was becoming more global, and while everyone was getting MBAs, I was studying international finance, international marketing, international law, international everything.

Ever since I started in this business, I have seen a great lack of diversity in the field — and it's hardly gotten better. My challenge with the public relations side of the industry is we still don't have the numbers. We still don't have minorities running practices, running P&Ls or running regional offices.

Right now, there is not one African-American running any of the top 10 PR firms; not one Hispanic, not one Asian. That's a problem. It baffles me to this very day.

For the most part, the same cast of characters that was running many of the top PR agencies 15 — even 10 — years ago, is still running them. It's still your typical white male.

When millennials look at an agency, before they even start interviewing, they check to see if there are people who look like them. Young people ask the question up front. "Where are those who look like me in your senior leadership team?" And if they don't see it, there is a high probability they will not entertain employment. Now, it's very different from when I was starting out. I'm a baby boomer. What was important to us was to get a good education, get a good job and build our careers.

The kids today, however, are asking these questions and won't join an agency unless they see that there are minorities who succeeded before them.

I'm much more hopeful on the client side, where you do have some people who are CCOs or CMOs. When it comes to practicing diversity, I think corporations do a much better job than agencies. I came out of the corporate world, so I can tell you that one of the things I would encourage a lot of kids — regardless of ethnicity and gender — is to go to the corporate side. I would say that's more preferable than the agency side, which is typically the place for entry-level people.

That's what I did. I found an incredible career path on the corporate side. I then did the opposite of what most people in the industry do: I went from corporate (client) to agency. I made that decision based on the fact that I found more creativity on the agency side.

Back in 1998, diversity wasn't talked about so much in the communications industry. But it was very much on my mind. I mean, I've been in the industry for 36 years this coming December. When I began my career, I would look around the room, just as I look around the room today, and see an incredible lack of diverse people. It was not an issue the industry generally talked about, but it was definitely an issue for me and for a number of thought leaders in the business. I continuously raised the issue — and eventually, they started to get it.

I vividly remember the moment I decided to start TLF. It was 1998. I was talking to Julia Hood, who eventually became the editor-in-chief of PR Week, about a number of things pertaining to the industry, and the conversation deviated to the lack of diversity and inclusion. I started hearing myself complaining about this — and I hate when people complain — and I sure don't like myself complaining.

"Julia, I gotta go."

"Kim, what did I say?" she replied.

"You said absolutely nothing. I'm going to talk to my lawyer and CFO," I remarked.

"Kim, tell me! What did I say?" she asked again.

"If I'm hearing myself complain," I said, "then I need to go do something about it." And that's how TLF was created.

The first year TLF awarded scholarships was 1999. It was phenomenal! That first year we had 10 recipients and a $2,000 scholarship for each. The money started pouring in! I mean, the response ... I had never seen an organization grow as quickly as TLF was growing.

I remember reaching out to my CFO and saying, "Robin, I think we have a problem!"

"What's the problem?" she replied.

"We have all this money coming in," I said excitedly. Her response was to give away more money.

"You can't just go below $20,000 a year, which the articles of incorporation states. Give out more scholarships."

We went from giving 10 scholarships the first year, to 20 to 50 every year after that, with the exception of the fifth, 10th, 15th and 20th year, when we awarded $250,000 to 100 ethnically diverse students who are majoring in advertising, marketing and public relations. It's always been a labor of love.

I started working at corporations as an intern while still in college, and this helped shape my perspective. I interned for IBM, Xerox and Dow Chemical (where I had two internships). Before I graduated, I had eight job offers.

It's no surprise, then, why much of TLF's funding goes to our internship programs. My second in command at my agency interned with me while she was at Howard. She has worked for me for 23 years. I've had several employees throughout my agency intern with me first and then ascend to high-level roles in corporate America and agencies.

Internships can be an incredible steppingstone, but only if the program is structured right. I don't claim that most of the current internship programs are structured well, but I think that arranging for minority students to get corporate internships is one of the most important head starts we can give to our young people. I have no doubt that my own success was due to the incredible internships I had in college.

Besides internships, there are many good programs out there — many more than when I was a student, but you can't get help unless you apply for it. I've seen billions of dollars in scholarships go unclaimed each year because kids don't apply for them.

While diversity is much more top of mind than ever before, companies are not making enough progress. I think the industry still struggles with implementing it. They're afraid of taking risks. They are not courageous, not bodacious. As a result, we're not seeing significant strides.

Our industry will be better off when leaders embrace diversity and inclusion as a fundamental business imperative throughout the enterprise. Be vulnerable. Be open. Embrace the present. Embrace the future.

If someone with my upbringing can make it, then any smart kid with drive, talent and resourcefulness can make it, if given the opportunity.

Torod Neptune

Torod Neptune is chief communications officer for Lenovo Group Limited. Mr. Neptune joined Lenovo from Verizon where he had overseen communications for each of its major business units before taking on a corporate marketing and communications role. A past president of the PRSA Foundation, he also serves as a member of the board of advisers for the USC Annenberg School for Communications and Journalism, Center for Public Relations, and the University of North Carolina at Chapel Hill School of Media & Journalism. Additionally, he serves as a board member of The LAGRANT Foundation. Mr. Neptune received a Bachelor of Arts in government and international relations with concentrations in the Middle East and Russia public policy, and journalism from the University of South Carolina.

I have always been enamored with great stories and great storytellers. Early on, the idea that people and companies could be the focus of stories intrigued me. Later I'd learn that powerful stories could be built around issues and causes, and this influenced me as I began to shape my career path. Throughout my professional journey, storytelling has been at the core of every role I've ever played.

My mother, a librarian, was a great storyteller. She instilled in me a love of books at such a young age, and I grew up practically living in a library. All that reading helped me become cognizant of the very big world beyond my very small hometown of Plymouth, North Carolina.

I was the youngest of five children: three brothers and a sister. Thanks to my mother's strength of character and determination, and the importance she placed on education, knowledge and hard work, each of my siblings went on to do unbelievably rewarding things. My sister, for instance, did her undergraduate studies at Princeton and attended medical school at Harvard; one of my brothers did his undergrad studies at Duke and then received his Master of Business Administration from Harvard. My remaining brothers also have done quite well in their respective fields of study and work. We each openly attribute our success to the upbringing and influence of my mother, and her love and dedication.

All these achievements are a reflection of a family raised with a strong work ethic, a broad and global perspective of the world, and the knowledge that good relationships are key.

From an early age I also was interested in journalism and politics. My mother built a very successful career as an elected politician in North Carolina. I was exposed to political campaigns and the importance of a compelling story, or message, as an up-close witness — and volunteer — in a number of my mother's campaigns.

These early experiences led me to study government and international relations and journalism at the University of South Carolina, with a concentration in the Soviet Bloc and the Middle East. It was an interesting opportunity to learn about these regions, which, despite having outsized influence on our own status in the world, were countries I knew little about. I felt we had to understand these countries in a global context as opposed to nationalistically.

Even with this growing interest in international affairs at college, I still maintained my interest in journalism, working both on my college newspaper and as a stringer for the local daily newspaper, The State, in my college hometown.

After pivoting from journalism as the sole focus of my college pursuits to public policy and government affairs, I graduated with a degree focused on international affairs, with journalism as a minor. I then moved to Washington, D.C., to work on foreign press and operations for the 1992 Clinton/Gore presidential campaign.

After the election I worked in public affairs, focusing on issues important to the private sector, and spent several years in some of Washington, D.C.'s, most influential public relations/public affairs firms.

Eventually, I was recruited to join Bank of America to work in the corporate marketing and communications organization. There I handled corporate reputation, media relations and local community issues. After serving in several roles with increasing responsibility, I ultimately became a senior vice president of corporate marketing and communications for the company's Worldwide Consumer Products division.

After the Sept. 11, 2001, tragedy, I felt the need to do something more meaningful and rewarding in my career. Congress also was starting to think about how to better prepare itself for the new reality of disaster planning and recovery, particularly from a communications and message vantage point.

To help develop this capability, Congress sought out private sector leaders who were experienced in crisis communications and real-time communications strategy. I was hired to help Congress develop its first post-9/11 and post-anthrax/ricin crises response plans. Up to that point, corporations had far more experience in crisis management than the federal government did, and certainly more than the U.S. Congress, so the opportunity made available to me was almost as ideal as they come.

After my time in Congress, I went back to the agency world. I was appointed general manager at Waggener Edstrom Worldwide, and tasked with leading its global public affairs practice in the U.S. and internationally. For the next six-plus years, I oversaw the practice from the

Washington, D.C., office. I counseled global brands and their C-suite leaders on corporate reputation, issues management and brand positioning at the intersection of business, public policy and reputation.

From there I moved to Verizon where I spent 4 1/2 years overseeing communications for each of its individual business units including its largest, Verizon Wireless. Eventually, I was selected to move to a corporate role, overseeing communications strategy, agency management and many of the typical functions that are part of the office of the CCO. All together, I worked at Verizon for eight exciting and challenging years.

Throughout my career, I've had the opportunity to work with some pretty amazing brands, and to support some incredible causes. Unfortunately, one thing that has been consistent throughout my career is the lack of diversity that permeates each of the industries I've had the benefit of working within.

As I have progressed in my career, my belief that this challenge might be *the* challenge of our time has only solidified. I would never minimize the progress that has been made in diversity — under the leadership of many peers and colleagues that I count as mentors — but there is so much more that has to be done in this important area.

There are some phenomenal organizations doing great work on tackling this issue including the PRSA Foundation, Page and the PR Council as well as The LAGRANT Foundation, on whose board I have the pleasure of serving.

We've been trying to get more diversity in agencies for years. But we found that in order to really get some traction, we needed to get the people with the checkbooks to start being very clear, and very adamant, about the way the agencies were staffing their accounts. I think that's what you're beginning to see now and will see more of in the future.

HP's CMO began sounding the alarm about this a few years ago, joined later by some other significant brands. They've all announced publicly and to the agencies that in order to win their business, the firms would have to commit to having diverse professionals handling the work. That's probably the most significant achievement we've seen to date.

As this trend continues, I think we will see some real meaningful change. It won't solve the problem, but the pressure will help focus the industry on real results.

Supporting this trend is an unbelievably compelling body of research. This research crystallizes many of the root causes and solutions that can — when combined with organizational commitment — help our industry address the recruitment-to-retention challenges, perhaps once and for all.

For example, some of the research we've seen over the last couple of years points to the role of issues like unconscious bias in impacting retention of diverse talent within our organizations. Earlier I mentioned some organizations that are doing great work around recruitment to help support the talent pipeline — and now we have real data on how to address the challenge of ensuring that diverse talent, once recruited into our industry, actually stays in our industry.

Fortunately, there are a growing number of programs springing up, both from agencies and brands, that are making serious advancements in all these areas. They are also increasingly turning their attention to building compelling career paths for diverse talent and showing them what those paths look like within a given organization.

Another research-informed priority in this area is the role that mentors play, both in the traditional and nontraditional sense. We know that the involvement of mentors is absolutely critical in helping guide the career paths of diverse talent within our organizations. But mentors are valuable throughout our careers, not just at the beginning of them.

As practitioners become more senior, we need to think about how to build a network of mentors that can help develop and grow our mid-level talent into senior talent. And increasing diversity in the senior ranks is one of the most important ways to boost retention. The mentor conversation is probably one of the most significant conversations we could have.

One last important emerging area I think we have to address is the rapidly changing skills and competencies required to be a successful integrated communications or marketing professional today. If we look at the skills required to be successful in our field, they are dramatically different than what they were even a decade ago.

Unfortunately, many universities are teaching PR students an outdated model of the role we play. That's a disservice we do to ourselves, and it exacerbates the recruitment and, ultimately, the retention problem. This is one of the reasons I decided to join the advisory board of two of the country's most respected universities, both with highly esteemed communications, journalism and media departments. The chance to influence and learn from academics who are equipping the next generation of practitioners was too appealing to pass up.

At Lenovo, even though we are a global company, we have the benefit of having fairly large operations in the Research Triangle Park of North Carolina, near some phenomenal universities. Our geographic location and my team's presence have afforded us the opportunity to build great relationships with some of the best universities in the U.S. We have been able to support a collaborative relationship that benefits both institutions.

Within Lenovo, if you look at any of the number of communications and marketing roles we are recruiting for globally today, you'd find we are not looking for candidates with traditional skills. Instead, we are aggressively looking to find candidates with experience and understanding in the areas of data and analytics, insights, digital and social media, content creation, advocacy, community building and an understanding of how to influence consumer behaviors such as considerations and engagement. Those are radically different skills than what I was looking for just five years ago.

But finding students who have been trained to think that way and who have those core skills is a real challenge.

As an industry leader, I fundamentally believe that taking on these challenges will require two things: courage and leadership. I believe it's that simple.

So I'm optimistic about the future of our industry and our discipline. But I'm also not naive about what being successful in the future will require.

That excites me on some days, and on other days it terrifies me. So what day is it today?

My hope is that today is the start of a much more diverse marketing industry, up and down the ladder of both corporations and agencies, and that in four or five years we'll look at diversity not as a challenge to overcome, but as an opportunity to embrace.

Catherine Hernandez-Blades

Catherine Hernandez-Blades is a corporate communications and public relations executive with over 25 years of professional success in optimizing operations, driving revenues, decreasing expenses and building high-performing, diverse teams. She is currently chief brand and communications officer at Aflac and previously held the office of senior vice president, corporate communications, at the organization. Hernandez-Blades received a Bachelor of Arts in mass communications from the University of Louisiana, Lafayette.

How did I get into public relations? It found me.

My whole life I wanted to be a broadcast journalist. By my junior year of college, I was producing a morning show in Lafayette, Louisiana. I was doing a little bit of on-air work. But soon I realized I didn't want to make a career out of it. I do admire those who do.

I rather fell into a corporate job. I became a copywriter, banging out press releases for a company called Stewart Enterprises in New Orleans. The company did about 250

mergers and acquisitions during my five years there, and
each of those events, of course, required a press release at a
minimum and massive communications support. I earned
several promotions there, finally being named manager of
community and media relations.

From there I was asked to take on the role of the
executive director of the Louisiana Seafood Promotional
Marketing Board. It was a gubernatorial appointment. My
job was to promote Louisiana seafood, a $2 billion industry,
which meant small budgets and large amounts of
accountability. One of the more creative opportunities came
in the form of seeking third-party partnerships. From
working to get Louisiana seafood into local products for
national chains like Taco Bell, to navigating government
bureaucracy, it was an education. You may ask — Taco Bell?
Keep in mind that the majority of those in South Louisiana
are Catholics. Taco Bell franchisees would literally watch
their business dry up on Fridays during Lent, as those are
days when Catholics don't eat beef or chicken. Several
related stories of how the gas stations across the street from
them were holding fish fries on Friday, taking all of their
business. Today we would call that disruption. It was our job
to help.

My office was housed in the Department of Wildlife
and Fisheries. You can imagine what it was like working
with all these wonderful gentlemen, all of them hunters and
fishermen. And then there was me — in my stilettos. So the
office photo resembled a little bit of "Duck Dynasty" or

ZZ Top during hunting season. But it was fun, even though I didn't blend. I knew I proved myself when fairly early into my tenure I heard one of the guys lean over to another when I was about to testify in front of a state legislative committee and whisper, "Don't let the high heels fool you!"

After my time there, I went to Fort Worth, Texas, to join Lockheed Martin. It was quite a change. I started out as director of marketing communications for the aeronautics business and eventually became director of international communications. From there I went to Manhattan Beach, California, to work for Raytheon, another defense contractor. I was the vice president of communications and public affairs for their largest business unit, Space and Airport Systems. Living at the beach, doing a job I loved, and working for A&D legend Jon Jones was a dream come true. Then, he passed away suddenly. An engineer's engineer, he truly appreciated the value of communications. He made all of us on his team not only better leaders, but better people.

Back then there were very few women in management roles at Lockheed and Raytheon. There were even fewer in leadership. This is why I've always admired leaders who promote qualified diverse candidates.

Today, Lockheed Martin has a female CEO, and she's fabulous. And Raytheon has more women than ever in senior leadership roles. Clearly, those early pioneers had a big impact. It's encouraging to see progress.

After Raytheon, I did a short stint in Silicon Valley for a company called Flextronics. I was the CMCO there for three years.

It was right after that — 4 1/2 years ago — I came to Aflac. I came in as the CCO, and seven months ago I also was assigned responsibilities for marketing. Now I'm the chief brand and communications officer, much like I was at Flextronics. It makes so much more sense to do it this way from an organizational structure and alignment perspective.

At Aflac, we have a CEO, Dan Amos, who is really supportive of women and a big believer in diversity. He's been CEO for 28 years. And he's been promoting women throughout his tenure, which is why there are several women in leadership positions today. In fact, we have six women on his leadership team and three on his board of directors.

At Aflac, we actually did an event on the importance of diversity with New York Moves magazine. They did a feature on our CEO, who took the unprecedented step of joining a panel of his female leaders in a room full of female college students. Bold and fearless!

The smart CEOs know that diversity is beneficial for a company. They get it. Dan Amos constantly says, "I already know what a 60-something-year-old white guy thinks. I need to know what other people are thinking. So I surround myself with other people to get different points of view."

At Aflac, one of our key audiences is the everyday consumer. It's no surprise that household purchasing decisions, including the decision to purchase insurance, are made for the most part by women.

It's really about tone at the top and promoting the most qualified people, or bringing the most qualified people into your organization regardless of whether or not they look like you.

A lot of people don't get this. But there's tremendous value to the company if you surround yourself with people who are different than you. That's how you get diversity of thought. And it also helps you compensate for things that you might not think about.

Sometimes it's as simple as tapping somebody on the shoulder and saying, "Hey, you don't want to run that ad. It's going to offend this segment of your market." You don't have to wait for the data. You just intuitively know because you think differently than the person next to you. Many business people aren't thinking that way. They're thinking, "Oh, these are the messages, we have to get the messages out, let's do a commercial." It's a recipe for disaster.

I hire to complement my competencies. I hire somebody very opposite of me to do things in their areas of expertise better than me. Diversity compensates for those skills you may not have. For instance, I just got a resource manager who came out of finance. Think about that: We moved a finance person to communications to be my resource manager. That's because she could handle those parts of the job where it's not a value-add use of my time or interests — like working on Excel spreadsheets.

It's interesting, the further you move up the corporate ladder, the further away you move from the things you love doing that brought you to the profession in the first place. By having someone on my team who can handle the things I'm not as keen on, I can concentrate more on doing what I'm best at doing.

Like a lot of women, I've had my share of challenges. While on a business trip in a former Soviet bloc country, I was with this colleague. Big guy. Suddenly there was this disturbance, and we were trying to get out of this public space where there was all this chaos. He turned to me and said, "Here, hold my hand." And I said, "I'm not holding your hand." But I did grab the back of his shirt and used him as a shield to move through the crowd. Fearless, not foolish! A few days later, he and I were having lunch. He said, "The man is supposed to pay." And I told him, "This is not a date. The director pays. In this case, that's me."

The trickiest thing is to remain open to all people when someone tries to belittle you or your talent. Nobody comes to work in the morning and says, "I want to do a really bad job today." These were some learning experiences that have made me a better professional.

It's all about appreciating people for what they bring to the situation that may be very different than what you do. And I think that's important.

There's no question that this industry needs to attract and retain more diverse young people. My alma mater, the University of Louisiana, Lafayette, has done a great job of attracting diverse students. I went there last year to give a speech and receive an award. The day I was there, their communications honor society inducted 15 people into it, and nine of them were African-American females.

It has to start at the university level, if not earlier. If schools aren't encouraging students who have a spark of interest and turn that into a passion, we won't see progress.

Corporations have to be dedicated to building a more diverse workforce as well. Most human resources departments in major corporations have a Diversity and Inclusion office or one D&I person at minimum that drives the company's efforts. Corporations need to "go bigger." A good example is Morgan Stanley. The company has set up an incubator for diverse women entrepreneurs. How phenomenal is that? Morgan Stanley!

So what's it like for me being a diverse practitioner in communications? Well, for one thing, I stand out, clearly. But in professional gatherings, I feel welcomed, not different or judged or anything like that. It wasn't always like that, of course. If only I had a dollar for every comment about my shoes, hair or clothing.

Throughout my career, my husband has been very supportive. But he would be the first to tell you, "I don't think any family members know what you do all day." I had a cousin ask me one time on Facebook, "I see pictures of you all over the place, but what do you do?" I replied to her, "I protect the brand and reputation of my company." The response was, "Yes, but what do you *do*?" The answer: a lot of corporate wonk stuff like contracts, budgets, etc. Her response: "Oh, okay, I get it now."

You know, I love this profession, I really do. But along my journey there have been ups and downs, zigs and zags, and all sorts of challenges. If I could, I'd go back in time and tell the younger me, "Don't be so hard on yourself. It's all going to turn out pretty well in the end."

Andrew McCaskill

Drew McCaskill is currently senior vice president, Global Communications & Multicultural Marketing at Nielsen. Prior to his current position, he held senior vice president roles at Weber Shandwick and at William Mills Agency. Mr. McCaskill received a Bachelor of Arts, English and political science from Morehouse College, and a Master of Arts from the Goizueta Business School at Emory University.

I originally planned to become an educator. In fact, I come from a family of educators. All four of my grandparents graduated from the same university, and my parents graduated from that same university. My parents met in the same building that my mother's parents met in.

One day, while I was an exchange student at Dartmouth, the head of Coca-Cola North America was speaking there. She was a black Dartmouth alumna. I went up to her and told her I was writing for the student paper, that I'd won some awards, I was doing well, but I was really homesick for Atlanta. She just happened to mention there was going to be one slot open at the Coke internship program. I followed up like crazy with the HR people, and eventually got the internship.

The summer internship went so well that they hired me on as a contractor. So I spent the last couple of years of college going to school and also working as a contract employee at Coca-Cola in brand marketing. At the time, I had no idea how big a deal that was.

At Coke, I worked on the team that was rebranding Sprite. They had done research to show that the target demographic was someone just like me, African-American males, age 18–25. They found that this group of men were trendsetters and tastemakers. So I naturally had some ideas on how to reach this group. It was the first time it occurred to me that your job could be incredibly personal and a lot of fun. And at that time, it was an almost alternative universe from a diversity standpoint.

At Coke I could walk through the halls and see all these people who looked like me. There were a lot of mid- and senior-level black executives who were very visible and very invested and interested in other people of color. We had formed a great network of people who wanted to help one another.

I was really lucky to start my career there. Besides being at such a great brand like Coke, Atlanta itself had tremendous access and opportunity. I truly believe it is access, opportunity and visibility that differentiates our majority counterparts from talented people of color — not our skill set or our ability to achieve. Far too often we're not given access to connections and opportunities, and we're just not seen or noticed.

One of the greatest lessons I learned early on was from a senior executive at Coke. I heard that she was a great mentor to several Morehouse men who had come through the company. So I got my elevator speech together, printed out my resume on really good paper, put on my best tie — I had like two — and went for it. I walked up to her and introduced myself the way Morehouse teaches you to introduce yourself: "Miss Jones, my name is Andrew McCaskill." Then I gave her my elevator speech and said, "I would really like for you to be my mentor."

Much to my surprise, Miss Jones said, "No." That was certainly not what I was expecting. My heart fell to the floor.

"Let me tell you why I'm saying no," she said. "As a mentor, I am probably overextended. But answer this for me: Why did you ask me to be your mentor?" I gave her all the reasons I thought she was amazing, and then she said, "I appreciate that, but the reality is that you asked me because I'm black. But you cannot afford to wait around to have a black mentor because there are not enough of us to go around. That's our reality right now." Then she continued, "You need to go out and find a mentor who is doing what you want to do, who can guide you in your career, who can help you make good decisions, who can help you decode things at work that perhaps someone who is not African-American may be better at doing than you."

This was such a revelation for me. It opened me up to the fact that I didn't *have to* have a black mentor. I should be really strategic about finding someone who had more in common with me than melanin.

That advice completely opened the world up to me. One of my greatest mentors, actually, was a man of Indian descent. He helped guide me through a lot of my career when I was working in tech. And the other one was an older white man who was in the agency business. I reached out to him from an email address that I'd gotten off of the internet. We started going to lunch once a quarter for four or five years. He guided me and navigated my career. And he never let me pay for lunch either.

And so, I learned: one, no one excels by themselves, and two, success is really a long game; you have to really think strategically about it.

At Coke I saw lots of people who look like me. We were very supportive of one another. But when I got to my next job there were only three black folks, and one of those worked remotely. I went from working at a large iconic multinational global corporation to working at a small family-owned business. The transition was good for me because the smaller environment gave me a lot of visibility to leadership, and the client load during the dot-com boom was more opportunity than I knew what to do with. At a small firm, everyone does everything. You can't afford to say, "Well, you only get to do this kind of work, and you get to do that kind of work." At William Mills Agency, if Drew built the deck and wrote the plan, Drew presented to the client — visibility, access, opportunity.

I fell in love with PR, especially the immediacy of it. In brand marketing, you could start a project in January and not see it come to market until maybe the next January. Whereas in PR, I could have an idea in the shower that morning, pitch a reporter the story by midday, and depending on the media outlet, I could see my idea in print within 48 hours.

PR firms tend to have their own culture. Teams are sometimes run like frat and sorority houses. You constantly feel like there's a pecking order or hierarchy — very cliquish. And that can be hard to navigate because so often your ascension in agency life is based on really subjective things. A lot of people who ascend the ladder in PR firms do so because they're very good at PR, and not because they're very good at managing people. Managing accounts and managing client relationships is very different from managing people. So there's a lot of unchecked power in PR firms. I was really blessed because my firm was in a very highly regulated, specific market: financial services technology. We were very lean and mean. It was good for me because in a small PR firm everyone does everything. It's all hands on deck.

I worked for a manager, a woman, who really loved the fact that I would come up with ideas that weren't already part of the plan. She gave me a lot of runway to explore new ideas, try new things. She also encouraged me to work smarter hours instead of longer hours. That made me more strategic and self-aware.

I hated writing pitch letters. I was a phone guy. I would pick up the phone, call a reporter and pitch them a story. I could get lots of results that way, and those results sort of trumped anything that would have kept me from excelling in that environment. My boss really understood that I was a carrot employee, not a stick employee. She knew how to really motivate me. If you pat me on the back for doing a good job, I'll do that job 15 times over. But if you give me the stick version of that, then I'm probably not going to perform as well.

As the financial crisis was beginning, I pitched my firm the idea of creating a crisis practice. So many financial institutions were in trouble; so many people getting bad press. And my firm had a lot of mortgage industry clients. So I got the opportunity to work directly with my CEO to support our financial clients in the crisis.

I took as many classes on crisis communications as I could find. I went to Louisville, Kentucky, for one; I went to California for another — I paid for that one myself. We were able to build out a crisis practice that really helped the firm financially during the crisis.

I was then promoted to the leadership team. I took over the internship program at the firm because all the intern candidates coming in looked exactly the same. My CEO said, "I don't care who does the work. I just want to make sure that we've got great people in here who are doing it. So mix it up as much as you want." Seizing that opportunity, the company started to get all of these amazing young black interns. It totally changed the way we thought about hiring.

I started infusing people from FAMU (Florida Agricultural and Mechanical University), from Morehouse, from Spelman, from Clark Atlanta University. Interns went to every team, all throughout the company. And then we started to get more and more resumes from those schools.

We started visiting those schools and hired a ton of young people of color while I was at that firm — a ton of them.

There are many, many young people of color who got their start in PR from our internship program. I don't take full credit for that, of course. I give my leadership credit for saying, "Wow, this is interesting ... We're hiring all these great people. The work is getting done and the perspectives on some of this is very different."

But you can't just change diversity by hiring interns or new professionals. You have to have someone who has the power to make decisions who is invested and interested in both the culture and diversity.

Once diverse people get inside the organization, it's really not the end of the journey for them. What most people don't understand about diverse young people coming into professional situations or coming into a new environment is we feel like it's our responsibility to adapt to the culture that's already there. In many ways that's true. But the people who are already there have a responsibility to help the new entrants adapt to the culture.

Sometimes I remind myself of this parable when I'm dealing with my own employees: A mouse and an elephant are in the same room, and the mouse quickly learns that it has to understand how the elephant eats, when it eats, what it eats, when it sleeps, what happens to it when it gets upset. Does it move around? Does it stay still? The mouse needs to know everything about the elephant just to survive. On the other hand, the elephant is completely unaware — blithely unaware — the mouse is even there, that the mouse is under all this pressure to survive or what is even important to the mouse and its survival in the room they share.

So what I would say to people in our industry who are in the majority is, "Hey, there is a mouse down there. Your coexistence would be much more successful if you both learn something about each other." The burden for the mouse's survival should not be entirely on the mouse; you are both sharing this space now. Think of how much more productive you both could be if you found ways to lean into each other's unique characteristics and assets — because that is really what diversity is — *thriving* together. The responsibility for survival is on both parties, not just the mouse.

The biggest revelation for me has been that sometimes, I am the elephant and not the mouse. I come to the table thinking, "I'm black, I'm gay, I grew up in the country, not just the South, but on a dirt road in Sandy Hook, Mississippi, a town of fewer than 2,000 people. *Nobody* has had to deal with more shit than me." However, I recognize that in 20 years of being in PR, most of my direct reports have been women. And I also come to the table with my own modicum of privilege by being a man in a lot of situations.

And with privilege comes a responsibility for retention and the survival of all the people with whom I engage. I try to think about that when I'm advocating for my coworkers, be they black, Asian, white, female or different-abled — whatever the case may be.

As an African-American, I bristle a bit when I hear people talking about "diversity of thought" and expanding the diversity umbrella. In theory, diversity of thought is a beautiful thing, but it's a very advanced concept. That's more Diversity 3.0, or Diversity, 4.0. Most organizations haven't figured out Diversity 1.0 yet, the diversity you can see.

If everybody in the room looks the same, you've got a problem. So organizations first have to think about those things you can see: ethnicity, gender, age, abilities. If we don't fix that, we're going to become obsolete. Here's why: Ninety-two percent of the population growth that has happened in the U.S. in the last 15 years has come from ethnic minorities: Asian-Americans, African-Americans and Hispanics. Of the most highly populated counties in the country, 21 are majority multicultural. Those 21 counties account for nearly 50 percent of the nation's GDP.

So whether you're talking about consumers or constituents, our demographics are changing fast. People of color view content through a very different lens than our non-Hispanic white counterparts. And if you're not equipped to be smart, engaging and authentic as well as culturally aware in your messaging and in your marketing, you will fail with consumers of color.

Consumers have more power today than they've ever had. They have the power of the ballot, the power of their wallet and the power of their influence. Consumers of color are incredibly influential. The democratization of the internet and digital platforms has completely changed the way consumers respond when they are not treated well or when they feel like they've been misrepresented, disrespected or left out of the conversation.

Consumers of color talk back to brands, and they use their voice. They coalesce in communities online and in digital spheres the way the protest movement happened in church basements in our parents' and grandparents' era. So now, if consumers are offended by your advertising, they will speak up. They will talk with you about it. They'll have their friends talk to you. They'll create a hashtag about it. And suddenly, you have a brand issue, one which may have been avoided if you had asked some people of color before you went forward.

That means having people on staff be the canary in the coal mine for you.

What are we doing as communicators if we are not mitigating reputation risk? You're doing a disservice to all your stakeholders if you are not creating teams that are reflective of the consumers or constituents you're trying to engage. You're essentially failing at your fiduciary responsibility as an executive if you don't have a team that can help you mitigate risk. So there's a lot of risk involved if you're not serious about how you engage consumers and consumer groups. If they take away their dollars, they could completely change a product category. They could take a piece of content off television. They could shut down a TV show, or shut down radio programming. That's a real thing. There are product categories that African-Americans and Hispanic-Americans over-index on. And if they change their mind about a brand in a product category, and move from one to another based on how a brand has marketed to them (or failed to market to them), that's going to be a big deal.

Consumers are now talking about why they buy products and why they chose to buy them from certain companies. In fact, 66 percent of consumers are willing to pay extra for products and services that come from companies who are committed to positive social impact.

The whole world in is awe of millennials — they're the Holy Grail for marketers. But you can't talk about millennials without talking about multicultural, because they are the most diverse generation we've ever seen, and they are looking at products and companies in a very different way than previous generations. They are looking for value. But they are also looking for values.

And a lot of that is wrapped around how companies treat people who look like them. We are talking about a generation that is almost 50 percent multicultural. And it's becoming more and more diverse, and more and more demanding of reciprocity in their relationships with brands and service providers — particularly among millennial women.

If African-Americans were a country, "Black America" would be the 15th largest economy in the world, right after Spain and just before Mexico. African-American women (married or single) are the primary decision-makers for almost all purchase decisions — and it's not just groceries. It's the car the family drives, the house the family buys, the neighborhood they live in. Latino women are similar, so brands have to be careful about how they engage black, Asian and Hispanic people — particularly women. If companies don't have women of color with a seat at the table and with a voice at the table to help in this process, our agencies and in-house teams are going to miss it.

Young people today are entering a profession that's very different from the one that I entered just 20 years ago. I would say to a young and aspiring PR professional that they live in a very different world, and a very different news cycle. Read the whole story and not just the headlines — it makes you a better ally to journalists. Hold yourself to a higher standard as it relates to what you do and what you say online. If you can't manage your own brand, then no one wants you to manage theirs.

Michael Sneed

Michael Sneed is Johnson & Johnson's executive vice president, Global Corporate Affairs, and chief communication officer, and a member of Johnson & Johnson's Executive Committee. In this role he leads the corporation's global marketing, communication, design and philanthropy functions. Previous to this role, Mr. Sneed was a company group chairman for Johnson & Johnson and a member of the Medical Devices & Diagnostics Group Operating Committee with primary responsibility for the global vision care franchise. Mr. Sneed holds a Master of Business Administration in business administration from the Tuck School of Business at Dartmouth College and a Bachelor of Arts Degree, cum laude, from Macalester College.

I've always known I wanted to do health care, because health care's in my family. We were fortunate. My family was solidly middle class. My role models at that time were my grandmother and grandfather. My uncle was a doctor. We knew a lot of dentists and other doctors. My grandmother was a nurse. She and her husband opened one of the first nursing centers focused on African-Americans. It was on the west side of Chicago.

So health care was very much front and center as a career for me.

I went to college as a pre-med student, because that's what I knew. I decided to focus on dentistry and did that for about 1 1/2 years, but really, I felt myself drawn more toward the business side of health care.

I was in my final year of college, thinking about what to do next. One of my professors, who's a great mentor of mine, suggested that I apply to business school. As I started that process my mom told me about an advertisement she had seen for a leadership scholar program in Black Enterprise magazine calling for students to apply for a scholarship in business school. It was sponsored by Johnson & Johnson, with an aim to bring more people of color into the organization. The program also included a guaranteed summer internship within the company.

I applied, was accepted, and went to Dartmouth College.

When I graduated, I wanted to stay in health care with a combination of business plus service to society. And Johnson & Johnson had all that. I had a terrific internship for two summers, and then went through the interview process to get a job with the company. And I got hired.

My career at Johnson & Johnson gave me the opportunity to serve in many capacities at various locations around the world.

After my first seven years at J&J, I moved to its over-the-counter pharmaceutical business and became the group product director for brands like Imodium, Children's Tylenol and Tylenol.

That ultimately propelled me into a role overseas. At first I was responsible for J&J's business in Asia, Latin America and Eastern Europe. My focus was opening new markets in Asia, particularly Japan and China. J&J started its own company in China: Johnson & Johnson Shanghai Pharmaceuticals. There we launched products like Children's Motrin and Children's Tylenol, which are the top brands in China today.

Then I moved to Switzerland for three years and started up our nutritionals business in Europe. In Switzerland, we built a company from scratch. I literally hired every employee. We were building businesses in the UK, Germany, France and the Netherlands, and I had to pull together teams of people from all these countries as well. I realized how important it was to make the effort to understand each of those individual cultures.

When I came back to the U.S., I ran our global nutritionals business. Then I moved back to our consumer group to run the North American business. That was a big opportunity with lots of complexity. We had turnarounds and high growth, and everything in between, and lots of supply chain challenges, but it was great. I loved that. And I did that for five years.

In 2006, I helped lead the acquisition of the Pfizer consumer health business. It was the largest acquisition J&J had made until that point: $16.6 billion. Once we integrated Pfizer, I moved from consumer to our medical device business as a way to broaden my experience.

I moved to Jacksonville, Florida, to run the global vision care business for J&J. We really got involved in the community. Our company was a supporter of Habitat for Humanity. It was a big initiative we had down there.

Then, in 2012, completely out of the blue, after spending all my career on the operating side of J&J, our CEO gave me a call. He wanted to talk to me about a role at corporate called Global Corporate Affairs, which also included communications. At the enterprise level I was able to get a view of the total corporation and work on driving our reputation. J&J had grown up with individual business units communicating on behalf of their individual brands and businesses, but at that point we didn't have an enterprise communication strategy or plan. But it was clear that the world was changing, and people were using their own platforms to talk about anything they wanted: companies, products, ideas. We soon figured out that they had the opportunity to talk about J&J, too, and not always in the best light.

And so we've learned that you have to be part of the conversation. And we've since been developing our own channels to start our own conversations. Our global corporate affairs team is over 400 people around the world. It's big, yes, but it's more about the impact they make. We're organized in a way where most of our communications people are embedded in our businesses. We also have communicators focused on supply chain, finance, R&D and diversity and inclusion. And it all comes from one cohesive overarching plan.

Along the way, there've been many people who have helped me. You need people who are going to be honest with you and tell you all your flaws. It's important to understand that you are going to fail, you're going to make mistakes. The key is to not make the same mistake twice. I've had a lot of people who were quick to let me know of the mistakes I made. And I was smart enough to know how not to make them again.

The person who brought me into J&J, an executive committee member at the time, was Wayne Nelson. He had come up through our McNeil consumer company, and he was very big on making sure that he got more people of color into the organization.

He was the one who had developed the J&J Leadership Scholar Program that gave me my Dartmouth education and my internship.

When I was working in Switzerland and traveling across Europe, my biggest difference wasn't my race, but the fact that I was American. That was what people were fascinated by. That was the curiosity — being an American.

In the U.S., I've always been aware of being African-American relative to the rest of the population. Whereas outside of the U.S., other countries have a much different view of race than we do. Europeans don't think about themselves as Europeans first; they're British, they're French. There were historical relationships between the Netherlands and Germany, or France and Germany. It was such an interesting dichotomy. You're asking a lot of people who aren't natural comrades, so to speak, to work together on behalf of a business. This is a very American mindset. It pays to read the history!

I think being African-American I was more attuned to the cultural differences than most. It helped me navigate the cultural landscape, whether in Asia or Europe. My radar around those things is more finely tuned because of the world I live in here in the U.S.

I was just at an event a couple of weeks ago to support medical students of color. This is a sweet spot for us. It's been something we've been doing for a number of years. It has been led by a number of our African-American medical doctors here at J&J. It's just part of the culture that we have.

It's very important that we retain women and people of color. We have recently piloted a mentor program with our Executive Committee members. Many of these mentees have been promoted or received broader responsibilities, and all have remained with J&J.

I mentor many employees around the world. I talk to them on the phone every quarter. We check in just to see how things are going or if there's any advice I can provide them. They help me, too, in terms of understanding what's happening in the organization. It's certainly one of my roles that I see as important, and I really enjoy it.

Particularly for people who aren't Caucasian, there are just a lot of unwritten rules, there are assumptions that people make, there's unconscious bias, which we talk a lot about at J&J.

I think being racially diverse in this field is an advantage. If you are a woman, if you're a person of color, you immediately get noticed and you stand out. So you have to be comfortable with that.

I think you have to embrace that awareness at times and take advantage of it. In the world of marketing, that would be called generating awareness. But then, once you have that awareness, you need to understand what you want your brand to be.

Early in my career, I made sure I didn't get stereotyped and pigeonholed into things that are just about diversity. I had to establish credibility on everybody else's terms.

J&J was supportive of diversity initially because they believed it was the right thing to do. Today, J&J understands that diversity is still the right thing to do and that it is a business imperative.

At my company I'm held accountable for bringing in diverse candidates, and we review those numbers twice a year. And we make sure that we have diverse slates. Culturally, we are not a top-down organization, so it's very unusual for us to demand anything. At the same time, I've told the group, look, I'm not going to demand it, but if I don't see things headed in the right direction, I will certainly start asking hard questions to make sure things get moved along.

Rosanna Fiske

Rosanna Fiske is currently vice president, corporate communications, at Wells Fargo, leading a communications team overseeing six Southeast U.S. states. Fiske was previously program director and associate professor of the global strategic communications master's program at Florida International University (FIU). Fiske earned both a Bachelor of Science in journalism and a Master of Science in integrated marketing, advertising and public relations from FIU.

I had been a reporter for four or five years and had learned how to cover different industries. I was freelancing for some publications; one was in construction/engineering. One of my sources was the CEO of Turner Construction, who helped me learn a great deal about the reality of reporting on a public company.

He asked, "What's your plan?"

No one had asked me that question before.

"What's your five-year plan? Everybody needs a five-year plan. Companies have five-year plans. What's your strategic plan? What's your personal brand? You need to have an idea of what you want your personal brand to be, and you need to have a personal board of directors."

And he said, "We're going to meet monthly, and we're going to talk about you, your career and where you're going." And because I was a reporter covering the industry, it was a very unusual situation, but I really embraced it.

What I really wanted to do is go to a warmer climate.

He said, "Look, we have an opening at our Southeast headquarters in Miami. It's very much an entry-level position, but I could put in a good word for you."

I was a very insecure twenty-something-year-old, and when I found out what the job paid, I jumped up for joy.

I took the job in Miami. I started as a marketing assistant and rose through the ranks in the same company. Part of my duties encompassed public relations and communications. When I learned that I would have those responsibilities, I felt I really needed to learn more about public relations. I started to attend PRSA events, National Investor Relations Institute (NIRI) events, and International Association of Business Communicators (IABC) events. I immersed myself in PRSA specifically because I saw a great opportunity in the Chapter and in volunteering with the people around me.

This is kind of a silly story, but it's a true PRSA story. After deciding to become a PRSA member, I went to my very first members-only PRSA event. I saw this woman who had the most phenomenal shoes. I'm a big shoe freak, so I walked across the room because I had to know more about her shoes.

"I'm in absolute *love* with your shoes," I said. And she said, "Oh, I saw *your* shoes and I'm in absolute love with *your* shoes." This was the extent of my networking at this event, when I learned that Linda was the principal of a boutique PR firm. We talked about becoming more involved in PRSA. Together, we co-chaired the education committee; we then co-chaired college relations; and then we co-chaired programming. It was a great opportunity for us to grow and to lead. We saw our Chapter grow as well, and turn into what is today's PRSA Miami — a much more diverse Chapter. Twenty-five years later, Linda remains one of my closest friends, and I have great shoes and PRSA to thank for that.

Some of the leaders in PRSA Miami started to notice our involvement and how we were leading our committees. One of them, Bob Ross, said, "You can really do amazing things. I've seen how fast your brain works, and just how great you are from an analytical standpoint. You really should consider PRSA leadership because analytical leaders like that don't come along very often." I've always been a big numbers person, unlike most people I have met in public relations who don't always have an aptitude for numbers.

Bob Ross has been a mentor of mine through my entire PRSA career, and he is always someone I can call on. Even if we disagree — and we often have — he always gives me something to think about. He has told me a number of times that the way I think about things would never be how he'd think about them. That's what made our friendship and mentoring relationship work. We always have made each other think.

Later I was recruited by a mid-sized agency called J.G.R. & Associates, which at the time was the Hill and Knowlton affiliate in Florida. We did everything from issues management to bond referendums to product launches to hospitality, travel, tourism, consumer marketing — just about every industry and specialty. We had some fantastic clients including American Airlines, Anheuser-Busch Companies, United Healthcare, the Costa Rica Tourism Board, Bloomingdale's ... some really, really great clients.

The CEO of the firm, Julio G. Rebull, Jr., also became a dear friend, and somebody from whom I learned a great deal. But more than anything, he taught me what *not* to do. I have to give him credit for that.

I went from there to Ketchum Miami. There I led the MCI and Charles Schwab accounts, and we did some great, great work. When the Ketchum office in Miami closed, I went on my own, and Charles Schwab became one of my clients. I worked with the managing director for international and the managing director for Latin America, who still remains a friend today. I did all of Schwab's work in Latin America and the Caribbean, and stepped in and out of work domestically as needed. When Chuck Schwab or any other senior executive was in town, I was part of the team that managed their visits. Working with Schwab allowed me to learn so much about the financial industry while also having a lot of fun.

Then 9/11 happened.

It shook me up personally and professionally. I was part of the crisis teams for two clients that were very much affected by 9/11. One had a big presence in Trade Center 1, and we lost team members. Going through that really changed me as an individual. You know how you do contingency planning for a crisis, and look at the many different aspects of crisis management and the many ways to make it work in every imaginable situation? 9/11 made us throw out every crisis book.

I felt so shaken and unprepared — and perhaps that was the selfish side of me — and I felt great sadness for everything that happened. I had been personally or emotionally touched by other crises or scandals I had dealt with. For example, I worked with the American Airlines team on the Cali plane crash. Two hundred and sixty-one people died, and four survived. Imagine 261 families being immediately affected so negatively and not able to do anything about it. I had a friend who was on that plane. He and his family were part of the 261 who didn't survive. As a crisis, it was a lot more personal for me. It ripped my heart out.

After 9/11, I felt that I needed to take a break from so much crisis work. I decided I needed to concentrate on giving back. So I became a professor of advertising and public relations at Florida International University. I also served as program director of the global strategic communications master's program. This was while I was PRSA chair and CEO, and it was very cool because I had academic freedom. I could say a lot of things as chair and CEO that if I weren't a professor I wouldn't be able to say. This brought a really interesting point to the mix — an academic viewpoint. Whenever we were advocating for the profession and commenting about hot issues in the press, I also was able to bring those to the classroom and discuss them with students.

Then I had the great opportunity to come back to the "real world" and work at Wells Fargo.

Diversity in communications in the past 20 or so years has come in waves. And where in the wave we are depends on leadership. When you have great leaders, there is a lot of effort and progress. Then the leadership changes, and it can go backwards. Then you get a new surge of leadership, and you see it move forward again. Then there is change again and the same thing happens. Hopefully the net return is that we have moved forward in diversity and inclusion. But then you hear the stories.

One of my team members, an African-American woman, previously worked at a multinational agency. One day, her boss walked up to her and said, "You're now going to be a part of this pitch because we need to show them that we can do diversity, that we can talk to the African-American market."

She looked at her boss and said, "But I've never done anything in the African-American market. Are you assuming I know how to do something in the African-American market because I am African-American?"

Her boss responded, "Who else would know how to do it? If you don't know, how would *I* know?"

That right there is an example of how much work leaders in our profession need to do to understand diversity and inclusion.

We've been talking about the opportunities in the diverse marketplace for I don't know how long. I remember having a conversation with a client in the mid-'90s about the Hispanic market and how in the next 10-15 years, the growth of that market was going to be such that it would be the largest ethnic market in the U.S. One of the main leaders said, "No, no, no, really the largest growing community is African-American, and we're going to focus our diversity component on African-American and no other ethnic market." It didn't matter that I was showing them U.S. Census data, peer-reviewed research and other supporting information that showed the projections making the Hispanic market the largest ethnic market. All the trends in immigration, the higher birth ratios, how the Hispanic population is younger, all the factors that define a market that would grow and grow and grow — yet nothing seemed to register with them. Fast forward 15 years, and I run into the same client at a conference. He said to me, "Can you believe that we're doing this conference regarding the

Hispanic market? Who knew the Hispanic market was going to be so strong today? Who knew that it would represent 20-25 percent of my portfolio? *Who knew?*"

We also have a retention problem in this industry. My current team at Wells Fargo is extremely diverse; about half were born and raised outside of the U.S. It's very cool to have that! The team is made up in large part by millennials. Whereas my generation had to work so hard to advance diversity, this millennial workforce sees diversity as a matter of a fact, a given. When they don't see the diversity, or when they don't feel that inclusion is important, they just pick up and leave to find it somewhere else. And if they have to switch careers, they'll switch careers; and if they have to go at it alone, they'll go at it alone. Diversity and inclusion is an expectation. It's not a nice-to-have; it's not, "Wow, look at our diverse team!" It's an *expectation* that there is going to be diversity and inclusion in the workplace.

When I was growing up in the public relations profession, I had to fight my way in. Talk about people opening the door ... I was *pulling* on that doorknob!

I wish that diversity was just ingrained in everything we do, as part of our reality every day; that there wouldn't be this overt effort of having to make diversity a key component.

I don't think we're going to get true diversity until we get inclusion. Inclusion is the name of the game. When we include people's very different perspectives — the way we look at things, background, education, socioeconomic —

the better the outcome: the more diverse the team, the more diverse the perspective, the richer the discussion and the more creative and innovative the solution. Who wouldn't want that? If you're not having a diverse team you are basically saying, "Innovation is not good for me. Creativity is not for me."

Discrimination is a barrier to any measure our industry makes toward diversity, inclusion or retention.

I was at an industry conference when a very senior-level, well-known leader came up to me and said, "Where did you get the name Fiske from? You don't look like a Fiske. A Fiske should be blonde and blue-eyed." I didn't respond.

When I was running for PRSA chair and CEO, there were several nasty and discriminatory comments thrown my way. "A Latina is never smart enough to make it to be a leader," and, "What do you know about leading an organization? You're supposed to be doing the landscaping!" Yes, I received these messages via voice-mail and anonymous letters.

My diversity is one of my biggest strengths. It's what makes me "me." My father was a photojournalist who traveled a great deal, so I grew up traveling. I was born in Havana, Cuba, and my parents' backgrounds are quite diverse. My maternal grandparents' background is Spaniard/Chinese and French/Basque. My husband was born in Portugal to American parents, and he was raised in nine different countries throughout Europe. So we tell people our kids are Portuguese, Cuban, Spaniard, American, French, Chinese Jews. We have diversity running through our veins!

Diversity is what makes me successful in my job as an executive. I am able to look at many different perspectives and understand many viewpoints because of my diversity. It has served me well in my line of work, where curiosity, innovation and strategic thinking are crucial. It has brought me many opportunities. It's helped me become a better leader. It's something that I'm proud of, and it's something that I love.

Cheryl Procter-Rogers

*Cheryl Procter-Rogers is a public relations and business
strategist and executive coach for A Step Ahead, a global
consulting practice. She received a Bachelor of Science in
English from Bradley University, a Master of Business
Administration in marketing from the Keller Graduate School
of Management at DeVry University, and a Master of Arts in
leadership and change management from DePaul University.*

I'd like to think that I was smart enough to find public
relations as a career in 1980, but that couldn't be further
from the truth. I had many interests early in my life and
wasn't sure I'd ever settle on one career choice. As early as
age 14, I could have been considered a serial entrepreneur.

My first business was as a young tailor — hemming
garments and adjusting waistlines at the age of 7 or 8. My
grandmother was a seamstress and taught me, so I could
make extra money in the summers. At first, neighbors would
give me items doomed for the dumpster, but once they saw
the quality of my work, I was given items they wore to work

and church. Around this time, my father taught me to type on an old manual Smith Corona typewriter we had at home. And with the help of a typing textbook he kept when taking courses at the local college, I eventually got up to 80 words a minute. This skill came in handy when I was seeking employment throughout my career. I moved on to making jewelry to sell at 10 and transitioned to a candle-making business in high school. All were successful; I just moved on.

I also enjoyed modern dance and ballet. I joined a local dance troop and performed around my hometown of Chicago and throughout Illinois during my high school and college years. I had considered going to New York to study with Alvin Ailey but realized in my senior year of high school that I didn't want to give up my other interests, and my parents weren't going to support that path. I just loved writing and found stints reporting as a youth for our local newspaper and school papers, so majoring in journalism was the obvious choice when I entered Bradley University in Peoria, Illinois. At the age of 15, I skipped the seventh grade and graduated high school in three years. Being born in August helped!

While in college, a career assessment suggested I might consider marketing, law or public relations. I was intently focused on journalism as a direct result of my love for writing and editing. Unfortunately, I was not focused when I first got to Bradley. I signed up for every extracurricular activity that met my fancy. I must have been in six clubs by the end of the first semester. It was a rough time academically. With the threat of expulsion looming, I got back on track by the second semester. So it was a total surprise when my journalism professor asked me into his office after class to hand me a drop slip for the class and a change of major form that was already filled out. He devastated me with the news that according to him, coming from an inner-city high school didn't prepare me for the rigors of the program and that home economics was a better choice for someone with my background.

There it was, staring me in the face for the first time in my life — racism.

Subsequently, I changed my major to English with a focus on earning my degree and proving him wrong. After graduating from Bradley, I used my writing and typing talents to land a position as an administrative assistant in the sales and marketing department of Sperry Univac Computer Systems in Chicago. I couldn't resist the temptation to edit and sometimes rewrite their business communications and proposals. These were the days when the reps presented you with a 12-page hand written document to type. I began helping with sales slide presentations as well. I built a reputation as the go-to person for effective communications. I loved it!

I was on the job about six months or so when an executive from Sperry's headquarters in Blue Bell, Pennsylvania, approached my desk to make me an offer to leave Chicago and take a position in the public relations department there. Someone had talked about my expertise, and he was willing to take a chance on a young recent graduate. Here it was again — public relations! I had to turn it down because I had plans to travel west to start a life in Los Angeles with my boyfriend, who later became my husband. I had already begun my search for job opportunities there when I received a curious call from an executive from one of the companies receiving my resume.

He had been forwarded my resume from human resources of his company and that while I was applying for a position outside his department, he wanted to make the case for why I should consider another option at the company. He was going to be in Chicago for a conference and would like to meet. I was so excited that I might have a job offer in Los Angeles, I forgot to ask what department. When we met, he had copies of my writing samples I had sent along with the resume. He had actually made notes in the margins. Was I in school or was this a job interview? He talked from his notes about what he liked about my writing and why he thought I'd be a good fit for his department. Finally, he would tell me what I failed to ask on the phone. I thought to myself, "Are you kidding me?" Here it was again — public relations! So my public relations journey, while delayed, began when I moved to Los Angeles and accepted the position of publications coordinator in the public relations department at the headquarters for the national black-owned and operated Golden State Mutual Life Insurance Company (now closed).

Golden State Mutual was a perfect fit for me. William (Bill) Pajaud, vice president of public relations, embraced my entrepreneurial spirit, challenged me daily and funded my academic pursuits and memberships in the Public Relations Society of America, the Publicity Club of Los Angeles and Toastmasters. As I grew, he promoted me and increased my responsibilities beyond publications. Because it was just he and an assistant in our department, I had hit the jackpot! I could wear as many hats under the PR umbrella as I could handle. Problem was, I didn't really know much about the profession.

University of California at Los Angeles (UCLA), offered a professional designation in public relations. The certificate program classes were held in the evenings through its extension. With the blessings of Bill Pajaud, I signed up. There were required courses and a variety of electives you could choose from. It was a two-year program that I completed in one year. I was just so excited about this profession and learning as much as I could. It aligned so perfectly with my personality, communication skills and entrepreneurial spirit. Each morning after taking a class, I'd get to work, sometimes before the sun was up, to craft a way to implement what I'd learned the night before. I was still writing the publications, but now I could venture into community relations, internal communications, media relations, and investor relations. I was energized by the endless possibilities this profession offered and wanted to make up for lost time. Whenever Bill said, "We don't have the budget for that," I'd find a way to make a win-win proposition for the marketing department. They always seemed to have huge budgets. I was creating opportunities to use what I'd learned. I now know I was designing integrated marketing communication strategies.

I continued to build my network through PRSA, the Publicity Club and Toastmasters. I became active in PRSA's Los Angeles Chapter and served on PRSA's national Minority Affairs Task Force, National Conference and professional development committees. A career-changing moment occurred when I met broadcast legend and public relations pioneer Chester Burger. I had many peer mentors such as Dr. Debi Miller, Ruby Miller, Dr. Marilyn Kern Foxworth, Helen Goss, Esq., Dr. Rhoda Weiss, Kenneth Carter, and Terrie Williams, but I had never considered securing a professional mentor.

I learned the value of mentorship one evening after a PRSA-Los Angeles program on the value of diversity in PR. Burger, the keynote speaker and a diversity champion, joined a few of us for dinner at a local restaurant. I ended up sitting next to "Chet" and recall how nervous I was initially. He put me at ease right away and asked about my plans for the future. As we talked, I literally felt as if I was the only person in the room. I later learned he treated everyone he encountered with a deep level of compassion, sensitivity and interest.

When he turned to me and said, "Cheryl, I would love to mentor you," I felt both honored and humble. Here was an industry giant that saw something in me he wanted to support and nurture. For the next 30 years, I consulted Chet on every major professional event in my career. He was my mentor and friend. In 2011, he called to tell me he had Stage 4 prostate cancer. I flew to New York and visited him in his apartment. I looked around at all the book titles from ceiling to floor, the tiny kitchen where he often prepared me tea, his makeshift office where the computers were always on and papers stacked high. I wanted to remember everything. I knew I'd never be in this space again. I knew I'd never see him again.

He taught me so much over the years. He taught me to always work with integrity and say you don't know when you don't know. He taught me that learning is a lifetime commitment. He taught me the value of storytelling — people will remember a story you tell before any data or information. He insisted that I be a generalist. Because of my personality and many interests, he didn't want me to be trapped by only taking on projects that speak to the black community or women. He would say to me, "You can counsel executives at the highest level and implement strategies beyond who you are. But you must believe it."

Golden State Mutual was a perfect launch pad for my career. When the marketing department declined to partner with some of my ideas, I developed partnerships with major community groups and corporations such as Anheuser-Busch, Coca-Cola, and local radio stations KGFJ and KDAY. Working with these partners, I led citywide

programs such as "Back to School With a Clear Head," and
"Operation Santa Claus," to support the needs of the black
community.

The success of these branding programs and other work
drew the attention of my public relations colleagues and
marketing executives. I was invited to breakfast one
morning by the regional marketing directors of Coca-Cola
and Anheuser-Busch. It was a breakfast that changed my
life. They loved the fact that we were having a significant
impact in our communities and that they were able to speak
to a coveted audience through the program we co-designed
and implemented. They offered, "If you start your own PR
firm — and we think you should — we'll become your No. 1
supporters and clients!"

I didn't have to think long. I started A Step Ahead
public relations and publishing company in 1986 with an
electric typewriter on our kitchen table, a bright future and
no funding. However, when you start a business with Coca-
Cola and Anheuser-Busch, it's pretty easy to get other
clients like Eastman Kodak, the Jewish Federation Council
of Los Angeles, IBM, Nissan, and others.

I quickly learned why, according to the Small Business
Association, 20 percent of small businesses fail in their first
year, 30 percent fail in their second year, 50 percent fail after
five years and 30 percent of those who make it to a decade,
fail in their 10th year! I'm proud to celebrate more than 30
years as a small business owner.

Over the years, I've had to make some hard decisions about my career and my business. I was recruited heavily on three occasions to suspend my consulting practice and enter a national or global enterprise. I was recruited in the early '90s to create a PR department for Nielsen Marketing Research. I was convinced by client Home Box Office (HBO) to join the corporate affairs team to help launch "Sex and the City," "The Sopranos," and other award-winning programming in the Midwest and West. It was such a rich time in television — I grew tremendously. And, finally, in 2009, I was recruited to create a proactive public relations and communications department for DePaul University in Chicago.

What was the common thread with each opportunity? I had autonomy, experienced professional growth, added new learning to my toolkit, and expanded my network. The one thing that sweetened the pot for me was each organization had an entrepreneurial culture. This is where I thrive, because at my core, I'm an entrepreneur.

But, why was I recruited so heavily? I believe it was because someone is always watching how you show up, how you treat others, how you deliver on your promises, how you strategize, how you perform under pressure. But most important, what others say about you.

The first time I suspended my business, I had many sleepless nights. I tossed and turned in agony — had I made the right decision? What if this didn't work out? Would I be able to resume my business? What would my colleagues think? What was I doing to my personal brand?

Needless to say, I couldn't sleep.

What I learned when I emerged two years later from the position at Nielsen Marketing Research made it easier for me the second and the third time I suspended my business. You see, each time I resumed my practice, I was up and running within 30 days with previous and new clients. Since launching my PR career in 1980 and my consulting and coaching practice in 1986, I've had few droughts and have rarely been impacted by an economic downturn.

My secret? I call it my "four Cs" for soft landings — especially when you're walking a tightrope like I have most of my career, and without a net: Capabilities, Career, Cabinet, and Community.

1. Capabilities

I continue to hone my communication skills, which includes being a better listener. I dial in to my emotional intelligence by gaining more self-awareness and try to step back and see myself as others see me. It is often difficult when I seek and encourage tough feedback from those that are close to me. I enjoy working from my strengths and have a philosophy that being a lifelong learner is an asset. I schedule time on my calendar each week to read an article, chat with an expert or reflect on what's important. I believe this provides a net for soft landings.

2. Career

I truly believe the only thing worse than a bad plan is no plan. This applies to my personal and professional life. I use the template for a business plan and review it monthly. Has my personal mission and vision changed? How is my audience responding to my messages? There must be a monthly effort to expand my network. Having a mentor or two is the lifeline for career planning. I've had as many as three mentors simultaneously over the years. I know that having a career plan provides a net for soft landings.

3. Cabinet

Having a small group of people in my inner circle to inspire me and challenge assumptions I make is critical for any success I achieve. Without those challenging me, I can be trapped by confirmation bias — only reading material, attending events, and associating with people who think and believe as I do. I need accountability partners that will insist I step outside of my comfort zone and see things from another perspective and help me reflect on what I've accomplished and what's next. My mentors have always been a part of my personal cabinet. These champions of my personal brand help provide me with a net for soft landings.

4. Community

I always make time to invest in my community. My definition of community can change from day to day and year to year. It can be my church, public relations community, coaching community, sorority, neighborhood, and civic organizations. I find it is a true test of my goal for work-life balance. When I give to these communities, I'm able to use my talents and strengths in new ways, which fosters innovation in my work. I gain new perspectives and hear great stories that help me grow as an individual. It also expands my network and provides a net for soft landings.

When I remain focused on my goals, the possibilities for success are endless. Having a plan and working my plan requires an investment of time and resources. Yes, I'm a risk taker. If I fail at something, it only means I'm in the game and that I'm challenging the status quo. I'm confident it makes me resilient, and having a net for soft landings has been the way I've been able to always bounce back. I encourage others to use the "four Cs" and design their own net for soft landings.

Racism is out there. Gender bias is out there. Confirmation bias is out there. I believe it is up to each of us to invest in our futures by investing in our most important assets.

Del Galloway

Del Galloway is currently vice president, communications, at Wells Fargo, for the Atlantic region. Previously, he served as vice president, communications, brand leadership at United Way Worldwide. Mr. Galloway received both a Bachelor of Arts in journalism and a Master of Arts in public relations from the University of Florida. He is also the first and only openly gay leader of PRSA.

Recently, I saw Ginni Rometty, chair, president and CEO of IBM, speak about the many life lessons she's learned as a woman advancing her way to the top of a male-dominated industry. One of her most powerful lessons spoke to me: "Never let someone else define you."

I embrace that statement. Hearing that through the lens as a gay man hit home. Throughout my career, I could have been marginalized. It would have been easy for people's assumptions, predisposed ideas or clichés to attach to me or anyone else who happens to be gay. I'm not burdened by labels. I want to be measured and defined by my performance.

I found my way to the world of public relations through a high school guidance counselor. I had completed an aptitude test, and based on my strong writing and verbal communications skills as well as what the test described as particularly strong organizational skills, my counselor introduced me to something called public relations — not a field with which I was familiar.

Even as a child, I invested myself in working with others on events and projects, school plays, and volunteer activities. Looking back I realize how those experiences sharpened my communication and leadership skills. All my life, I've been bringing people together for a common cause.

After graduating from the University of Florida, I received a job offer from Young & Rubicam, an internationally recognized advertising agency. It had an office in St. Petersburg, Florida, with a PR department. I was an account executive in title, but I was pretty much at the bottom of the ladder. I was excited, though, because I was able to put my skills into practice. And it was wonderful so early in my career to be associated with such a respected global brand.

We received clippings each day, and I would review them and separate the clips by client. It was a *slow* process. Then I would prepare a media coverage report. In those days success was measured by the number of press clippings we'd generate — what we now consider outputs, rather than the far more important outcomes where we examine: Did we move the needle? Did we influence behavior?

Instead, we'd just put a big pile of clips in front of the client and say, "Success!" Our value was measured by the volume of clips.

As I look back at my 35 years in this business, I've been fortunate to practice in the agency and corporate worlds as well as nonprofit and education. When I left the agency world, I went to work at a business unit of AT&T — AT&T American Transtech — which happened to be headquartered in my hometown of Jacksonville, Florida. It was the largest private employer in the city, with more than 5,000 employees and 16 locations around the world.

I was hired as a media relations manager. Eight years later, I was the director of corporate communications for the entire business unit. That was heady stuff. I attended monthly meetings at AT&T's headquarters in Basking Ridge, New Jersey, exchanging ideas with the heads of communication for the 18 other business units of AT&T. I was in my early 30s, the most junior person in the room. I now look back and think, "Wow! That was a big job."

AT&T's public relations organization was headed by Marilyn Laurie, a trailblazer in the field, who was the highest-ranking woman in AT&T worldwide. I admired Marilyn for many things. She had absolute bedrock ethics and a gift for crisply sizing up a situation.

I was fortunate to reconnect with Marilyn years later through PRSA. She was being honored and I, at that point, was leading PRSA. So I had the good fortune to work with her again. She was an inspiration to women and men alike, and sadly we lost Marilyn way too soon when she passed in 2010.

After eight years at AT&T, I went back to the agency world and joined Husk Jennings — which later became Husk Jennings Galloway + Partners. I was hired to create a public relations division. When I joined in 1995 we had 16 employees. When we sold the agency to a Canadian firm 10 years later, we had 52 employees, and we'd quadrupled billings. It was a wonderful experience.

Suddenly, for the first time in my life, at 46 years old, I didn't know what the next step was. I didn't have a plan. I didn't have a place to go to in the morning.

I discovered that you can fill a lot of nothing with a lot of nothing. I needed to get back into the game. I learned about an opportunity in Washington, D.C., where I had long done business. I remember thinking, "Gosh, D.C. is a cool city! I can see myself living there."

I took a one-year assignment with the Corporation for Public Broadcasting (CPB), the holding company for PBS and NPR. CPB wanted to roll out a national advocacy campaign to help society understand and appreciate the value of public service media. I was tasked with leading the initiative.

After that, I was appointed head of communications and public relations for a global nonprofit, United Way Worldwide, where I stayed for five years.

I then moved to Wells Fargo, where I am currently.

I led PRSA as president and CEO in 2004, and I'm the first and only gay person to lead PRSA.

I've been a member the Society for roughly 25 years. Like any organization: You get back what you put in. I've invested myself in PRSA, and I've gotten back tenfold the return on my investment.

When I led the Society, we made diversity and inclusion a full-fledged committee, with staff and financial support. It had previously been a task force.

There are many different ways to look at diversity: diversity of ideas, gender, age, race, ethnicity and other diverse characteristics — and when we acknowledge and embrace these differences, it makes for an even richer experience, one that reflects the society we serve.

We need public relations people bringing all those perspectives to the table. Public relations people are the glue, the bridge between an organization and its stakeholders. We are uniquely positioned to offer diverse perspectives, enabling us to make more informed decisions that reflect the constituencies we represent and serve.

As a public relations professional and a gay man, I see that an important contribution I can make is to help pave an even smoother, more productive road for others — gay or straight.

What's been unexpected and surprising for me is that my being gay, showing up as my true authentic self has been valued. The organizations I've worked with see that I am able to bring a rich perspective to the business.

I'll share a personal story. It's when I came out to my mother. It was a powerful moment of truth.

I was 23 years old and had just completed graduate school at the University of Florida. I was sitting at the kitchen table with my mother. After hemming and hawing I said, "Mom, I'm gay."

She looked at me and said, "What does that mean?"

And while she certainly knew what it meant, she wanted me to express it. I said, "It means I'm attracted to men." And she said,

"Ok, so does that matter?"

That was *such* a powerful moment. She let me know immediately that her love for me is unconditional. What a gift for any child!

My experience as a gay man in business is probably the exception. I experienced success and was supported. Sadly, that's not the case for many, and that's a key reason I want to help others on their career path.

At AT&T American Transtech in the early '90s, a woman was appointed as the first-ever head of a business unit at AT&T, and she relocated to Florida from New Jersey. My function had previously reported to the vice president of marketing. The new leader said, "You're going to report to me, because I value public relations and I need you as my trusted adviser."

That woman — Monica Mehan — changed my life and changed my career because she created a safe space for me to be me. It was within that safe space that I let her know that I was gay. She'd host parties and dinners and celebrations in her home, and my partner would always join me.

From that point forward, I showed up fully myself. And if anything, there have been times in my career when being gay and bringing that perspective has been valued.

I remember at the agency pitching a piece of new business. Part of the demographic being targeted was what we now know as the LGBTQ community. I was able to speak about nuances from a consumer perspective, from an LGBTQ perspective.

And while I certainly don't attempt to present myself as representing the LGBTQ community writ large, I was able to bring a perspective to that meeting that they wouldn't have otherwise had. Ultimately, because we understood their market, we won the account.

The whole idea of being true to oneself, to bringing your whole self to work, was discussed at a recent Town Hall at Wells Fargo. Someone asked a top executive how she defines leadership. She answered, "I think one of the most important words in the English language is authenticity. The gift to be yourself, because when you are yourself it gives others permission to be themselves. Therein lies the opportunity for genuine connection. Number two: curiosity. Be curious. Be curious about a customer, be curious about your family, be curious about the world. And number three: Celebrate others. It's not about you, it's about them."

Authenticity is important for all of us — particularly young, gay students or entry-level folks. I encourage them: Go about the business of being you. Life is difficult enough to navigate without burdening yourself by hiding. The shadows are no place to live your life. Live authentically. Live in the light.

Rochelle Tillery Larkin Ford

Rochelle Ford, Ph.D., APR, is the dean of the School of Communications at Elon University. She most recently served for four years as a professor and the chair of the public relations department at the S. I. Newhouse School of Public Communications at Syracuse University. Previously, she taught as a professor for 16 years at Howard University in the school of communications. Currently, Dr. Ford co-chairs the Page's diversity and inclusion committee. Ms. Ford received a Bachelor of Arts in journalism/public relations from Howard University; a Master of Arts, public relations and journalism, from the University of Maryland, College Park; a doctorate, journalism, from Southern Illinois University, Carbondale; and a graduate certificate, higher education/higher education administration from Harvard University.

"I think there's this thing called PR," my Dad said to me one day; he was working at AT&T at the time. I always was interested in journalism. I love writing; I loved reporting and writing news. "You should talk to this woman who has that title at my company."

So I met her. She did marketing communications, and a little bit of internal comms. She told me about this industry and I said, "This sounds kind of cool!" So when I went to Howard University for its journalism program, I majored in public relations.

At the same time, I got involved with a program called INROADS, a management development program. I was paired with Nationwide Insurance and did four summer internships at Nationwide, writing, editing and working with marketing communications, internal/employee and community relations.

During my freshman year, I got involved with Howard's Public Relations Student Society of America (PRSSA) Chapter, and rose up the ranks. In sophomore year, I went to my very first PRSSA conference up in New York. On one of the panels was David Drobis, then chairman and CEO of Ketchum in New York. He was talking about what it was like to work at an agency.

Then I raised my hand. "Well, this is all wonderful," I said, "but can you tell me what you're doing about diversity at your agency, and who do you have who's diverse among your leadership team?" He answered, "So, yeah, it's something important we've got to do better."

Afterward, I went up, shook his hand and he asked for my resume. I was shocked.

"Thank you for asking that question," Dave said, "It's an important question you asked." He sent my resume to the Washington, D.C., office, and I was hired to intern part time that spring. I was one of the youngest interns they had ever hired.

After graduation from Howard, I decided I wanted to study to become a college professor. I went to the University of Maryland for my master's degree and studied under Lauri and Jim Grunig, two of the most amazing scholars in our field. I don't think I'd be who I am without them.

I had also gotten married and just had a baby at this point. I was only 23. One day, the Grunigs told me that the University of Tennessee at Martin had just announced an opening for an instructor. The school was looking to bring on diverse talent with master's degrees, and as an incentive, UTM would pay for them to earn doctorates while teaching there.

So my husband and I moved to Northwest Tennessee. While teaching there, I enrolled at Southern Illinois University because there were scholars doing the same type of research — situational theory of publics — that I was doing at Maryland. And so I would drive the 2 1/2 hours to Southern Illinois.

However, when I started, both scholars had left SIU, and I had no one to advise me. So the director of the journalism school, an advertising professor, said that he'd take me on as an advisee as long as I change the topic of my dissertation from situational theory to researching the pigeonholing of blacks in public relations. This diversity issue was plaguing both the advertising and PR industries. I came out of the university on a different trajectory than when I entered. I always said I wasn't going to become a diversity expert. But this research served me very well throughout my career.

What I found in 1999 in my dissertation was that older practitioners felt overwhelmingly pigeonholed into doing work related to race, when they were qualified and willing to do other types of work. But they weren't given the opportunity. They also felt they were not getting compensated fairly for the work they did. This was quite different from the younger practitioners doing race-related projects. This younger generation felt differently. They felt they were compensated more fairly and called themselves multicultural experts.

This is still going on today, especially with black-owned agencies or consultants who would like to be able to do general market projects that offer greater income. But they aren't being given that work by clients. Clients still don't look to them as being able to complete general market accounts. But if you look at the American market, it's a multicultural market, and these are multicultural experts. Fortunately, the practitioners working in-house, on the client side, are not experiencing the same level of pigeonholing as was the previous generation of African-Americans.

There is an improvement, but the struggle is real. There are a disproportionate number of PR practitioners of color who are working as freelancers, independent consultants, entrepreneurs, who own their own businesses. They're primarily brought on for projects related to race.

People say we have a problem attracting diverse students to the field. I don't think that's true. The reality is there are more students of color entering college who are interested in PR, but don't know the fullness of the industry's opportunities. They're taking PR classes; they're majoring in it. There's definitely some interest there. It's not a pipeline issue. The pipeline is there. The question is, is the pipeline clogged with unconscious bias? Am I only going to recruit people I know? If I'm used to recruiting from Newhouse or other prestigious, predominantly white, institutions, or in a particular sorority, then there are not going to be people of color. Too often, recruiters will ask for only the best minority talent, but won't apply that same standard to the Caucasian students. Taking those approaches demonstrates unconscious bias resulting in a perceived pipeline problem.

If recruiters expand their pool to include City College of New York, San Diego State, Jackson State or Howard University, they're going to get a lot more brown faces, a lot more Latinos, a lot more first-generation students from other countries.

It's like fishing. If you only have a hook that will attract a certain type of fish, then you're not going to get diverse talent into your agencies or your departments.

And once diverse talent is there, they need to be treated right. I feel very fortunate to have had the opportunity to intern where I did. I felt welcomed, I felt appreciated, and I felt supported. I have fond memories of those environments.

If you look at my experience when I was at Ketchum in 1990, the agency was supportive of the Black Public Relations Society of Washington, D.C., that was being founded by the PR pioneer, Ofield Dukes. So I had a very positive feeling they were supportive of people who looked like me. They were also supporting the professional organizations that would help us excel.

Not all my experiences were positive. Right after I graduated from Howard, I was invited to a national PRSA conference reception by Hal Warner, one of the organization's past national presidents, who was a mentor of mine. So I show up and the people at the door asked, "Well, who are *you?*" They said I was not supposed to be there. My name was not on the list. They wouldn't let me in, although others were walking in without checking first if their names were on the list. I just happened to be black in a place where there were no other black people. No other black people in that room. None. Zero. Just me.

Then Hal comes out and says, "Oh, Rochelle! You made it!" The people at the door were shocked. The rest of

the night, people would talk to me while Hal was beside me.
If Hal were away from me, people would not talk to me.

However, building relationships across cultures or race
can help in tough situations. When I taught in Tennessee,
one of my white students on the collegiate rodeo team said
to me, "I heard you're traveling to the airport tonight." He
said it was dangerous for someone like myself to go through
this county or that county. "Do you got one of those new car
phones? Because if you get stopped, you call me, you don't
call the police, because I know how to handle them boys."

You get it from all angles, from everyplace. Still, today,
with a doctorate and as a senior administrator, people will
come up to me and say, "My, you are so articulate! I've never
heard a black person speak like you do."

Most people don't realize they're acting like this. It's
unconscious. These are micro-aggressions. People often
don't know that they're saying things that are offensive.
Often it's not intentional. If you are a Caucasian person, and
want to understand what it feels like to be the only white
person, show up at a black church one day. Go to a soul food
restaurant in a part of town that you would normally never
travel to. See how people look at you and see how you feel to
be the only white person. And just try to be authentically
yourself. And see if some of the things that happen to
minorities end up happening to you.

I think that society has moved the conversation about
acceptability of women in the workplace much more
expeditiously than it has for minorities. But I would never

say that the struggle is over for women. The pay in nearly every industry for women is appalling.

Today we're having a conversation about holding PR agencies accountable and forcing them to change. Clients must demand that they're not going to spend our dollars at these agencies unless they put diverse people in mid-level and senior positions to work on our projects. This has to come from the client side demanding they need a team that reflects America.

I also think clients and agencies ought to be making public commitments about what they're doing to recruit and retain their talent. We — including the PR professional and trade associations — need to hold each other accountable. We need to be willing to make a public statement about what our commitment level is going to be, and what we're willing to do if we're meeting the mark or not.

Currently there is no industry report card, or any real visible commitment on the part of agency or client communications departments, when it comes to holding each other accountable. Hardly anyone does it. And that is problematic.

Ofield Dukes, my mentor and sponsor, was one of the first people in this industry to put pressure on agencies to hire black people. In fact, Ofield Dukes made me a young leader in the Black Public Relations Society, had me working on Bill Clinton's inauguration and placed me in my first job out of college. It was at the firm Arthur J. Schultz and Associates.

"Art, you're considered the most influential boutique agency for D.C. politics," Ofield told the owner of the firm. "And you've got no black people on your team. You should hire Miss Tillery."

And Art did.

Marvin Hill

Marvin Hill is a corporate communications lead and national communications manager for Humana. Additionally, Mr. Hill is a part-time faculty member of the University of Phoenix – College of Humanities and Sciences, School of Business, as well as a Page Up member. Mr. Hill received a Bachelor of Arts in journalism from Indiana University, Bloomington, and a Master of Business Administration in management from Purdue University, Northwest.

I first studied journalism at Indiana University. My first class was a photography course, and my professor pulled me aside and said, "Hey, I think you have a pretty good eye," and I said, "Okay," and that turned into a 15-year newspaper career, working for newspapers across the country as a photojournalist, photo editor and director.

My first full-time job was at the Arkansas Gazette in Little Rock, Arkansas. The Gazette was in a heated competition with the Arkansas Democrat, so there were two competing morning papers, two newspaper boxes right next to each other on the street, where readers could make the choice of buying one or the other. This fierce competition enabled me to hone my skills, to be competitive among my peers, spotting and racing to news situations first, documenting the moment and learning as much as I could.

Life as a photojournalist was hectic and rewarding, but I wanted more. I wanted to be a leader. I not only wanted to create and drive my own work, I wanted to lead a staff and have more of an impact on the newspaper business. Traditionally, you have to work at small-town newspapers before getting to larger operations. So I showed my stuff and worked my way up the ranks. I was motivated to become a photo editor and director of a department within the newspaper.

The sale of the Arkansas Gazette, my first full-time employer, was a sobering sign to me that journalism and newspapering were also about revenue and profits and not just about changing the world or your community.

So to make the necessary change of course from the newspaper industry toward business and corporate communications, I went back to school to get my M.B.A. That M.B.A. led me to an opportunity at Humana.

I worked in human resources at Humana for about five years while polishing my skills as a corporate recruiter, and I helped lead a leadership development program. Then the communications officer at Humana, Tom Noland, whom I met at the start of my Humana career, said, "You know, Marvin, at the right time and when you're ready to come back into communications, just let me know." And that was the start for me in corporate communications.

I recently joined Page Up, and as part of Page, my leader connected me with a mentor, and she's been fantastic. I've been on calls with her where I'd tell here about a conference I was attending and she immediately started making connections and before I knew it, I not only went to the conference but I met a CEO of an organization that I wanted to meet. This mentor just made things happen for me.

Mentoring and sponsorship are so important for anyone who is young in the business. But even as you grow, it's still important to connect with well-connected mentors in the industry, and if you can find a really good one, they can make your career journey so much easier.

There are other people who have helped me, encouraged me, pushed me and inspired me. And those have been my peers, my fellow African-American, Hispanic — and white — peers, who have been in the struggle as we helped each other build connections, learn the business, find opportunities and ultimately to be the best that we can be.

At Humana I was on the ground floor of launching network resource groups. And the first one we launched was the African-American resource group. Humana now has nine of these employee-driven groups that enrich the culture and drive innovation at the company.

It's a burden sometimes to be the only African-American in the room and be the only one to represent your culture. It seems like that's the case 90 percent of the time. It's frustrating. I continually ask myself why there aren't more African-Americans, Hispanics, Asians — or just people of color in general — in PR and business. It's also an opportunity. Ultimately I think it's up to the leaders in this industry (whatever their ethnicity) to make inclusion and diversity a priority and to find ways to incorporate diverse talent into their ranks.

And then I meet people of color who have really made it in our industry and inspire me to keep striving for excellence. Like Rochelle Ford, dean of the school of communications at Elon University, who got me connected to Page and Page Up, and others who have "made it." When I engage with leaders like Ford, it encourages me and makes me feel like I can break through any ceiling.

I want the PR and communications industry to mirror the people and communities we advertise and market to. Agency and corporate leaders should actively engage with communities and work together to cultivate, recruit, hire and retain diverse talent. Throughout my career at newspapers and in corporate America, I've always supported diversity and inclusion initiatives. I've incorporated diverse people, opinions and ideas into my daily work. When I worked at newspapers I looked for opportunities to incorporate diverse sources; for example, when we wrote a health care story, we tried to include an African-American or Hispanic doctor as a source.

Expanding diversity within the PR industry or any industry isn't easy. The effort can be driven faster by leaders who are innovative, committed and inclusive. Diverse voices and insights can enhance the industry and improve the way we understand and relate to consumers.

As a diverse leader, I approach problems differently. Where one of my peers might see a problem, I see an opportunity. And my perspectives are not necessarily a product of being African-American. It's because I was born and raised in Gary, Indiana, and because I went to Indiana University, and I grew up with a younger sister, and so many experiences that make me who I am. And if you tap into all of those things, and if you make me feel included, comfortable and empowered, wow, you're going to get everything I have to offer.

I think the efforts to drive diversity within our industry should be holistic, not just for the younger generation coming into the field but also for mid-level leaders already in the industry who would gain value from an initiative, a mentor or from organizations like the PRSA Foundation, the Museum, or Page.

As I continue to advance my career, I focus only on the future. I can't focus on the fact that others have risen to leadership roles faster than me or that I am "the only one" in the room, or the building. Yes, the journey has been frustrating at times, but the lessons learned, the guidance of mentors, and random acts of support have made the journey worthwhile.

So I think the journey is a lot harder for people of color within the PR and communications industry. Every organization is different. Every leader is different. And that framework has created the opportunity for this book, and is a reason why the PRSA Foundation exists — to help drive diversity within the industry. At the end of the day, I want to use my capabilities to make the biggest impact on my organization and the customers we serve. I think I've done that in many regards, and I understand that the path to success and excellence isn't a straight line. Organizations need to celebrate courage, to welcome and include diverse people, diverse opinions and diverse voices.

Patrice Tanaka

Patrice Tanaka is a serial entrepreneur who has co-founded three award-winning PR and marketing agencies: Patrice Tanaka & Company; CRT/tanaka; and PadillaCRT (now Padilla), the largest employee-owned PR agency in the U.S. at the time, with 200 employee-owners. Currently, Ms. Tanaka is founder and chief joy officer at Joyful Planet, a business and life strategy consultancy she founded in 2015 focused on individual and organizational purpose. Ms. Tanaka received a Bachelor of Arts in journalism from the University of Hawaii at Manoa.

Asians are the majority in Hawaii, about 40 percent of the population, so I never thought much about my ethnicity, growing up in Hawaii. And when I moved to New York, I was focused on my career. I wasn't focused on being Asian.

And then I started getting invited to conferences for women of color. At first I didn't realize why I was being invited. It took me a while to realize that as an Asian-American, I, too, was a woman of color.

I just wasn't focused on that aspect of my identity. And then I understood, "Oh, I'm a person of color, I get it."

I think of myself as an Asian-American, not just Japanese-American, because that's a bigger, more significant percentage of the population.

And, even better, I like being considered a "woman of color" because that's an even bigger percentage of the population.

At one time I used to attend Black PRSA meetings because I felt that people of color should band together to form a bigger community. I was often the only Asian in that group. I've also been involved in a lot of different organizations in the Asian-American community, and in many more organizations focused on women, because I believe we need more women leaders, including in PR, seated at every leadership table.

In any setting, I will usually gravitate to women of color there because, one, I'm a part of that community and, two, I want to make sure that my sisters feel comfortable and welcome.

I went to college at the University of Hawaii. At first, I was an English major. But I quickly realized that I didn't want to teach English when I graduated, nor was I equipped to write the great American novel. And since this was the Watergate era, I thought, well, maybe I should think about journalism. So I took a class, fell in love and switched my major to journalism.

PR was not on my radar at that time. The University of Hawaii didn't have a major in that field then. It does now. When I graduated, I started working at a small newspaper in Hawaii, and one of my assignments was to fly to Maui and do a story on this new, world-class resort, Wailea, that just opened. I flew there and the PR director for the property gave me a helicopter sightseeing tour of the resort and the island. It was so cool!

I remember saying to myself, "God ... I wish I had her job!" And, surprisingly, a year later that same job was offered to me. At that time, however, I wanted to move to New York, a childhood dream of mine. I decided, however, to take the job at Wailea and learn this profession called PR. But I was afraid of getting stuck on Maui, so I made a vow to only stay for two years.

Two years to the day, I quit without a job to move to New York City. I didn't have an apartment; I didn't really know anyone. I didn't even know uptown from downtown. But I knew that everything would turn out fine, and it did.

Six weeks after relocating from Maui to Manhattan, I started working at a small PR agency for — I didn't realize at the time — one of the worst bosses in the industry. I was just so happy to be living and working in New York that didn't even matter! I fulfilled my dream. So here I am in my early twenties, working at this small PR agency with six people. Within three months, four people left. All of a sudden, I am the most senior person at the agency ... apart from the CEO.

My boss and I were so different that we actually worked well together. She only liked to pitch and bring in new business. And I was only interested in servicing clients. I was able to help her grow her PR agency over the next seven years. We became a very attractive acquisition target and Chiat/Day, a big advertising agency, acquired us. Suffice it to say, working for my boss pre- and post-acquisition was a very challenging experience.

But I learned a lot. And that's what I tell young people: There's a lot you can learn from a really terrible boss, especially what *not* to do and how *not* to treat employees and clients.

Every time she did something that was particularly egregious, I would say to myself that if it were *my* agency, I'd do exactly the opposite.

So when I finally did start my own agency, I knew exactly what to do because of those seven years of seeing firsthand what *not* to do. In hindsight, it was a very good learning experience for me.

When our agency was acquired by Chiat/Day, we were very excited because they were a hot creative ad agency. Our PR agency was also known for being very creative and coming up with big ideas, which is what I always loved about our profession.

It's like creating magic, isn't it? You can create something from an idea you think up. And then you can bring it to life via a campaign!

For instance, we were working for Korbel Champagne. It's not easy getting media coverage for beverage alcohol products. Reporters didn't want to be perceived as promoting alcoholic beverages. So our creative way around that was to create an "irresistible" news hook — corporate America's first-ever Department of Romance, Weddings & Entertaining for Korbel, covering all the occasions when you would celebrate with the bubbly. The press loved it and so did our client. We helped Korbel grow from 800,000 cases to 1.2 million cases over a four-year period when the champagne/sparkling wine category actually declined 12 percent.

After we were acquired by Chiat/Day, I was running the subsidiary as general manager. During that time our biggest client came to us and said, "We love you guys! You've really helped us to grow our business, but we're going to consolidate all of our business with another PR agency as a cost-saving measure because our senior executives are worried that a recession is imminent."

I had three people working on that account full-time. And I knew that if I went to my boss at Chiat/Day and told him that we were losing our biggest client, he would make me terminate those three people, immediately!

So I didn't tell him that we were losing our biggest account until I could come up with a solution to avoid having to fire those three dear colleagues. But the only solution I came up with was to spin off our PR subsidiary and set it up as an independent PR agency. As the new agency's CEO, I could then choose not to fire those three employees. So that's how we started PT&Co. in July 1990.

Our clients all followed us. There were thirteen employees, including me. We started the firm as an employee-owned agency, owned by the 13 of us involved in the buyback. What we didn't know at the time, however, was that July 1990 was the official start of the recession of 1990–1991.

Within six months we lost half our billings.

I believed that the only way out of this hole without terminating any staff was that we'd all have to take a pay cut, equaling a 50 percent reduction in overall staff costs. And we'd all have to totally focus on rebuilding the lost business. Over the next 12 months, we worked so hard to rebuild our business that we actually grew 100 percent! We were right back up at the billing level we were when we first started the agency 18 months earlier in July 1990, and with all 13 employee-owners intact.

The recession was a critical bonding period for PT&Co. We didn't give up on one another. We didn't give in. We didn't let anyone go. We knew that if we hung tight and hung together we could weather the storm of the recession.

It was all about protecting our workplace "community."

In 1993, one of our clients, The Coors Brewing Company, agreed to fund a gathering in Vail, Colorado, led by a woman who wanted to start a nonprofit to provide leadership development to mid-career, Asian-Pacific-American women. The woman, Martha Lee, called to invite me to attend this gathering in Vail. At the time I was totally focused on my career and rebuilding PT&Co. It was just a crazy busy time of endless work, and the last thing I had time for was to go to Vail for the weekend and discuss whether there was a need for an Asian-Pacific American women's leadership institute. But because my Coors client had funded this gathering, of course I went. I tried to get out of it by telling Martha that I don't want to take up a valuable spot if she could only invite 17 women.

I explained to her the way that I look at my own self-identification is not first and foremost as a Japanese-American or as an Asian-American. I think of myself first as a woman. Then as a female business owner. Then as a New Yorker. Then as a person in PR. Then as someone who was born and raised in Hawaii, and *only then* as an Asian-American and as a Japanese-American. Being Asian-American is way down the hierarchy of my own self-identification, I explained to Martha. "That's precisely why you should be at the conference," she said. And I thought, "Darn!"

I attended this Vail gathering with other Asian-Pacific American women from across the country, including Hawaii, plus me, a Hawaiian now living in New York. Hearing these Asian-American women speak about their experiences, growing up in areas where they were the only Asian in their class, in their school and in their neighborhood, was eye-opening for me. They said they always felt like the "other."

They never saw other Asians in positions of leadership, including Asian women.

I see myself as a woman of color. I am a sister to Asian-Americans, Latinas, African-Americans and all women of color — a beautiful rainbow coalition of women of all ethnicities. It feels comfortable, strong and powerful!

Diversity is important, but if you don't have real inclusion, then diversity is just window dressing. So I believe the focus on inclusion is key: how we can make people feel part of the culture, part of the action and part of meaningful decision making.

There's a lot of focus on diversity and inclusion now, but the proof is in the pudding. We need to track the PR industry's progress in terms of diversity and representation of people of color in the senior ranks. Unless we look at growth in these numbers over time, it'll be hard to tell whether the industry is making any inroads on diversity and inclusion.

When I think about a career in PR among all the possible careers, PR is one of those careers where you can actually live your life's purpose. Any impact that you want to make in the world, you can find a PR job that will allow you to do that.

For purpose-focused millennials, this should be hugely appealing in attracting them to the PR profession.

I love speaking to students. I try to reassure them by saying that you do not have to be the most brilliant or the most talented person to succeed. But you must be willing to work harder and persevere longer than most people are willing to do. And if you do that, you will probably end up succeeding or winning. Unfortunately, a lot of people give up too soon. And really, in our profession, in any profession, passion, perseverance and resilience always win the day!

I also tell young professionals not to be afraid of failing. I've failed so many times in my career. But the most important thing is to get up and keep going and trying different ways to succeed. You need to learn from your failures so that you can figure out how to succeed. I tell them about our Dyson client, Sir James Dyson, who built 5,127 prototypes over 15 years before he finally succeeded in creating the DC07, the world's first bagless vacuum. He failed 5,126 times until he finally succeeded.

And I tell young women, in particular, to please, stop thinking you "have to be perfect." An HR executive once told me, "You know the difference between men and women applying for the same job at a company? If a woman can do nine out of the 10 things required by the job, she feels unqualified if she doesn't know how to do that tenth thing. If a guy can do four out of the 10, he thinks he's qualified," she said. Women need to take a page from the guys in that respect.

Asian-Americans are told by their parents to be perfectly professional in the workplace. Don't reveal anything personal, don't get emotional, do your work and don't get into anyone's business. This advice, however, prevents others from getting to know you as a "whole person."

And unless people get to know who you really are, like and trust you, they're not going to stick their necks out for you. I think the more people know who you are, like and trust you, they feel more comfortable to vouch for, advocate for and sponsor you. It's always a mix of knowing the personal and professional side of someone that makes us willing to go to bat for them.

So I think that if you're a person of color and you're trying to remain purely professional on the job, that is not a good strategy. We have to bring our whole selves into the workplace and be known for all of that richness and strength. That is our superpower!

For me, personally, a woman, a person of color, an Asian-American, someone who is height-challenged and more introvert than extrovert, I've had to push myself a little harder to make myself visible and vocal because I don't want to get lost in a sea of white people doing all the talking. I want others to have a sense of me as a person and not just as a member of a monolithic "model minority" group.

Young people of color must do that — stand out and have the courage to be seen and be heard. Human nature is such that we're always more comfortable working with and championing people we know, like and trust.

And if you don't know anything about someone because they're trying to be too purely professional, it's hard to want to include them.

Jon Iwata

Jon Iwata is the former chief brand officer and senior vice president of IBM. He led IBM's global marketing, communications and citizenship organization for a decade. Mr. Iwata is the architect of several of IBM's most recognizable brand platforms including e-business, Smarter Planet and Watson. Currently, he is Executive-in Residence at Yale School of Management. He received a Bachelor of Arts degree from the School of Journalism and Mass Communications, San Jose State University.

I'm a Californian. I entered San Jose State in 1980 as a journalism student. Watergate was a formative experience growing up in the 1970s, and like many others, I was captivated by Woodward and Bernstein. I thought journalism was a noble field.

But in my second year, walking by a corkboard advertising internships, I noticed IBM was offering an internship in "corporate communications" right there in my hometown. I didn't know much about IBM, but I knew they were a big computer company, and I was intrigued that they were recruiting journalism students. I applied for and got an internship, the first of three.

My eyes were opened. I was plunged into the world of computers and technology, which I found fascinating. And the work allowed — required — me to hone my writing skills. I decided to switch majors from journalism to public relations.

Dr. Dennis Wilcox, who led the PR program at San Jose State back then, was one of those professors who can reach your head and heart. His PR case studies class was infamous for being demanding — and rightly so. Our study of Johnson & Johnson's management of the Tylenol crisis made a deep impression. I learned from that case, and others, that PR requires rigorous thinking and a moral compass. I found that to be a powerful, appealing combination.

My third and final IBM internship was with the company's research laboratory in San Jose. I worked for an extraordinary manager, Kay Keeshen. More than anyone, Kay taught me how to be a professional. As I neared graduation, Kay offered me a regular position. I gladly accepted.

So in 1984 I became an IBMer. I was part of a tiny department so I got to do a little bit of everything, from composing news bulletins about employee promotions and organization changes to writing speeches for the lab director. But the core, and what stoked my curiosity and passion, was learning and writing about science and technology.

Some of the subjects were mind-numbing. Once I was assigned to write about "photo-chemical hole-burning." I must have spent a month with the scientists leading this work. They were patient, answering my interminable questions and trying one metaphor after another to help me understand their work. It was a struggle, for them and for me. (Years later, in 2014, the lead scientist shared the Nobel Prize for Chemistry, in part for the work I labored to comprehend.)

In hindsight, I see that those first five years at IBM Research taught me how to make the complex understandable and relevant to others. It's a muscle that grew and grew and that served me well throughout my career. And I learned that Step One is to dive in and learn the subject yourself. I've never found a shortcut. You can't delegate understanding.

After a few years in the research lab, I started receiving opportunities in other parts of IBM, all of which required a move to the east coast. But I had just gotten married — to a fellow native Californian — and the idea of living and working in New York was a little scary.

Then I was offered a two-year assignment at IBM corporate headquarters in Armonk, New York. It was quite an offer: Spend two years at the top of the company, and if we didn't like New York, I could come back to California, guaranteed. That was 1989. Two years turned into nearly 30, all of it at corporate headquarters, under four CEOs.

IBM's commitment to what today we call diversity goes back to the origin of the company. In the first half of the 20th century, IBM hired its first disabled employee, established schools to prepare women employees to become managers, and promoted a woman to vice president. It opened factories in the South and, despite resistance, demanded that they be nonsegregated. IBM was the first company to adopt a nondiscrimination policy — more than a decade before the Civil Rights Act became law.

As I learned, this is just what you do at IBM. It's built into the management system. We have strategies and goals for hiring, developing and mentoring. It starts at the top, and we're held accountable for results.

When I was appointed senior vice president, I became the executive sponsor of IBM's Asian diversity community — thousands of IBMers of Asian descent in the U.S. It was a formal responsibility, which I was expected to take seriously; and I believe I did.

I've been a board member of Page for a long time. Some years ago, we were discussing diversity in public relations and communications. What more can we do to help women and underrepresented minorities enter the profession and progress into leadership roles? In the past five to eight years, we've launched several programs at Page that have helped address this need.

One is Future Leaders. It's helped CCOs identify people of high potential — of course including people with diverse backgrounds. Scores of promising professionals have experienced the program and several have become CCOs. When I was chairman of Page, we launched Page Up, a complementary organization of Page. Page Up allows a much larger group of high-potential leaders to network, learn and grow.

Both programs have given CCOs powerful ways to provide development, training and exposure for diverse members of their teams.

Of course, these programs help people who are already in our profession. But what about high school and college students? Do they consider public relations and communications a career goal, or even a profession? We have work to do to clarify and elevate what our profession is and why it matters. Importantly, we have to lean into what it's *becoming,* not what it was.

I don't believe that public relations and corporate communications should be taught in journalism schools — despite my personal journey, which began in journalism school. At one time it made sense to teach PR alongside journalism and advertising because they were variations of "mass communications." But with the rise of social media, mobile devices, and the explosion of data that enables hyper-personalization, it's time to decouple PR and communications from journalism. Our field and disciplines belong in business schools, or perhaps schools of public policy and government. Doing that is not only appropriate and better aligned with corporate structures, it should also attract more top talent into our profession.

In terms of women representation and inclusion, one hypothesis is that some women take themselves off of the career track to have children and families. We did see that to some extent at IBM. Of course, it's wonderful for women who want to do that. But we also learned that many women want to come back to work at a later stage in their lives. So we established programs where we kept track of women, kept in touch and made them feel welcome to return to IBM. We can do the same in the public relations field.

Throughout my IBM career, I was blessed to have had many mentors; most were informal relationships. The best mentors got to know me and provided feedback, guidance and "straight talk." They pushed me out of my comfort zone at important moments.

The three IBM CEOs to whom I reported directly were not only my bosses, they were also mentors; and they continue to be.

Lou Gerstner led the historic turnaround of IBM in the early nineties. Lou promoted me to senior vice president and head of communications. That was in 2002 and I was 39. (I didn't know it at the time, but I was later told that I was the youngest senior vice president in the history of IBM, with the exception of Tom Watson, Jr., the first CEO's son.) I had my doubts. Lou did not. I got a note from him: "No matter how far you go, never stop learning." Lou and I still talk. In fact, when I declared my intention to retire, he quickly reached out to me and said, "If you want, come by and I'll give you some advice." Of course, I did that as quickly as I could.

I worked for Lou's successor, Sam Palmisano, for a decade. On the first business day of 2008, Sam called me into his office. He announced that he was combining communications with marketing and CSR, and that I would lead the new integrated organization, effectively making me chief marketing officer in addition to chief communications officer. By any measure, this was expanding my responsibilities more than tenfold.

I don't remember what I said in response to this news, but likely I was silent and wide-eyed. I do remember what Sam said to me: "Jon, you can do it." That was Sam speaking to me as my mentor, not as CEO of IBM.

Ginni Rometty succeeded Sam in 2012, and I reported to her until my retirement in 2018. Ginni invited me to lead the corporate strategy committee in her first year as CEO, and twice reappointed me to that role. More discomfort, more learning. Ginni is doing a magnificent job leading another transformation of IBM. She has not only been a great boss and mentor, but as IBM's first female CEO, she is also a source of inspiration.

There are many reasons to make a commitment to diversity and inclusion. It may be the "right thing to do." It's also the smart thing to do.

No segment of society, however you define it, has a monopoly on talent. And if you believe that your competitive advantage starts and ends with outstanding people, then you do what you can to get more than your fair share of great people. And then you create an environment, a culture, that brings out their best, not only from women and minorities, but from the quiet people, the loud people, the people who work and think and express themselves differently. This is the difference between representation and *inclusion*, and that's another mountain we have yet to scale. But if you want to win, then you have to be relentless about it, all of it. That's true for IBM and it's true for our profession.

Jessica Casano-Antonellis

Jessica Casano-Antonellis is vice president of communications at Disney Streaming Services, and previously held the dual titles of vice president of communications and diversity and inclusion program lead at Vimeo. Ms. Casano-Antonellis holds a Bachelor of Science in business administration with a concentration in marketing from San Francisco State University.

Diversity was just not always on people's radar.

I remember one specific incident that occurred during my time on the agency side of the business: I was meeting with a client who seemed very open to my talking about what it was like being gay and being married to a woman. Later on that week, the director on the account at the agency told me to refrain from talking to clients about my sexuality, noting it was inappropriate and *could* make them uncomfortable. I doubt the client felt that way, but I sure did after that conversation. Thankfully that director didn't have a long shelf life at the agency.

Things are much, much better nowadays. Today, every company knows that D&I is a critical part of operations. And I can't imagine that it's not part of every company's core values. In fact, I have found the PR industry to be big on D&I and very accepting of all types of people. It's a great career for everyone: women, people of color and people who are identifying as queer or anywhere else on the LGBTQ spectrum.

In fact, I advise everyone in PR who identifies as LGBTQ to come out in the workplace. I've been out my entire career in PR and have always considered it a strength I bring to the table, offering up a different perspective in the workplace. Nowadays companies are looking to increase their diversity numbers, and being out is an asset. Men have had their own advantages for years. This is *our* time as women to have our advantages, too. That's why I'd say it's high time to come out and leverage it.

I got my undergrad degree in marketing from San Francisco State University.

In the mid-2000s, I went to work at a high-tech PR agency in New York. I started as an entry-level account coordinator in 2005, and by the time I left eight years later, I was a director running multiple accounts and key player on the New York senior leadership team.

There were a lot of reasons why I stayed that long: the team, the clients, my boss. My boss was incredible. We built up the consumer practice together, advising media clients on their digital strategies, and even had the opportunity to serve as the face for a major travel search engine. It was exciting work.

At the same time, I remember being *so* stressed out back then. I was *constantly* stressed out. In a way I found it thrilling being so utterly stressed out (and still do today)! So I stuck with it, and accepted all the challenges, even when I felt underqualified and in over my head.

After the agency, I went over to lead communications at a major video-sharing platform, reporting directly to the CEO. It was a thrilling opportunity and I learned a lot from my boss. But after some executive turnover, there came a point when the senior leadership team was all male, and that began to bother me greatly.

In this kind of culture, it was not a surprise that lots of women employees were feeling frustrated since only the men were making decisions. The tipping point came when a few women engineers quit.

That's when the CEO decided it was time for a change and created a D&I initiative and asked me to lead it. That itself brought on a whole other set of challenges, because this role was in *addition* to my regular job in corporate communications. It was overwhelming.

At the time, the program was strictly grassroots with zero budget, so I relied heavily on my personal network to consult and help me as much as they could.

I really learned a lot from that experience, starting up a D&I program from scratch.

We surveyed employees to see what suggestions they had for our retention efforts. One of them was training and development for staff, mainly around recognizing unconscious bias. Another part was mentorship: We paired people together based upon their personal goals, interests and career paths.

Another part was getting employee resource groups off the ground. They became very active. We also put together entire handbooks of how they should be run, in line with our organizational objectives.

We had employee resource groups for women, LGBTQ, people of color and one for people passionate about making the world more accessible (a11y) for people with disabilities. The group worked closely with our product management and engineering teams to improve the accessibility of our product features.

After nearly four years at the video company, I was recruited by another video company that Disney had just announced it was acquiring majority ownership of.

Today I'm part of the communications team within The Walt Disney Company's Direct-to-Consumer and International (DTCI) segment and lead comms for the company's direct-to-consumer initiatives including ESPN+ and the upcoming Disney DTC service.

It is incredible getting to work for a company that puts such attention and emphasis on D&I. I recently joined a peer coaching program for senior women in tech that has been great, and also part of the larger PRIDE ERG.

While I don't work in a dedicated D&I capacity today, it's something I continue to remain passionate about and will always champion.

All in all, PR is a great industry for people who like a challenge, are adaptable, have a creative mindset and consider themselves strong communicators — having strong executive functioning skills is also pretty important. There's a lot of multi-tasking going on in those early days. That's one of the reasons I loved being in at agency for so long, working on so many different accounts and getting to learn everything from Fujifilm cameras to high-tech IBM servers to the MTV VMAs to providing travel tips for KAYAK. My days were diverse in terms of the clients I represented and I loved it! Coming in-house, it's been exciting to take on different roles as well. My main job has always been corporate comms, but my role has expanded over the years and I've had the opportunity to take on a variety of different functions as well: events, video production, internal comms, D&I, to name a few. I still love the challenge and never turn down an opportunity to take on something new.

Emile Lee

Emile Lee, senior vice president and global head of communications at Dun & Bradstreet, is a seasoned corporate communications executive with 20 years of international communications experience. He specializes in corporate and strategic communications, executive communications, message development, public relations, media relations, employee communications, international communications planning and issues management. Mr. Lee received a Bachelor of Arts, political science, from the University of Toronto – Victoria University.

Blind luck is what got me into this business. I actually never thought of this as a profession until it landed in my lap. And as it's turned out, the field has been fantastic for me. I can wax lyrical about communications all day!

Communications is not a career option for many young people in the Asian-American community. As far as your atypical helicopter moms and dads are concerned, you're going to be a lawyer or a doctor, or maybe an accountant.

That's pretty much it. Everything else is kind of a failure in their minds. Your parents never really told you that marketing, let alone communications, would be a viable career. In fact, there's no word or phrase in Korean that properly describes "corporate communications." When I tried to explain my job to my parents, they'd just nod their heads, but really had no idea what I was talking about. So, aspiring to be a corporate communications professional was not in our culture.

I went into college thinking I was going to be a lawyer, but that changed very quickly in my sophomore year. Ultimately, I was hired right out of school to work in South Korea for an engineering firm, based primarily on my native English skills. But it really didn't work out. So I left there and went to look for another job. I happened to land at a Hill & Knowlton affiliate office in Seoul. They were looking for native English speakers to help manage their multinational clients like General Motors, Delphi Automotive Systems and British Telecom. I honestly knew nothing about public relations and communications, but I thought, "Why not?" It's certainly better than the job I previously had. And I dove right into it. I loved it. It's been my career ever since.

Since the mid-nineties, I've had a variety of positions, primarily B2B but also a good number of years on B2C as well. After a number of years on the agency side, I worked mostly in-house — nine years with SAP, close to three years with Johnson & Johnson and several others — and I've been here at Dun & Bradstreet for two years. I've also worked in management for a number of agencies and startups. I've loved the variety of all these different positions.

With every step, I allowed myself to be open to different experiences in order to broaden my understanding of the field, particularly the ways in which communications can impact a business. For instance, at J&J, we were using PR not just from a brand reputation standpoint, but creating strategies to sway public opinion on purchasing decisions. We were able to measure our impact in a way that business people understand, how it impacts the business, and to demonstrate this in tangible ways that the leadership can appreciate.

As a function, we've certainly come a long way from measuring our results based on column inches and the like. But however we measure, we have to be better at that as an industry to showcase how we contribute to the goals of that business, division or company. We're getting there, though.

Diversity in business today is critical, and most certainly for communications. Everybody needs to know how to reach new markets. If you don't understand the different cultures, languages, ways of doing business — even the differences between men and women and how to communicate with them effectively — you are not going to be able to do your job successfully. If you don't understand or feel that you can communicate to all audiences regardless of sexual orientation, race, gender, culture, language and religion, then, well, you're doing the company a disservice.

I didn't think too much of being from an Asian heritage while I was growing up in Canada. Then when I started going abroad, I got a huge appreciation for all the differences there are in the world, differences we need to understand if we are to be effective in our jobs.

In PR we need to do a better job of diversity. I hate to say it, but it's still very white dominated in both in-house and on the agency side. Are we doing better? Yes. Do we have room to improve? Absolutely.

Some corporate functions have more diversity than others. Here at Dun & Bradstreet, we've had an aggressive focus on gender and LBGTQ equality and have seen solid progress, and have even been recognized for our efforts. Like most companies, we are not perfect, but we're getting there.

I think the communications industry is probably more on the bleeding edge of gender diversity and LGBTQ diversity, but certainly the minority aspect of the diversity mix is still lacking across the board.

There's a lot more that needs to be done. Gender-wise, we're doing much better than a lot of our functional peers. We have more women within executive and management ranks. Now we need to take it to the next level, and address LGBTQ, cultural and racial diversity as well.

The more diversity we have, the better our function becomes. We can have diverse thinking and different viewpoints, and when we all collaborate, we come up with better results.

As an industry, we need to do better at how we recruit from colleges. We have to position PR as a good career choice for minority students. We need to do better in the interviewing and recruiting processes to ensure we have the right levels of diversity in the mix.

We also need to make sure we are leveraging diverse leaders in the field — like Jon Iwata and Michael Sneed — so that we can dispel the typical racial stereotypes that still exist. We need to make our successful minority — women and men — more visible within the industry and outside it. That would help a lot in promoting the field as a career to consider and even aspire to for diverse college students.

Another idea: Why not have the various minority PR associations — Hispanic, African-American and Asian-American — collaborate. This way we can all learn from one another and encourage more of an understanding across racial lines.

As for advice I would give minority students and young professionals, here's what I would tell them: Find a mentor — or three — both within your current company (who can also act as an internal champion) and from the outside. I've had the fortune of having mentors throughout my career who absolutely helped, encouraged, coached and made me a better leader, professional and human being.

And don't just find mentors from your area of expertise. While this is critical for sure, you will be a much more well-rounded professional if you learn from others with diverse backgrounds and career trajectories. My mentors feel like a

United Nations roll call of sorts with diverse backgrounds, languages, cultures, ethnicities and business backgrounds. I've had mentors from China, Australia, Singapore, Great Britain, Germany, Canada, Brazil and the U.S. who worked in various functional areas and executive ranks, from sales to marketing, human resources, technology and, of course, communications. And every single one of them helped me in my career.

Go international. If given the opportunity, work abroad, as it will open your eyes, experiences and perspectives on working with, communicating to, and living with cultures and languages different from your own. Not only is it fascinating in its own right from a personal development point of view, but you will honestly be living an M.B.A. as opposed to being stuck in a classroom learning about it. The experiences you gain will absolutely accelerate your learning curve, abilities and capabilities, strategic thinking and sensitivities that will make you a better communicator and leader.

Let's be honest, while America is certainly a melting pot and still the world superpower in many respects, we are decidedly still American, regardless of whether we are African-American, Latin-American, Asian-American or otherwise. In an environment and era where technology advancements have broken down time zones and borders, the better your ability to be able to target, empathize, understand and communicate to global audiences and cultures, the better you will be at what you do.

Take risks and get out of your comfort zone. Don't take the safe route. Just go for it! The more knowledge, know-how and experiences you have, the further — and faster — you will go in your career trajectory. Don't worry about promotions or getting that vice president job title before you are 30. The more diverse your experience, the better your long-term career trajectory will be and the more doors you will open as a result.

I lucked into a career in PR. And after joining a PR agency in the lead-up to Y2K, the president of my firm asked if anyone wanted to volunteer to pursue business development and account management opportunities with the technology sector, as more and more companies were preparing for Y2K. No one volunteered as technology wasn't well understood at that point and no one wanted to pursue something they were not familiar with, especially B2B technology. But I jumped right in, and it was huge in my development as a result.

I took that kind of "experience first" thinking for all of my career moves. I still do that to this day, as I am a big believer in continuous learning. I've taken jobs where the roles were ill-defined and different, and stepped way out of my comfort zone. It's the same whether at a 15-person startup company, a boutique crisis and issues management firm, or at an established Fortune 100 company for a division on the verge of collapsing. I've looked for opportunities where my experiences could help, volunteered to expand my responsibilities and immersed myself in projects outside of what would be considered core communications responsibilities, to take on projects related to customer experience, sponsorships, brand, partner and alliance marketing. Why? The experiences I gained from each of these opportunities made me a better communicator and business leader as a result.

Embrace your difference, whether that is gender, ethnicity, sexual orientation, culture, language or otherwise. The mere fact that you are a minority is what makes you special. Inherent in being a "minority" is that you are "different." And different is a huge advantage, so embrace it. All the diverse personal experience, perspective, upbringing and wonderful qualities that make you, *you*, also will enable you to bring diversity of thought and ideas to the table when developing a strategy, a campaign or a project, and everyone on your team will be the better for it.

Nyree Wright

Nyree Wright is a trusted adviser and widely recognized public relations executive with strategic counseling/marketing expertise in the crisis, corporate reputation and consumer practice areas. Currently she is principal at NW Consulting, L.L.C., after serving several years as senior vice president at MSLGROUP. Prior to MSLGROUP, Ms. Wright was vice president at TMG Strategies. She received a Bachelor of Arts in communications from Rutgers University and a Master of Arts in corporate and public communications from Seton Hall University.

PR was not a career I just fell into. It was what I chose. During high school I belonged to a program called INROADS, a program specifically for diverse students founded in 1970. It's a competitive program for which you have to apply and be accepted. Many high school students of color have begun there in preparation for working in a corporate environment. I began the internship program my sophomore year of high school and I was paired with Chubb, an insurance company in Murray Hill, New Jersey.

It was my first exposure to a corporate culture, where effectively interacting with executives was crucial. In addition to being introduced to the skills needed to work in such an environment, they emphasized professional etiquette. I had to wear suits, skirts and blouses. (I come from a traditional West Indian family where on Sundays we dressed up to go to church, so I was very much used to that.) But I would not have transitioned as successfully from school to corporate life had it not been for the many programs in which I participated, such as INROADS.

Five years ago I ran into one of the women who I shadowed at INROADS here in Washington, D.C., and she remembered me. It was such an unexpected yet welcoming experience. We had kept in touch through college and maybe into my late twenties but then that fell off. She was still working at Chubb.

INROADS would pair high school students with a corporation. In New Jersey we had AT&T as a partner, Johnson & Johnson, Chubb — all those large corporations. On-site there was a liaison between INROADS and us, who would basically help guide us.

At Chubb, I worked in underwriting. It entailed plenty of numbers crunching, paper pushing, filing and sitting in on meetings. It wasn't the most interesting work, but I learned how a corporate environment works from answering the phone properly to participating in a meeting with senior executives.

I majored in communications at Rutgers. The School of Communication and Information at Rutgers covers both communications and journalism, and while I originally thought about studying the latter, I quickly discovered I enjoyed marketing and PR, so I focused on that.

I was a member of PRSSA the last three years at Rutgers. During my last two, I worked at the Rosen Group on the New York Auto Show, where, upon graduating, I landed a job.

After the Rosen Group, I attained an entry-level position in the corporate communications department of Prudential. My main focus was on the Prudential Foundation, the representative network and financial services.

With my internship experiences, the transition between college and work wasn't anything I wasn't prepared for.

I believe my transition to corporate life was easier because I had gone to a mainstream state school such as Rutgers. I was used to dealing with all kinds of people being the majority — Caucasian, Latino, Asian, Indian, et al. I don't believe I would've evolved as quickly, understanding "need-to-know nuances," had I attended an HBCU.

While I was at Prudential, I started going for my master's in corporate and public communication at Seton

Hall University, and then left Prudential and went to Ogilvy, where I finished it.

So I was at Ogilvy for a little over two years, and loved it. I came in as an account executive and I left as an account supervisor. I went up two, three levels in three years. At the time I didn't appreciate that as much as I do now, because I didn't realize how rare that was.

I believe it's a disservice when employees are not promoted according to ability but must wait a year or three — or whatever the minimum number of years policy mandates — to rise from one tier to another. Promotions shouldn't be limited by cycles or time. If the person is going above and beyond, they ought to be rewarded. Period.

I was at Ogilvy when it was growing by leaps and bounds. We had business coming in every which way and I was given a plethora of opportunities. I think it was a combination of raising my hand and having the capability, and the agency needing people to service accounts. It was the perfect storm. The more I did, the more I was given. The more I succeeded, the more work was assigned to me. The more I was offered, the more clients I managed.

I worked on the Qwest account, when Qwest and US West merged. That's actually how I got into crisis communications. I also worked on Sun Microsoft Systems.

HD Vest Financial Services was my biggest client and the one that helped make my career at that time. It was a small financial services firm based in Irving, Texas, and the owner and decision-maker was a guy who was enamored with my work. They launched the first online tax service, before H&R Block did. We managed the entire national campaign. We won awards. Eventually they were acquired by Wells Fargo, which was their goal all along.

This was all happening around 1999 and 2001 — when tech was crazy, and then crashed and burned. Ogilvy had to go through layoffs and I made it through three rounds. Word spread that another one was coming, so I negotiated a package and left.

I was already interviewing and accepted a job at a crisis communications firm, the McGinn Group, in Washington, D.C. That was mid-August. I moved out of New York and started a new job in September of 2001, right after 9/11. While I was at McGinn, we were acquired by MSLGROUP. After four years, the relationship with MSL ended, and MSL made offers to people they wanted — and I was one of them.

I continued to specialize in corporate reputation and crisis: breast implants, the Purdue/Oxycontin issue, the GMAC lawsuit, you name it. The biggest one was the GM bankruptcy, as we were the communications hub for them. We even built a separate office to handle it. It was absolutely chaotic! I'm sure I lost two or three years of my life in that position. They had a hub in Detroit and one in Arlington, Virginia. That would probably be the second most impactful phase of work in my career: working pre-, during and post-bankruptcy.

Not to be dramatic, but it was somewhat life changing, it really was, in a number of ways. It changed my understanding of business, my understanding of the restructuring of a company, and gave me an understanding of how that affects people's lives, jobs, media and how to cover a crisis. I was actually one of the managers of that communications hub. We were in the trenches.

Rick Wagoner, GM's CEO, was in our office almost monthly. We would meet on Sundays. He had meetings on the Hill. It was really, really intense. I mean, even for that time, for me, it was a lot. It was my life. I traveled a lot, back and forth to Detroit, worked late hours, weekends — nothing was off limits.

Dan McGinn, for lack of a better phrase, had an infatuation with diversity. He was able to successfully navigate his way into the C-suite and meet with CEOs rather quickly. He would talk to them about the importance of diversity and the changing landscape of their customer base around the world. A lot of work that I did while I was at McGinn was putting together presentations to C-suite executives and CEOs, talking about diversity, talking about the changing numbers, the execs on their business, why diversity was important. Blah, blah, blah. I spent a lot of time doing that. It was very helpful to the firm because, quite frankly, I was the resident senior person of color.

He looked to me often for engagement on those matters, which was good. But the other side of it is, I think I got pigeonholed in that for a little while. And while it was interesting work, I never aspired to be the girl who does *only* multicultural PR. That's never been my thing. It never will be.

I wouldn't exactly use the word "stuck," because, like I said, it was very legitimate work. His agency made plenty of money counseling on those topics. But after a while I was like, OK, I can contribute, but I'm not going to be held in this phase doing "multicultural" work.

This scenario plays out frequently as the number of diverse voices in agencies is limited. They're looking to open new avenues for business. It's like, "Lets cobble together the people of color we have, and we'll have our focus group of two to get their opinion." It's such an old and archaic way of doing things. It completely blows my mind how often it still happens.

The diversity situation on the whole though has improved, in that there are mentors in the industry now who have made a concerted effort to help our younger people. But when I was coming up, there was not a "me."

Now I have several peers and colleagues, in different agencies and corporate communications entities, to whom young people can look. There are significantly more of us who exist and who make a concerted effort to help groom our young people.

That said, I still don't believe that there is a real authentic commitment to diversifying the PR industry. It should be done, as with any other industry, because that's the world we live in now. And the companies and services that go after these consumers should reflect the consumers they go after, especially media companies.

Minorities are the biggest consumers of media, whether they watch on their phones, laptops or TV. The growth of the market is through the roof percentage-wise. Yet all marcomms agencies continue to do things as usual based on their very limited knowledge being non-diverse.

Time after time you see companies apologizing about something that they did wrong in a commercial, an ad or in a tweet because the people doing it are a room full of Anglos who have no idea how to communicate with the audience they are going after. That's because it's not coming from the top down. You do have some leaders who I think are sincere, but there is a funnel that is happening at the middle management level. There are several decision-making folks on the vice president level who have their own biases. And they have the power to help make hiring decisions. That's where we are having real issues — that level, that funnel. They are the ones who need to understand the importance of going after our talent.

I'm speaking from experience. I've seen it with my own eyes. There are certain schools they go to first for interns. There are certain types of candidates they engage. It's just blatant. They don't even realize it.

If the industry itself doesn't make a real sincere effort to go with the times and address the change in landscape, and by that I mean: Put resources behind it, change will be forced upon it. I can't tell you how many times I've been asked to build a multicultural this or that. Wherever I was, whatever the agency or company, was anybody going to give me a budget? Was anybody going to give me resources? That has to be part of the equation. And in order to get a return, you've got to make an investment. Making a real investment in talent needs to be made sincerely in order to see positive changes happen.

David Albritton

*David Albritton is currently executive director, product
development and international communications, at General
Motors. Prior to that he was vice president and chief
communications officer at Exelis. Mr. Albritton earned a
Bachelor of Science in general engineering at the U.S. Naval
Academy in Annapolis, Maryland, and a Master of Science in
management at the Naval Postgraduate School in Monterey,
California.*

I actually came into public relations by happenstance. I
started my career as an officer in the U.S. Navy after
graduating from the U.S. Naval Academy in 1988. I spent my
first 3 1/2 years serving on a ship that sailed to many places
around the world during multiple deployments, which
included a stint where we were gone 14 out of 17 months.

After I transferred from that ship, my next assignment
was two years of graduate school in Monterey, California. As
I was preparing to graduate with a master's degree in
management, I was supposed to go back to sea duty for two

years, which at that time in my life I wasn't looking forward to doing. I loved the Navy, but I wanted to pursue a new career field that didn't require me to be away from my family for so long. One of my best friends had transitioned from ship duty and became a Navy public affairs officer (PAO) stationed at the Navy's Chief of Information (CHINFO) Office in the Pentagon. When I inquired about his experience as a PAO, he was enjoying it immensely and invited me to visit him to determine if this was a career I'd be interested in.

When I visited, I really didn't know much about the public affairs profession, but I was very impressed with what I'd learned from the key leaders I got to meet including the two-star admiral who ran Navy public affairs, the legendary Kendall Pease.

Soon after the visit, I submitted an official career transfer application to the Navy, and thankfully I was one of 10 officers — out of more than 40 applicants — that was selected by a PAO review board.

Ironically, my first assignment as a PAO was at CHINFO. But before I reported to the Pentagon, I spent nine weeks at the Defense Information School (DINFOS), which at the time was at Fort Benjamin Harrison in Indianapolis. It's basically what we used to call a "knife and fork" school, where we were taught the basics of public relations: how to write press releases, how to engage with media, how to be a storyteller and many other related skills. It was a great eye-opening experience and opportunity for me to basically learn the craft before beginning my new assignment.

I was first assigned to the Plans and Policy section for a few months, before transferring to the Navy News Desk, which I equate with putting a fire hose in your mouth and opening it up full blast. The volume of issues dealing with personnel in the Navy, or real-world operations, exercises, technology, etc., was just massive. A ton of different issues came across my desk on any given day, and I learned so much about the strategic side of the Navy. It was fascinating. I was very thankful that I had some wonderful teachers at CHINFO, like Stephen Pietropaoli, who was a Navy commander at the time and in charge of the "Desk," who later achieved the rank of one-star admiral and ran all of Navy public affairs. All of the junior PAOs on the Desk would sit in his office daily when he was talking to reporters and we listened closely to how he told a story, how he responded to questions, and very importantly, learned what he didn't say about particular issues. And he would spend time with us and teach us why he responded the way he did. He would put it into strategic context for us.

But after about a year on the Desk, I also had the amazing opportunity to become the Flag Lieutenant/Aide to Admiral Pease and it was there that I furthered my education about strategically tying the responsibilities of public relations to the actual day-to-day business of the Navy, and I got to engage with military and civilian officials at the most senior levels. It was, by far, one of the most educational and rewarding opportunities I've had in my career.

My next assignment was over in London at the headquarters for U.S. Naval Forces Europe (NAVEUR). Our command owned everything operationally for the U.S Navy, from the northern tip of Norway to the southern tip of South Africa, across Europe and the Mediterranean, plus the northern half of Africa.

It was a huge operations area and I traveled wide and frequently to participate in a diverse mixture of real-world operations and joint NATO exercises that ranged from the war in Bosnia to U.S. Embassy personnel evacuations in Western Africa to peacekeeping training exercises in the Baltic region to media embarks on U.S. aircraft carriers and submarines in the Mediterranean.

I had some phenomenal experiences that I would never have had elsewhere, and learned a lot about how to operate remotely and sometimes independently as a PAO, while also interacting regularly with very senior military and government officials from around the world.

But in mid-1997, something happened that changed my life and the trajectory of my career.

Sam Falcona is a former PAO who had retired from the Navy and taken a job as the director of public relations at Sears, Roebuck and Co. in Chicago. One of his former Navy bosses was my then current boss at NAVEUR and he called him one day to say that his boss at Sears, Ron Culp, the senior vice president and chief communications officer

(CCO), was coming to London on holiday with his family and asked if he would take care of him.

So my boss, Captain Steve Honda, gave that assignment to Lieutenant David Albritton, who met the Culps and spent the day giving them a tour of NAVEUR, which included a detailed briefing about our operations across our region.

After an amazing day together, I said goodbye to the Culps. I never thought I'd see them again since in just a month and a half from then I was going to be promoted to lieutenant commander and go on to finish out my Naval career and serve for more than 20 years.

But it seems that fate would have other plans for me. I got a call from Sam a few weeks later saying that Ron really liked me, and asked me to send a resume since there might be a job opportunity at Sears to consider. But being a Naval officer, I didn't have a resume, so had to construct one based on the ones some of my buddies had written. Days later, they invited me to fly to Chicago to interview for a PR specialist job at Sears Automotive Group, an invitation I accepted mostly because I hadn't been back to the U.S. for over a year and I thought it would be a nice vacation — in addition to my paying homage and being respectful to Ron for such a wonderful gesture.

To my shock, I was offered the job as soon as I returned to London; and it was one of those jobs that was nearly impossible to turn down.

The job had responsibilities for all 700-plus Sears Auto Centers and more than 300 National Tire & Battery (NTB) stores across the U.S. But even more intriguing to me was the responsibility of owning public relations activities for all of Sears' NASCAR properties, which included the NASCAR Craftsman Truck Series, the Diehard 500 race at Talladega Motor Speedway, and support of both Craftsman and Diehard as official tools and batteries of NASCAR. I've always been a huge NASCAR fan, and it was phenomenal to believe that Sears would pay me to go to races and give me full access to every part of the track on race day — including the drivers' meeting before the race.

With about 10 years of Naval service at the time, I was at the halfway point before I could retire, so I thought that it was a good transition point to consider a brand new civilian career. I then moved to Chicago to work for Sears. Just eight months later, I got promoted to be PR manager for Sears Automotive, and a year after that, I got promoted to senior manager. In addition to Sears Automotive, Craftsman and Diehard, I added responsibilities for the Kenmore appliance brand, Weatherbeater paint, plus all Sears Hardware stores and Sears Dealer stores. I'd gotten promoted twice in two years — Sears was going great, and in my mind the decision to leave the Navy was a good one.

Over this time, I was privileged to be able to get to know Ron a lot better, and it was then that I decided that my career aspiration was to one day become a CCO like him.

About 2 1/2 years into my tenure at Sears, I got approached by a headhunter for a senior manager opportunity at Compaq Computer Corporation in Houston. I decided I'd ask Ron his advice about this, and Ron, being the fantastic leader that he is, was more concerned about me and my career than he was of the investment he'd made in me at Sears.

He told me some very specific things that I carry to this day. Number one: "You have to be strategic. Learn how to equate what you do in public relations to how it adds value to the business operations of the company. Become a business partner first — a public relations practitioner second."

But also, from a career perspective, this would be a strategic move because at the time, while Compaq had a global director of communications, they did not have a vice president. So the senior manager job, even though I was already a senior manager as Sears, was equivalent to a director job in terms of level of responsibility of what I would support at Compaq.

So, much to my surprise, Ron recommended that I take the job. And I did. I left Sears and went to Compaq in Houston. And at Compaq, I was lucky enough to meet yet another key leader in my career: Roger Frizzell.

Less than a year into my tenure at Compaq, Roger became the senior director of global communications at Compaq. We had tremendous success. And then one night — I remember it clearly — it was a Sunday about 10:05 p.m.,

I get a call from somebody on my team who said, "Look at the news," and when I did, I learned that HP and Compaq were going to merge. As scary and uncertain as that proposition was, it turned out to be a great career opportunity for me, since following a year-long proxy fight, the merger finally closed, and on day one of the new company being formed, Roger promoted me to director of communications at HP, as he was promoted to vice president. I had responsibilities for all consumer and commercial desktops, notebooks, handheld devices and networking equipment at a time when computing technology was changing every minute. It was very exciting.

I spent about four years at Compaq/HP, but during my last year, my family relocated to the Washington, D.C., area since my wife took a new job in the federal government. Roger was very supportive in allowing me to do my HP job from Washington, but as a former Compaq employee, it was becoming clear that the new HP culture wasn't as accepting of us. So, after a recommendation from a former Navy PAO colleague, a headhunter approached me to become the vice president of communications at United Way of America, the national leadership organization for all 1,400 local United Ways. It was a very interesting and rewarding experience and I loved the people there, but after being there for about two years, I yearned to get back into the corporate environment. I'd been recommended to a headhunter by another colleague and ended up accepting a job at Raytheon Company as a director of communications in their Washington, D.C., office, supporting global business development and government relations, and various product communications, among other things.

Pam Wickham was the CCO at Raytheon and another phenomenal practitioner of public relations that I've been lucky to work for like Ron and Roger. Having been a Naval officer, it was great to go back into the defense industry. I knew the products, I knew the mission and I knew the culture of the military customers, so it was easy for me to fold back into that environment. It was a great experience, and my career was thriving at Raytheon.

One day I got a call from a person I served with on the advisory board at the University of Florida. It was Angela Buonocore, the CCO of ITT Corporation, who asked if I'd be interested in a vice president of communications position at ITT Defense. At ITT, I'd be able to prove that I could be a change agent, and create some much-needed structure into the communications department for the defense business. Angela was also an amazing boss and public relations expert that I really enjoyed working for. I really learned a lot from her.

In that role, I also got the opportunity to work for and with one of the greatest leaders I've ever come across in my career: Dave Melcher. He had just retired as a three-star general after spending 32 years in the U.S. Army and was now the president of ITT Defense. As I look back over my career, that was probably the best job experience I've ever had — and I've had some phenomenal job experiences. Dave was a leader who understood communications to the core, and he truly believed in building and fully leveraging every member of the team to accomplish the mission. But beyond that, it was the tremendous team that he built and the numerous business transformation activities we worked on together that were such an amazing learning experience for me under his guidance.

In January 2011, we found out that ITT was going to split into three entities within a year, and ITT Defense would become a stand-alone Fortune 500 company. I said to myself, "ITT has been around for 50 years. In less than a year we're going to have to create a new brand, create a new brand identity, launch it globally and sustain it." Personally, it was a scary proposition since I was going to be tasked with leading the effort and I hadn't ever done anything of that magnitude before in my life. Angela's experience and expertise in communications was extremely helpful, but I was extremely impressed by the way Dave pulled the ITT Defense team together and we successfully launched a new company, Exelis Inc., in just ten months.

It was truly the pinnacle of my career from a couple of perspectives.

First, I was completely honored to be promoted to become the Exelis chief communications officer. I'd finally achieved the professional status that was inspired by Ron Culp just 13 years earlier, but it was enabled by what I'd learned from so many great professionals over the years. But I also relished the opportunity to launch Exelis with an amazingly talented group of communicators on a team that I built almost from scratch. In fact, out of my six communications directors at Exelis, three of them (B.J. Talley, Courtney Reynolds and George Rhynedance) have gone on to become CCOs themselves, with a fourth, Leah Lackey, being in the CCO pipeline. I'm so very proud of all of them.

So we successfully operated Exelis for 3 1/2 years. But in January of 2015 we learned that we'd had an overture from Harris Corporation to buy the company, which ultimately came to fruition in May 2015, when the merger deal was completed.

It was sad to realize that everything that we'd built up as a team at Exelis in those 3 1/2 years was going away. But Harris already had a chief communications officer, so I was going to be a free agent for the first time in my career, without a defined career opportunity to step into like all of my previous jobs since I left the Navy. Plus, a lot of the job opportunities I was seeing were not in Washington, D.C., which meant I had to consider what that meant for my family in terms of possibly relocating.

But then yet another phenomenal career-changing situation happened. Mark Reuss, the executive vice president for Global Product Development at General Motors Co. in Detroit, was a member of the Exelis board of directors and I'd gotten to know him fairly well through many engagements with the board members. As the Exelis-Harris merger was completed, he said that I'd done a great job at Exelis and would like for me to consider coming to GM. The next day I got a call from an HR executive at GM and was invited to come to Detroit to interview for a yet-to-be-identified position. Ironically, I'd just recently met the GM chief communications officer, Tony Cervone, a few months before at the Page Spring Seminar and I was completely impressed with him.

Fast forward to September 2015 and I began working for GM as the executive director for Global Product Development Communications.

But to get to that point, for the first time in my career, I had to have a really tough conversation with myself in terms of "who" I am as a professional. I had just come from being a CCO at Exelis and I had just been offered an executive director job at GM working for a CCO. I had to get past my own ego and say, "Get over yourself!" As a good friend who is an HR professional told me years before, "Titles are free." Despite the less senior title, this was a huge opportunity in front of me, since I'd be going from a $5.5 billion business to one that's over $155 billion! But the thing that really moved the needle for me was Tony's willingness to accept me commuting from Washington, D.C., to Detroit, which as of 2018 I've been doing ever since. And I'm continuing to learn as well, since Tony is an amazing public relations professional and a legend in the automotive business.

That takes me from day one to now. As I reflect on all of the great leaders that I've had the privilege of working for, as well as all of the fantastic people on my teams across many organizations, I truly believe they've all collectively been *the* reason I've gotten where I am today.

One of the strong messages I convey to people is: "You will never get anywhere by yourself. You have to have people in your life who are there to tell you how great you are, but you also need those people who are willing to tell you that you have mustard on your shirt."

I was deeply honored to be asked to be included in this book, especially since I know about the challenges the public relations industry has with respect to diversity and inclusion. I applaud our industry for recognizing that we do have challenges, but in my opinion we have too many disparate efforts that aren't tied together, so we're not reaching the critical mass of people who could benefit from these efforts collectively.

When you think about the African-Americans, Hispanics and Asians, all the people of color who work in our profession, there is not just one organization or one entity or one conversation going on. So where do those people turn?

And as it relates to hiring and advancement opportunities inside companies, it's the people inside those companies that are making those decisions, not the people outside. So, until we can find ways to educate and influence the people making the hiring, firing and promotion decisions inside the company, we won't be 100 percent effective.

We have to educate every diverse professional on what a successful career track is and how you can effectively manage that. It's not just showing up every day and doing your best work. You have to understand how to become a better business partner and equate what you do in public relations and communications with how the company makes money. As you get more senior, that is fully expected. I tell people all time, as much as I am a PR practitioner, I am more of a business partner. The conversations I have are more about what's going to help the business versus media engagement and pitching stories. Every day, I remember Ron Culp sitting me down and having that very same conversation about needing to be strategic and needing to understand more about the business.

Ron Culp talked about this in his first book, "Business Essentials for Strategic Communicators," that he published with his fellow DePaul University professor, Matt Ragas. I've given out probably 50 copies of that book to communications professionals in many organizations. It shows how and why every public relations practitioner should understand the basics of the business. It's a great how-to guide that I tell people to keep on their desks and refer to it all the time.

So, particularly as it relates to people of color, I give this book out a lot. You can get from here to there, you can go from PR specialist to PR manager, but how do you become a director, and then a vice president? What are the skill sets you need to develop? What is the knowledge base that you have to have to get there? A book like Ron's and Matt's helps.

There needs to be a more unified conversation among all the organizations about the diversity issue. How can we create the best practices on what's successful? How do we get the right feedback? How do we monitor this? How do we track a person going through the pipeline and watch how they're progressing? And how do we ensure that everyone is reaching back and pulling more people in, especially as organizations morph and evolve, and hiring practices change?

And then, it's also critical to have mentors and other professionals in other functional disciplines who can help guide, counsel and advocate for you. I've taken that on as one of my personal charges, and I love doing it. And I'd love to see more people doing that across the board.

Judith Harrison

Judith Harrison is currently senior vice president, Diversity &
Inclusion, at Weber Shandwick, a global public relations
agency. Ms. Harrison was formerly senior vice president,
human resources, at Ruder Finn. Her recruiting and HR
career was preceded by years of public relations and marketing
communications practice at companies including Burson-
Marsteller, Arthur Young, CBS and Media General. She is
president of the PRSA Foundation and president of New York
Women in Communications. Ms. Harrison is the only woman
of color to hold either position, and the only individual who
has held both simultaneously.

I discovered public relations unintentionally. I was
following my dream of being a jazz and pop singer, which
was exciting, but didn't pay the rent. I went to an
employment agency for what I saw as nothing more than a
"day job," and they sent me to Burson-Marsteller. I had
never heard of public relations. I was placed in what they
called sales promotion at the time, which is now known as

creative. It was a traffic job, basically, making sure each part of every project met internal and external deadlines.

For a time, I put in full days (and more) there, then went out and sang in clubs or recorded in studios, usually well into the wee hours. Then I would go back to work on just a few hours of sleep. This is why God gave us our twenties.

I had spent my life immersed in music. I started piano lessons when I was 5 with my aunt, a classical pianist and opera singer. When I switched to pop and jazz, I learned from some of the best people in the industry and it was wonderful. I never stopped loving music; it was the music business I couldn't stand.

Meanwhile, I loved the energy and creativity at Burson. The work had unexpected depth and intellectual challenge, and the work hard/play hard ethos was a natural fit for me. My "day job" had become my real life.

After four years at Burson, I went to Arthur Young (which is now Ernst & Young); then CBS, where I managed promotions for mini-series and other non-series television; and Media General, where I directed marketing communications for their media buying and barter divisions, and launched a new division, Professional Inventory Management.

After 11 years of working for others, it felt like the right time to experience independence. So, I did, and it was great for a while. I had clients like the Italian Trade Commission, for which I worked on a fashion exposition with top designers including Giorgio Armani, Paula Fendi, Valentino Garavani, Gianni Versace, Gianfranco Ferre, Krizia, Ottavio and Rosita Missoni and Laura Biagiotti. I worked with clients ranging from the American Cancer Society to the International Art of Jazz.

And then the recession hit, and suddenly every freelancer in town was chasing the same three clients. The good times stopped rolling.

When the market started to come back, I was unable to find a place as a PR or marketing communications practitioner. Ironically, I found a related opportunity: recruiting at a search firm specializing in PR and marketing communications. I had a deep understanding of the industry and the positions I sought to fill, so there was rarely a learning curve in terms of skills required for successful hires. Given this knowledge and my wide range of industry contacts, the professional pivot made sense.

I enjoyed recruiting for a while, especially when I had the opportunity to interview smart, interesting, forward-thinking people who loved their work.

Some of my favorite interviews taught me invaluable lessons about strategic thinking, how various industries worked and the sometimes surprising impact of agency and corporate cultures on the lives of employees. Some of my clients were great sources of life lessons and inspiration, too, though not always in a positive way.

One taught me the extent of the PR industry's hypocrisy about diversity in the '90s. She had a small consumer agency with 30 or so employees, 29 of whom were white. A favorite client of my manager, she was slated to give a keynote speech about diversity at one of the industry's leading annual gatherings. When my manager told me this, I asked what she had done to increase or advocate for diversity in her business or the industry. The answer was: nothing. Her theory, I was informed, was that "cream rises to the top." With no interest or experience to draw on for her speech, she asked my manager to ask me for stories about my life that she could use. In one of the most uncomfortable moments of my career, I looked at him and said, "If she wants to know what life is like for people of color in this business, she should hire some and take them out to lunch."

I learned much more positive lessons from some of my clients, especially Chen Sam, who was best known as Elizabeth Taylor's publicist, in addition to working with Audrey Hepburn and a range of high-profile fashion and beauty clients. As my client and mentor, Chen taught me invaluable lessons about client service, drive and resourcefulness by example as well as discussion. After years of women being told to "think like a man," and black women having to walk a higher tightrope most people pretended didn't exist, Chen was like water in the desert in teaching me the power of embracing my authentic self. Had she lived, I would have been her deputy in a celebrity fragrance-licensing business she was planning to launch, and my life would have taken a completely different turn.

Although I enjoyed recruiting, I needed to do more, but had no desire to go back to practicing PR. I had read a lot about how HR was becoming more of a strategic partner with corporate leadership. It was no longer seen as a place where papers were pushed and ideas went to die. It was beginning to have real influence, according to business thought leaders in Fortune, Harvard Business Review, etc. I thought it could be an interesting way to use all that I had learned and stretch myself in the industry I knew best. In 1997, I left the search firm to become vice president of human resources at Ruder Finn.

I'm so glad I did. Ruder Finn, a leading independent agency just before the dawn of the consolidation gold rush, was a great place to dive into existing practices, help launch new ones, and get the occasional incredibly interesting side gig. My first assignment there, given to me by David Finn himself, was to find a press secretary for his friend, Kofi Annan, who was about to become secretary general of the United Nations.

After nine years, I was ready for a change. During that time, I'd had the privilege of chairing the HR Roundtable of the PR Council, where I met all of my PR agency peers. This network led me to Weber Shandwick. I was hired by the agency's parent business unit, Constituency Management Group (CMG), to lead a shared services North American recruiting team for Weber Shandwick and other agencies, and to lead HR at FutureBrand, CMG's branding agency. All of the above are owned by Interpublic Group.

This entailed working two days a week in one office and three in the other, and sometimes commuting between both several times a week. Rather than take years off of my life, I brought in a trusted colleague with whom I had worked at Ruder Finn years before to handle HR at FutureBrand, which enabled me to work on one job, out of one location.

While focusing on creating and leading a great recruiting team, I started thinking more about the importance of diversity and inclusion (D&I), and the number of years our industry had been giving it lip service without significant action or accountability. I started reading about D&I best practices and arranging meetings with D&I leaders at companies that were making progress. After inundating my manager with multi-page memos about what we should be doing in this area, she asked if I would like to take on the role of D&I leader, which we would create. It was a no-brainer.

Once again I found myself balancing two full-time jobs: recruiting leader and D&I leader. One had to go. Another no-brainer. I enjoy leading recruiting teams, but diversity and inclusion is my life's work and legacy.

Along this journey, I've had amazing experiences, but have faced some of the challenges that can come with being a black woman in an extraordinarily homogeneous industry. Although there is undeniable bias in this business, it can be unconscious and definitely not as in-your-face today as it was years ago. When I started out in public relations, there were people of color who were told they could not work on

certain pieces of business because the client wasn't "ready."
We've come a long way since then. To wit:

Years ago, I worked in marketing communications at a
leading firm. The HR manager had a huge Confederate flag
on her wall. It was roughly the size of Montana. And she was
the only HR person there. I saw it as an interesting
indication of the attitudes in that company. Unfortunately, I
was right. Every day was an exercise in being
underestimated, unappreciated or misunderstood.

The stress of being in that environment for three years
actually made me physically ill. And when my doctor said,
"You need to leave. Just get out," I did. Ordinarily, I would
never have left a job without having another one lined up,
but it was worth it to avoid the serious surgery I was heading
for if I stayed.

I also worked for a company whose headquarters in the
South seemed to have been modeled on the mansion in
"Gone with the Wind," servants and all. When I went there
to meet the executive team for the first time, lunch was
served in the formal dining room by a maid dressed to bring
to mind Hattie McDaniel, who won an Oscar for her
portrayal of Mammy, Scarlett O'Hara's painfully devoted
domestic. I was beyond mortified, and it looked like she
was, too. The ugliness of that deliberate adherence to
stereotype and musings about what that woman's life might
have been like if not circumscribed by prejudice, stayed with
me for a long time.

Despite much progress, our country and our industry have a long way to go. In survey after survey, diverse PR practitioners report lack of equal access to jobs and opportunities to advance, being looked at with a sense that they don't bring as much to the table (a point proved every time someone talks about "lowering the bar" in a conversation about diversity), and being frequent targets of micro-aggressions.

Unconscious bias is at the root of unequal access to job opportunities and advancement for many multicultural professionals, and affects every aspect of business operations: sourcing, interviewing and hiring, talent development, choices about who is included in brainstorms and new business meetings, who runs accounts, and how inclusive thinking shows up (or doesn't) in our work.

Widely shared myths based on unconscious bias do daily harm to individuals, undermine group interactions and crush the innovation that diverse and truly inclusive environments can create. For example, the "angry black woman" trope, prevalent throughout media, transforms black women who speak with the normal range of human emotion into avatars of anger. One of the most infamously egregious examples is Alessandra Stanley's 2014 New York Times piece, which starts with, "When Shonda Rhimes writes her autobiography, it should be called "How to Get Away with Being an Angry Black Woman." To this day, many black women I know in this business, including senior executives, are very careful about the way they phrase their thoughts to white colleagues because they don't want to have their words discounted or not even heard because of the myth.

The psychological and emotional energy it takes for these women to think about what they want to say and how to say it in a way that can be heard by people who may assume anger is the background music of their lives is exhausting, demoralizing, counter-productive and potentially soul-crushing.

Everyone should be educated about unconscious bias and micro-aggressions. People can be thoughtless, condescending and hurtful without realizing it. Many people of color in this business speak privately about having experienced this. There have been times I have been spoken to as though I were an idiot in search of a village. But I know it's not about me. And I learned a very long time ago not to allow it to affect my sense of self in any way.

We need to be explicit about the behaviors we need to model, to exhibit what's acceptable and what isn't. Teaching people how to interview is critical because that's where careers and organizational change begin.

Early- and mid-career diverse practitioners often look for senior people of color as role models, but there aren't nearly as many as there should be. And if young people feel that there isn't a career path for them or they're not welcome, there's really no point in their staying. And so they leave. This is why retaining and developing diverse staff is one of the most important and urgent issues the industry faces today.

Diversity and inclusion is not an HR initiative. It's not an initiative at all; it's a strategic imperative, a leadership function, and everyone's job, every day. An organization's leaders must be accountable for diversity, equity and inclusion (DEI). Creating a diverse workforce and an equitable, inclusive environment in which people of all backgrounds can thrive is a job that starts at the top and belongs to everyone. Leaders need to make their senior managers accountable for creating inclusive workplaces. That means having DEI councils, having people engaged continuously in diversity, equity and inclusion — all the time. And I'm not talking just about people of color. Diversity without inclusion and widespread engagement is meaningless.

For many, many years I've heard accepted "wisdom" about not having enough diverse students in the pipeline. I do not see great difficulty with the entry-level pipeline. What I see is that we are not sufficiently intentional about bringing diverse people into the business, retaining them, and developing them into organizational and industry leaders.

This is connected to the notion of cultural fit: who "fits in" with the business and who doesn't. This is a very homogeneous business, racially and socioeconomically. People who do not come from the common background and understand the unwritten rules often have a bigger challenge getting in the door and becoming embedded in the group.

Business is moving faster and faster. This can make an unintentional underpinning of recruiting a search for people who are plug and play, limiting the considered talent pool to the usual suspects with whom potential colleagues are already familiar or easily comfortable because of shared experiences. While I understand the impetus for this thinking, it's unacceptable. It's not going to change the face of our business or give us the amped-up creativity an inclusive environment provides. If we want to communicate and engage with a world of stakeholders whose demographics are changing faster than ever, how can we possibly expect to do so authentically, appropriately and resonantly if we don't have people on staff who are representative of the evolving marketplace? It makes no sense.

The industry needs to do a better job promoting itself. We need to talk about the skills that are needed and the types of work we do that are beyond what some people may think of as traditional PR. If we want to attract the smartest students with a wider range of majors and interests, we need to tell them about the intellectual challenges and cutting-edge possibilities in this field.

We should be reaching out to high school students, too. The competition for great college graduates is intense. The earlier we can create engagement, the better off we will be.

My dream legacy is that my role will be obsolete because diversity and inclusion will have become such an integral part of who we are and what we do as an industry that it won't require a designated leader. It will be as natural as breathing.

Terry Edmonds

*Terry Edmonds is an executive speechwriter and
communications strategist. The former chief speechwriter for
President William Jefferson Clinton, Mr. Edmonds retired as
an executive speechwriter for IBM in 2018. He received a
Bachelor of Arts in English language and literature from
Morgan State University.*

When I graduated from Morgan State University in
1973, I didn't know anything about public relations. There
weren't any courses in public relations at Morgan or at most
universities at that time. I'd never even considered PR. I had
set my sights on a career in journalism. But even that was a
long shot. I think there was one journalism course at
Morgan State at that time, and I don't even know if I took
it.

After graduating, my goal was to scour the media
landscape in Baltimore. I went to every TV, radio and
newspaper in Baltimore to see if I could get a job as a
reporter, writer, on-air person — whatever I could do. But

those doors weren't open, and they weren't opening for me, for whatever reason. It was the early '70s and diversity in journalism was in its infancy. Public relations was a lot more receptive, and I quickly realized that journalism and public relations were very close cousins. One can't live without the other.

I got my first public relations job as a PR specialist with United Way of Central Maryland. That's where I learned the rudiments of public relations — how to write a press release, how to put together a newsletter, how to even become a photographer and do some graphic design.

United Way was very collegial and mission oriented. In fact, it resonated with my soul because from a young age I was interested in human service and helping others. It was a perfect fit for me because it let me do two things that I really wanted to do: writing, which is the primary skill needed in public relations, along with the opportunity to work on a mission to help others. I knew I had started out on the right path for my career.

In my early career I changed jobs many times. In addition to being recognized for the quality of my work, it wasn't that hard to get noticed as one of the few African-Americans in the profession at that time. And the appreciation for diversity was starting to grow. Within my first 10 years in the profession I had maybe five or six jobs. From United Way I became a public relations specialist at a local brewery. I was the first public relations director at the Maryland Science Center in Baltimore's Inner Harbor. I then moved to the Maryland Mass Transit Administration doing public relations for the city's bus and subway systems.

I was the first in my family to graduate from college. My mother was a waitress and my father was a truck driver. So I didn't have any professional role models in my immediate family. My mother was always a strong supporter of my interest in literature and writing and both my parents were very supportive and proud of the rise I was making in the profession.

As a public relations specialist at Maryland Blue Cross and Blue Shield, I tried my hand at media relations, another aspect of public relations that I hadn't done before. These were the days before the internet. Fax machines were rudimentary. Many times I recall having to hand deliver press releases. The profession has changed so much. I think it was much more personal back in those days. The idea was to get in front of the reporter's face, try to establish relationships, and make a personal pitch for coverage rather than just faxing or emailing a press release to the assignment editor. I did a lot of traveling around town, walking up steps and cajoling my way into newsrooms. It was a challenge and kind of fun doing it that way.

I didn't sense much adversity as an African-American PR professional in Baltimore. After all, Baltimore was a majority black city, and I think that we were gradually coming of age racially. Even though there were still not many African-Americans in public relations, people were beginning to accept diversity within the profession.

After Blue Cross, I became the first public relations director for the Baltimore ad agency, Trahan Burden & Charles. I was the only African-American professional in the agency. My job was to promote both the agency and its clients. But I think that after a while they decided that they wanted a more prominent person. After all, I didn't have many connections in the corporate arena. I do think that maybe there was a little bit of discomfort for them having an African-American in the position, so I transitioned out of that. But it was a great experience. I didn't harbor any ill will about it. I felt like it was just another move, another experience.

In the early '80s I went to Washington, D.C., to work at an African-American think tank called the Joint Center for Political Studies. That's where I really got more interested in politics and government. The organization was focused on monitoring and advocating for better economic conditions for African-Americans. They published monographs and white papers, and convened conferences focused on the plight of black America. They also published a book every so often listing every black elected official in the country. That really whet my appetite for the political world.

I went back to Baltimore to work for Congressman Kweisi Mfume. I had worked on his campaign for Congress, and when he won, he asked me to come and work for him in his Capitol Hill office. I became his press secretary. Working in the national political arena for the first time was an eye-opening experience. Our offices were in the ornate

Longworth Office Building. I helped the congressman compose his floor statements, his newsletter to constituents, and I wrote press releases.

After that I had several stints with small professional services firms around the Washington Beltway. These were mostly government contract companies hired to promote public sector initiatives — mostly health related. Earlier in my career, I also had the good fortune of working with a firm that is commonly regarded as a pioneer in the field of social marketing: Porter, Novelli and Associates. Again, I was the only African-American man while I was there.

I think more African-Americans would be in the profession if schools and colleges made greater efforts to recruit and prepare them. Many African-Americans don't consider public relations because they are not aware of the vast number of opportunities that exist. I think that's why I initially never considered it, in addition to the fact that there were no serious efforts to train African-American professionals back in the day.

Mentorship is also very important. It was an essential part of my success, especially in the early years when I was just learning the profession. Some of my early mentors were white. I am forever grateful to a man named J. Joseph Clark, who was the PR director of United Way at the time I worked there. He saw my potential and challenged me to reach it. I was also fortunate to be mentored by an African-American businessman named Raymond Haysbert. As one of the owners of Baltimore's Park Sausage Company, he led by example and was always willing to offer good advice. Other mentors who have helped me throughout my career included Dan Porterfield, who is now president and CEO of the Aspen Institute, and several civil rights luminaries, namely Vernon Jordan, Earl Graves and Marc Morial.

The highlight of my career began in 1993 when I joined the Clinton administration. I had been working for a Washington Beltway professional services firm, and was getting restless, when someone suggested I send my resume to the Clinton-Gore transition team. So I did.

I didn't expect anything to come of it, but my resume apparently popped up in the office of Donna Shalala, the secretary of Health and Human Services (HHS). I interviewed for a job as a speechwriter in her office. I got the job.

After two years of working as her deputy director of speechwriting, I was encouraged to apply for an opening at the White House. Of course I was flabbergasted, and I'm thinking, do I even want to apply for this? But I did. I got the job as a junior speechwriter for President Clinton and eventually worked my way up to be the chief speechwriter for the president.

Bill Clinton is a great leader, mentor and human being. As perhaps the most loquacious president in history, he kept his cadre of speechwriters very busy. The job took over our lives. And remember, this was before email. We were probably the first administration to get computers. We did have beepers, but we didn't have cellphones back then. It was a 24/7 job — sort of like being a fireman. You would get a call in the middle of the night and you had to come into the White House because of a crisis. The president needs to make a statement in one hour. So it was that kind of lifestyle. It was the most exhilarating, exhausting and rewarding experience of my life.

I started working for President Clinton in 1995 in the middle of his first term, and I worked for him throughout his entire second term. I even worked for his '96 reelection campaign. When you're a White House political appointee, as I was, you're precluded from doing campaign work. So they asked me if I would give up my White House job to work on the '96 campaign. It was implied that if Clinton won I could go back to the White House — they couldn't guarantee that, of course. But that's what I did. I got a chance to travel with him during the '96 campaign and help with his acceptance speech at the Democratic National Convention in Chicago. I was eventually promoted to assistant to the president and director of White House speechwriting, the first African-American to ever hold that title.

As chief speechwriter, I traveled extensively with the president on Air Force One.

Traveling and working on Air Force One was an especially unique opportunity. It's almost like being in your living room. There is a conference room in the middle of the plane and spacious legroom at every seat. The speechwriters even had our own little office in the back of the plane. I don't know how they did it, but you could fax things from the plane to the ground. To me that was amazing. I also remember that there was a private phone at every seat. During my first trip on Air Force One, I was informed that I could call anybody I wanted. I called my mother and said, "Guess where I am? I'm calling you from Air Force One! I am on the president's plane." And you know, she was overjoyed. And so was I that I was able to do that.

My assignment with the Clinton White House was a great inspiration to a lot of young people, and to my church, my community and even the African-American press. Ebony and Jet magazines did stories on me, as did the Baltimore Afro-American, The New York Times, The Washington Post and The Baltimore Sun.

After leaving the White House in 2001, I had several other interesting career experiences including serving as chief speechwriter for NASA Administrator Charles Bolden.

Throughout my career I have had many opportunities to speak to young people about what it took to rise from Baltimore's inner-city projects to the White House, and more than 40 years in public relations and speechwriting. Encouraging young people to fulfill their dreams remains my passion.

Damon Jones

Damon Jones is a global communications executive and reputation strategist who has served for 21 years at Procter & Gamble. In his current capacity, his responsibilities span corporate media relations, financial communications, influencer engagement, crisis prevention and rapid response, and social media, digital strategy and execution. He also served as director of press relations for the Democratic National Convention Committee in 2008. Mr. Jones received a Bachelor of Arts in communications, journalism and business administration from Xavier University.

My aspiration as an undergrad student was to be a journalist.

So my degree is in journalism; and it wasn't until I took a communications course later in my college career when I was, like, "Oh, there's this stuff called PR!"

I pursued print journalism and stayed in Cincinnati. There was this company called Procter & Gamble looking for people with journalistic skills to work in their PR department. I was, like, "Well, I wouldn't mind sticking around here! Let me give it a shot."

Also, I had discovered during that time that I had an interest in the business side of broadcasting. I'd done a number of interviews while I was a student, and was always intrigued by the business end of it. I had done an internship in the sales department and said, well, it's not quite sales, but just knowing how stuff happens from a financial perspective was always an interest.

From that perspective, I kind of fell into PR. I really enjoyed it. And it's been 21 years since.

My first job at P&G was doing traditional publicity for Tide, Mr. Clean and a couple of other cleaning brands. Now what do people really need to know about laundry detergent? Learning how to build brands and understanding the elements that went into that was a really good experience. I had to learn the story behind the story, and then be challenged in creative ways to get that story out.

So while my job was mostly a lot of traditional publicity work, events, "Media Relations 101," we had a number of interesting issues to deal with very early on in my career. I was intrigued by the complexity involved in running a successful business and the impact that communications could have on it. Over the course of my time with P&G, I've had opportunities to work in marketing and other parts of the business. But I have always been in love with the communications aspects. And that's where I decided to stay.

I was intrigued by what we were doing on Tide and Mr. Clean. We were rewarded for both our strategic thinking as well as the creativity. I enjoyed the variety of the work. I guess I wasn't expecting as much variety as that. It's one of the things that I love about communications: You can be dealing with an issue one day, and an opportunity the other day. And then there are other days when the phone rings at 5 p.m. and there goes your weekend.

I've always wanted to have different life and professional experiences. I thought I'd be at P&G for three years and then move on and do something else. But here I am, almost 21 years later. When I counsel younger people about looking for jobs, I say to talk about the experiences you want to have and then rely on people to help you get there. But don't define it by saying, "I want to do this for three years. I've got to be in this company, or I've got to be in this location," because life may take you on a different path. In my own career, for example, I've been in six cities and four countries on three different continents. Yeah, I wouldn't have anticipated that at all.

When people find out that you're good at something, sometimes projects will find you. But you have to be able to articulate what it is that you bring to the table, and then seek to match that up. But don't use labels like, "Well, I only do this or I do that," rather than, "Here are the skills I have. How can I apply those skills to different challenges that businesses or organizations might have?"

I've been fortunate enough to work for a number of individuals who have talked to me about the importance of carving out time to reflect on my career experience. What did I really like about that experience? What didn't I like? What are the lessons I learned from that? And then it's important to be open to sharing and having those discussions with people in a safe environment. It really allows you to benefit from the perspectives that other people have. That's something I don't think we spend enough time thinking about.

A number of the jobs that I've had at P&G weren't jobs that I even knew existed. But as people get to know you, they'll figure out what you enjoy and they'll help to match you up with different jobs. That's how I became involved in a number of nonprofit activities. If people understand what you're good at, how you work, what you're passionate about, then some of these opportunities might present themselves to you.

In our industry, we talk often about the value of networking for your career and personal growth. You also must be in a position to be open and receptive to whatever feedback you get.

I haven't done as a good a job as I would have liked in finding champions outside my company. I have a lot of agency partners who've become mentors to me. And they've been relationships that have grown out of experiences working together. But it is something that I can see being a challenge if you're not in a position where you're able to work with different people in different industries. You're going to have to work hard to put yourself in a position to do that. And so it's going to require you to invest in the time to make connections. You're going to have to work for it.

There is a low percentage of African-Americans and an even lower percentage of African-American men in our industry. There's always a challenge to ensure that your skills are seen in the broadest sense, because African-Americans are so few and far between, and it's easy for us to get pulled into projects that have to deal with diversity or multicultural issues.

And that can be a challenge if that is not a passion of yours. Do not let yourself get pigeonholed in places where you don't want to be.

The challenge in looking for colleagues in the business who looked like me was something that I struggled with. There were moments when I questioned whether I could be successful in an industry where people don't look like me. I don't know how significant a barrier that has been to my success, but it has been a challenge.

It forced me to build bonds with people and really look for that mutual support.

There was an agency at P&G pitching for business. My team was in a room getting it all set up. I happened to step outside of the room for a moment, and the agency people called me back in. They said that the AV equipment wasn't working. So I went back into the room and fixed it. Then someone from the agency said, "OK, we're going to get started now. Thank you for fixing that. You can leave."

I saw the reactions of the agency people who knew me. And it was just one of those, "Did that just happen?" moments. Needless to say, they did not get the business.

I don't know if there have been times when I've been specifically excluded from opportunities just because of my race. I've been fortunate enough to work with people who value the diversity and the expertise that I bring. Some of that comes with having a blue-chip company behind you. Being on the client side, you don't run into it as much. But you do feel pressure to perform at a higher level.

In PR, we deal in perception. Our business deals with how different people perceive the brands, the companies, the institutions we represent.

I think it goes beyond the whole "diverse people bring diverse perspectives and the more ideas we have the better we are." It's about nuance; and it's nuance based on actual experience. Whenever an agency walks in the door, they're not only pitching their experience, they're pitching the individuals they have to work on our account. Those individuals need to transfer their prior knowledge, experience and expertise into the current situation.

We need to look at so many of the decisions that we make through so many different lenses. As great as any group of individuals is, they all bring diverse perspectives. And race is a hugely important aspect of what we're dealing with in our country right now. It is a lens through which people are looking at politics and brands and corporations.

I think over time there won't be such a thing as multicultural PR. It will all just be the way brands engage and operate. When you look at all of the brands that have had missteps, they prove the value of having diverse people at the table. That's where I think companies and brands and agencies really need to make sure that they are not just having diverse perspectives but are able to integrate that perspective in an effective way. Flip-ups happen too easily. And they can happen because of the lack of diverse perspectives.

From an industry standpoint, I think the whole blend that we're seeing between paid, earned and owned as it relates to traditional PR continues to mean that we will need a very diverse set of skills. All of those things are melding together, so we're going to have to redraw the lines for how we typically organize corporate PR departments and agencies.

When I started my current role, we had a person on our team who was doing a lot of our visual and multimedia design. The way the process worked was we'd go off and we'd prepare a brief and we'd write a press release. And then we'd give him the press release and say, "Go design me some visuals to go along with this press release."

And what we realized was we were missing the visual inspiration as part of the creative process. So I think we'll be seeing a blending of all of those skills much earlier in the development of communications campaigns, and that way we get greater levels of creativity and integration.

Whether you are a traditional media relations or a digital person, whatever your skill set may be, you'll also be bringing with you certain points of view. That can be very helpful to us in forming insights about our audiences, whether millennial, multicultural, Gen Z, what have you.

I think we're going to have to develop that talent in different ways than we do now. We typically seek out people who are like us. We can judge good writing and good media relations because that's how we grew up in the industry. But now we've got to learn new ways of spotting talent. And then we may have to grow and develop that talent to build different skill sets.

The last person that I hired on my team was someone with an agency background, most recently was working with Tumblr, and has never worked in a traditional corporate environment. I had to help him learn how to be more effective in a corporate environment. But candidly, I hired him specifically because he had *not* worked in a corporate environment. So it's about taking that unique perspective of his, nurturing it and making sure not to erase those skills that we brought him in for.

There are all different types of diversity. Age has been very important because we need to communicate to the boomers at the same time we're talking to millennials. And while you could target in some ways — I mean your Facebook page is your Facebook page, the article in The

Wall Street Journal is an article in The Wall Street Journal — you're going to need to speak to all those audiences. So I think age diversity sometimes is underplayed.

There are people who write short-form content versus those of us who grew up mastering the art of long form. They are very different skill sets. We need to nurture that. Some of them are younger, some of them are older, some of them were born in other countries. We must fully embrace all their differences.

People recognize that they need to have the diverse-looking faces around the room. But there are still challenges in making sure all of those voices are heard equally.

I talk to people about how to develop younger, and in this case, multicultural talent. If Procter says, "Hey, we want a diverse team," then yes, we need our agency partners to bring us that diverse team. But we share in that responsibility to grow and develop them so they reach their full potential.

One of the things that I don't think we've gotten right is that I see many fragmented diversity initiatives. We need to connect these programs a lot better than we're doing. We need to focus more on the development at the mid- and more senior-career-levels, not just the recruitment.

How do we partner with certain schools of communication and develop classes of talented individuals? What is the equivalent of mid-career development opportunities that are agency or company agnostic? I think we could benefit from more of the cross-industry networking, and developing talent in more senior levels. I see a lot of it at the entry level, but just not enough at higher levels.

My advice to young people starting off in this business is to be open to feedback, to let people know that "Hey, I want to get better." This is why they feel good giving you feedback even when it's tough feedback. And they know that you're grateful for it, as opposed to the excuses, "Oh, that's why I did it that way." And it's hard sometimes in creative industries when it could be perceived that you are attacking their ideas. What you're doing is bringing forward a different point of view. Being open to feedback was probably the single best piece of career feedback that I've ever received.

You can get feedback from all sorts of people, not just your bosses. If you're receptive to that, in words and action, it opens up relationships and makes people more comfortable with you. And frankly, people will then become more vulnerable with you. Because if you can be more vulnerable, this leads to much more powerful interpersonal reactions.

As a more senior communications practitioner, the core product that I bring is advice and counsel. If I'm in a room with my CEO, I am only useful to the degree that he wants me in the room. When he no longer wants my guidance and counsel, I'm bringing no value.

The soft skills are incredibly important in our business, especially for our diverse talent, because a lot of those generational connections aren't there; that experience isn't there. When I'm mentoring, in fact, I would say that 75 percent of the time is spent on those soft skills.

People take knowledge and trust advice from people that they know and like. So getting to know people very well will help your work become more effective. I think that goes to developing close relationships with your colleagues and your clients and your staff.

I also advise young people to seek out as many new experiences as possible. Recognize that there's always more to be learned than just doing the job that you're asked to do.

If I could go back and give my younger self some advice, it'd be to have more fun along the way. Enjoy the work. Enjoy the people around you. Enjoy the ride.

Sheryl Battles

Sheryl Battles is the vice president, global diversity, inclusion and engagement, at Pitney Bowes, with responsibility for strategy and communications in those areas. She has been at the company for over 25 years. During her tenure, Ms. Battles has provided strategic communications counsel to the CEO, COO and other designated senior management in a range of communications areas, particularly in financial communications, thought leadership, crisis/issues management and diversity communications. She earned a Bachelor of Arts in human biology from Stanford University.

I grew up in a small town in Texas. My mother was an educator with a master's degree. My dad worked in a manufacturing environment.

I always say to people that my first communications job was communicating to my parents — after getting a Bachelor of Arts in human biology from Stanford — why I would not be going into medicine after I graduated. My educational focus at Stanford did, in many ways, prepare me to do a lot of what I do now. My area of concentration was using the media to implement health care systems. That taught me how to think about really complex topics, and be able to articulate them in language an audience could understand.

One of my projects was to script and produce a TV show to get people to stop smoking. I also developed a soap opera for a radio station around cardiovascular health. So, while it was all in the science realm, I was using communication to get the message through to the audience.

In my first job, I actually ended up having a very good relationship with my boss's boss. It wasn't by design. It was because he happened to have a daughter still in college who was a few years younger than I. She was interning for the summer. I identified with her as another young woman trying to learn about the working world, and I kind of took her under my wing. We became friends. But there were some others in the office who were dismissive of her, feeling that she was there only because she was the kid of some high-ranking executive. But I treated her as a human, as someone who had some good ideas. Well, my boss's boss took note of the relationship. Apparently, she went home each day telling him about how smart I was and what I was working on. So I had someone who was providing this whole different perspective of who I was. Had it not been for her, my boss's boss would never have known who I was, let alone the work I was doing. As a result, he was very supportive of me and my work in the company.

One of the things I did before working at Pitney Bowes was to run my own firm. I was very young and it was very challenging. My clients included a real estate developer, travel agency, a stockbroker, a municipality, and I did pro bono work for a church.

Throughout my professional journey, I worked for a variety of companies in different industries, different sizes. Early on, most of them were privately held. I've had the opportunity to learn all aspects of public relations and communications. And I sought those opportunities to practice my craft not only at work; I also sought them through volunteer opportunities as well.

I'm proud to have had such a rich variety of experiences — everything from media relations to internal communications to litigation communications to special events to strategic philanthropy to financial communications, diversity communications, executive communications, speechwriting — I've done it all.

Every organization is made up of people. And how you interface with people will determine to some extent your opportunities. Some of the conversations that most impact you in life happen in rooms where you are not, but your personal brand is. So when your name gets on the invite list for a meeting, there's some image or perspective of you that pops into people's heads. Your brand enters the room before you; and once you are there it influences the lens through which people assess your behavior and hear your ideas. After the meeting, people will walk away and say, "Yeah, I was just in this meeting with her, and she did XYZ." Perceptions about you and your value are shaped by all of these interactions, as people seek to see how your brand and your behavior are aligned.

Part of how you make connections that matter is through results. And it can be a Catch-22, because first you've got to have opportunity to show what kind of results you can deliver. Then when you do deliver, you've got to deliver results that add value. Then, hopefully, there'll be other opportunities coming up with your name on them.

It's really important that your network is multilateral. I have great relationships with everybody in the building, from the lady who makes the coffee all the way up to executive row. Networking is not just getting to know those you think you can learn from; you also need to network with people you think can learn from you as well. That means everyone has the potential to make a difference in your journey, no matter where they sit in the organization.

Every day, you have the opportunity to make it happen. And even now, later in my career, I'm getting to learn and do and think about very different things. That's been key throughout my life and career.

Being a person of color has overall been a good experience for me. But there have been challenging moments. I remember getting a call from an agency to come in for an interview. I walked into the reception area; I was pretty excited. I was in a new city. I couldn't wait to go after this opportunity. The receptionist asked who I was there to see and told me to have a seat. Then I heard the click clack of the heels of the woman coming to meet me. But when she realized that I was the person she was going to interview, the smile on her face practically disappeared. Then she extended her hand to me and said, "Oh, you looked so good on paper."

You can't judge an organization by the actions of one individual; you really can't. But there was something about how the receptionist looked at me, in addition to the interviewer's statement, that provided a clear indication that this was not an inclusive environment.

There's a lot of research out there about the business value of diversity. Years ago Pitney Bowes funded research at the Wharton School about the performance of diverse teams. What the research showed is that teams with more aspects of diversity among them might take a little more time to get the project done because they had to get used to each other's communication styles, work styles and preferences. But in the end they came up with a better solution.

The differences in experiences, approaches and thinking led to innovation and better problem solving. Thinking differently about what is possible and the way things work is what is reshaping industries and redefining the way we live. The question that organizations have to deal with today is their openness to embracing difference in order to produce better results. That is the power of diversity and inclusion. Inclusive organizations make room for different voices, perspectives and experiences to be respected, heard and make meaningful contributions to results.

When you look at the demographics of the world, we are in the most diverse interconnected marketplace in the history of commerce. So there is diversity coming from geography and culture, there is diversity of generation, there is diversity in terms of gender identification and orientation, there is diversity in terms of ethnicity, there is neurodiversity and disability, and it goes on and on and on. So whether an organization is actively seeking to include more diversity within its walls or not, it has to deal with the diversity of everyone outside of the organization that it needs to connect with, whether it's customers, decision makers, policymakers or regulators, or the talent that it needs to keep going further into to 21st century.

The communications industry has what I call both a pipeline issue and a promotion issue. The pipeline is who's coming in, and do we have a critical mass of diverse talent that looks at the communications industry and says, I am interested, and I am in. The promotion issue is a question of unlocking opportunity for those who are already in the industry. We're looking for more diversity in leadership in the communications industry. Part of the answer is sitting right there in our organizations today. While this is not unique to the communications industry, the closer you get to the top, the less diverse it becomes. As an industry, we have to ask ourselves what's happening in our industry today to prevent more of our diverse talent from making it to the top? Are we getting the most out of everybody in the room?

What can happen with diverse talent tends to be due to one or some combination of three factors. One is visibility: Who knows you're there? Another is opportunity: Do you have an opportunity to demonstrate what you know, how you think and what you can do? And the third is senior advocacy: Who is actually going to be your advocate in that room when a decision is being made about the next opportunity or promotion?

I was raised to believe that for people of color, everything you say and everything you do will be assessed and analyzed by a higher standard. It was common for parents to say to children, "Look, you are going to have to be better than anyone else when you walk in that room." It's something that I've carried with me all my life. Yes, I am known as an overachiever. And if that's the worst thing that you can say about me, then I have done a good job. If I could go back and tell my younger self what to say to the woman who implied I was more desirable on paper, I would answer, "That's nothing compared to how much better I am in person!"

Lisa Chen

Lisa Chen is the head of internal communications, distribution and go-to-market, Google Cloud. Previously, she was a senior director of employee and executive communications at Sabre and a vice president of change communication at ADP. Prior to that she worked with diverse companies including Mars Chocolate, Rolls-Royce and US Airways. She's lived abroad with work assignments in Belgium and the UK. Additionally, she is a Page Up member of the Page Society. Ms. Chen received a Bachelor of Arts in liberal arts from the University of Virginia and a Master of Arts in communications from Johns Hopkins University.

It has always been my goal to feel like I can be myself at work. I want to believe that there is an equal standard for people who appear to not be like the rest in the room, as I often represent a different background than those around me.

When I first walk into a meeting, sometimes the first thing that hits me is that I'm the only person who looks like me. But I typically forget that quickly. I know that the value I bring as a communicator is equal to anybody else. And just like everyone else in the room, I have to earn the right to be listened to and for my opinion to have impact. It may be harder if there is bias in the room. But it's not something that has been in the forefront of my thought process throughout my career. I focus on what I have to offer: my experience and perspective.

To be fair, I haven't always thought this way. In one of my earlier corporate jobs with a powerhouse female CCO, I spent the first couple of weeks trying to dress like the senior women in the room. I was focusing so hard to look like them and blend in with the team. But you see, I'm a very colorful person, and one day when I was in the boardroom with the entire executive team the morning of a major announcement, thinking about whether I should be wearing beige or neutral colors or not, I realized that as a person of color I already did have the most color in the room despite what I wore. And so, instead of worrying about superficial things like if I'm wearing bright, vibrant colors, I needed to think about how I'm contributing. And I stopped worrying about blending in with the other people around me; it was a futile attempt.

That's just the start to how I may be perceived as different. Since my last name is Chen, people are often thrown off when they first meet me. They're expecting an Asian-looking person in appearance. Instead, in walks a black woman. Technically, they see an African-American with Chinese heritage from my father (African-Asian-American). When new people first meet me, they are always trying to figure out what I am. I can see the reaction. I can see shock and confusion. I work past that. And as I get to know people on a personal level, I happily explain my heritage — just not when we're in the boardroom, as I don't believe anyone else explains their heritage upon introduction.

Throughout my career I've seen diversity programs that are great, and some that I perceive as non-value added. So I've been a bit cautious about them until I understand their vision and remit. Early in my career I worked at a company — a very small think tank — and there was a group of diverse employees who were trying to make the case for diversity in an environment where we were clearly in the minority. And what was frustrating and made me turned off by it was that the leadership did not appreciate the cause that these diverse employees were trying to argue — essentially, not enough to put any investment or leadership support behind it. Rather than try to hit my head against the wall, I decided that this was not a place I could flourish in, if they could not understand the benefits of supporting diversity.

In another company, the diversity programs were well established, but they had the reputation of being social events, party time. They received liberal funding. There was leadership support, but nobody really knew how diversity was affecting the bottom line, and there was overt resentment, including derisive comments, from those who felt they were included in these groups, which made it uncomfortable to celebrate my participation.

I think the perfect example of that I've experienced was at ADP. Yes, there were fun times around events such as Black History Month, Hispanic Heritage Month, Pride Month and so forth. There was that social and celebratory aspect. But they also shared and demonstrated how these groups contribute to the company's business success: recruiting, retention, brand awareness, partnerships. And those are the types of groups to which I want to contribute.

These successful groups make it possible to know people who are from different parts of the business. There is a real advantage when you are brought together and it's cross-title, cross-business unit, cross-location, and it's an internal network that you can draw upon that allows you to learn from others, make connections or actually help others learn.

In my career, I have felt more different being a woman versus being a *black* woman, per se. I've been in all-male environments, and while it's not overt sexism, I've felt like I'm not part of the boys' club, and it takes work to fit in with the crowd. In those circumstances where I don't feel naturally included, I try to find a few individuals with whom I have something in common. I'm not trying to win over the entire group. I'm trying to get to know a few people more substantively and build from there.

I would be remiss in saying that I had not heard things that were borderline racist, or offhand comments that lack sensitivity to diversity; I certainly have. And when it's happened, I addressed it individually and got to the heart of it. Usually we learned from the experience. I'm fortunate that those challenging conversations have always yielded a positive outcome and rarely is there discomfort on my part after the discussion.

Diversity and inclusion issues are gaining more visibility now. The situation isn't necessarily getting worse. But in a social media type of world, considering how quickly things move, when people make blunders, it's likely because they didn't have a diverse panel of people reviewing certain ad campaigns, marketing strategies or social media posts that are going out from senior leaders. Perhaps it's not that there are more incidents, they're just more public and more visible. What shocks me is that there isn't faster change to make sure that there is a diverse internal team reviewing things that go external, because it can be a huge, huge, risk to a company's brand. That's the bottom line. Some of the mistakes that I'm seeing out there are just astonishing to me (and shareholders)!

Sometimes there's absolutely no sensitivity. And I have to wonder if there weren't diverse voices that felt they had a safe space to speak up about it. I think that's something that needs to be evaluated, because psychological safety in group environments may prevent someone from saying, "Hold on! I think there may be a problem. Let's take a minute and think about this, discuss it, test it." If you're a diverse person in that room and you don't think you can speak up, or you're not listened to, what's the point of being there in the first place?

Increased diversity continues to be a huge opportunity in the PR/communications field. I'm oftentimes still the only person of color in the room. We have to try to understand the motivations for why people like me choose this field.

Many of our parents were first-generation college graduates. And traditionally, a lot of our families were pushing us into professions like medicine, law, accounting — careers that are very straightforward and don't have as much subjectivity. You know, if you aced your exams in med school, then you're going to become a doctor and you can work from anywhere and work independently quite easily. If you're accepted in a corporate environment, having your voice heard, your writing/project management respected and your ideas appreciated is more subjective.

We need to study how to provide an avenue for people who are first thinking about what they are going to major in, in college, and then see what opportunities are there for them. Future professionals need to see diverse leadership teams in the companies that they're exploring so that they know those positions are possible for them as well. The leaders should also be seeking future communications talent at the high school level in programs like INROADS, a program that facilitated a four-summer HR internship for me at Fidelity Investments. It was an invaluable experience; however, there was no mention of corporate communication opportunities, and the field was never discussed versus careers in engineering, finance and sales. That program has excellent opportunities for young people to be exposed to minority professionals who were at the top of their game — and at the top of the communications game.

At Page, I am encouraged by the inclusion of diverse members. I think they have been forward and transparent about the desire to be more diverse. But to be successful, they've got to start with people who are junior in their careers, support them on a path, and help get them to those positions that make them Page Up and Page-eligible. You can't start when somebody is at a director level at a company. You have to start earlier.

We should look at the programs that are successfully reaching students at a high school level, like STEM. You've got to start in the middle school to high school range. One way to present this field's value to these kids might be to talk about the many racially insensitive marketing mistakes we talked about earlier. We should explain to these future communicators why things like that happen — that the right filters were not put in place — and how we need more diverse people in the business to stop these disasters from continuing. That's a good way to show the value that a diverse perspective could have in preventing these things from happening in the future. I mean, you've got a generation that is very used to having its voice heard through social media. This generation understands all the things that could go wrong — all the dire consequences — when a company posts or tweets or airs a racially insensitive message.

When I was first starting out, I had absolutely no role models in the business. I did not see a woman of color in leadership until at least seven or eight years into my career. But I was fortunate to see a lot of strong women in the communications field in general, though I always found it ironic that there was often a man at the head of the corporate communications function. There were some exceptions to that, but, yeah, it definitely let me know that there were opportunities, and I did feel like there were really no limits to how far I could go. But again, for someone to bring your whole self to work, it's something that needs to be improved.

Another essential key to my success has been having sponsors and not just mentors. A mentor is a person you go to with the good, the bad and the ugly. The sponsor is the person who most likely just sees the good. They are in the room making decisions that affect you when you're not there, like promotions and project assignments. The sponsor is the one who'd say, "I think you should give this project to Lisa. I think she can handle it."

I've had a lot of sponsors in my life, some that I know of and some that I might not have known of at the time. And they all have come from different backgrounds. I've had Caucasian males, Hispanic women, leaders who were raised in other countries, etc. Just knowing that there are people who are going to speak up for me is very reassuring. With sponsors, you need to be clear on your goals and clear on what you can offer so that those opportunities can happen for you. But with sponsors, sometimes you will never know that they are advocating for you — so view all senior leaders as potential sponsors; always bring your A-game.

Today we are starting to recognize there's no single straightforward way to get to the top. There are curves and turns and people behind the scenes. It's a combination of things. You have to work hard, but you also have to work smart and understand how the system works. I don't think you should change yourself for it, but I think you should figure out what parts of the system you want to follow and lean into. And if there are parts of the system you are not fond of, there's no reason to change for that.

I hope that in my new position at Google I am able to serve as a role model for junior communicators coming in and for them to realize that there is a place for them as they move up in their career. I'm at a pivotal point in my career, a place where I know it's not just what I take from a job or what I take from mentors, it's what I'm giving back.

And that is very important to me because there have been so many people instrumental in getting me to where I am today. It's been a team effort. And so it is my responsibility to do that for others.

D&I is a part of all of our jobs. It's making sure that my leaders are communicating their expectations around D&I,

and what I am doing to bring diverse talent into my organization by being a role model. I want to discover what my own biases are, overcome them, and ensure that I'm doing things objectively and taking the opinions of others around me into consideration when we are hiring new talent.

Beyond having diversity, we need to feel like our voice is heard and appreciated; that we're included. I've learned about inclusive environments; there have been plenty of times when I may have assumed that everybody knows what I'm talking about, whether about culture, music, politics or some rock bands from the past. I have a funny story about not being familiar with Freddie Mercury — and admitting it out loud. My well-intended colleagues never let me live it down. Rest assured, now I know him quite well. It makes me keenly aware that in almost every situation, somebody's going to be left out, and it's our job as communicators to say, "Are you with us? Do you understand what I'm talking about? Do you have the context?"

Being a diverse communicator may make me a more intuitive communicator. I have been in situations where I had been left out, and I am constantly trying to figure out ways that everybody in the organization, from the entry-level employee to the senior leader, can feel that they belong. I think I have an antenna for that based on the experiences that I've had.

There are studies that show that having diverse leadership teams and boards yields companies that are more successful financially for their shareholders. But in terms of just wanting to have an environment where people can bring themselves to work in their full self, so they're giving their best ideas to problems, challenges or consumer issues, I think people want to get the best of their employees and they want their employees to feel engaged. And if you don't feel included and you are not engaged, I don't see how a team is going to get the best solution.

The moment that you feel like you're welcome, contributing and creating value, that's when the magic starts. That's when we feel like we can make a career out of our job or a specific company. When we bring our whole self to work it benefits shareholders, leaders, colleagues and ourselves. It's a win-win for everyone, and I'm committed to sharing that more broadly.

Mike Fernandez

*Mike Fernandez has served as a senior executive with five
large U.S. companies including Cargill, Cigna, Conagra and
State Farm Insurance. In 1996, he became the first U.S.-born
Latino to serve as a chief communications officer of a Fortune
500 company when he was tapped for that role at US West.
Most recently, he was the U.S. CEO of Burson-Marsteller. His
early career was in politics where at 23 he became the youngest
person ever to serve as a press secretary to a United States
senator, when Ernest F. "Fritz" Hollings hired him. Mr.
Fernandez received both a Bachelor of Arts in government and
a Master of Science in accounting from Georgetown
University.*

It was October 1983 in Des Moines, Iowa. The annual
Jefferson-Jackson Day Dinner was drawing lots of activity
and notice as the 1984 Democratic presidential hopefuls
looked to gain some early advantage in Iowa's first-in-the-
nation caucuses. I was there with my candidate and boss,
Senator Fritz Hollings of South Carolina, who remarkably

came in third in the straw vote that evening behind
Minnesota's Walter Mondale and California's Alan
Cranston, and as a consequence became *the* story the next
day. The Day One story was how Fritz Hollings had
surprised the pack that also included Senator and heroic
astronaut John Glenn of Ohio, Senator Gary Hart of
Colorado, Florida Governor Reuben Askew and civil rights
activist Jesse Jackson. David Yepsen, the political writer for
the Des Moines Register asked for a one-on-one interview
with Senator Hollings and we obliged. In the prep for the
interview, the Senator and I talked about taking the high
ground, being upbeat and saying that the evening's result was
a sign that our message was resonating with an increasing
number of voters. But reporters do not always ask questions
in the way you hope they will. Mr. Yepsen started with,
"Senator, that was quite a showing last night. Why didn't
you do better?"

Rather than staying positive, my guy went south.
Hollings muttered that Mondale had won because he
brought people in from neighboring Minnesota — his home
state — and that Cranston had come in second because he
had secured a lot of early union support and brought in labor
supporters from out of state. And then he supplied the line
that would drive the Day Two coverage and test my mettle
as press secretary for the next three weeks. He said the act
of bringing in supporters from out of state "was like bringing
in a bunch of wetbacks."

My phone lines lit up. This was not a normal media crisis. As one of a very few Latinos on Capitol Hill in those days, I found myself in a situation where I had to manage my out-of-touch boss who not only had offended a growing population of voters, he had inadvertently offended me.

And yet I felt an obligation to help my boss both navigate and mitigate the situation. We developed an apology and I put him on the phone with and scheduled one-on-one and group meetings with virtually every national Latino leader, where he expressed that he was sorry about his insensitive choice of words and that he desired more and direct dialogue to better understand the issues that mattered most to the Latino community. Hollings would drop out of the race after getting just 4 percent in the New Hampshire primary, but he would go on to be an influential vote for immigration reform when the Simpson-Mazzoli bill came to the floor of the U.S. Senate in 1986.

What kept me focused then and throughout my career were words of encouragement from my grandfather, Guillermo Fernández. One: *Keep learning.* That aspiration included me being the first in our family to earn a college degree. But it was much broader; it was about probing to better understand the world or a given situation. And two: *Never forget who you are and where you came from.* This second thought was multifaceted as well. It was about taking pride in who you are; it was appreciating the unique perspective that one's upbringing permits; and it was never forgetting one's humble beginnings as you interact with others. In short, bring your whole self to a job and strive to understand the perspective of others.

While working on Capitol Hill, the learning would continue both on the job and in the classroom. I enrolled at Georgetown University and through night and weekend classes earned a Master of Science in accounting so that I would better know the language of business. That, combined with my political and government experience, would set the course for a career helping organizations grow and navigate challenging issues.

After several years working in various public relations and marketing positions at Eastman Kodak Company, I was hired into my first chief communications officer role at US West, the leading telecommunications player at the time in 14 Western and Midwestern states. The person who hired me was its CEO, Solomon Trujillo, who at the time was only one of three Fortune 500 CEOs who were Latino. Key to getting the job was my marketing experience in a highly competitive industry, my understanding of technology and my work with Fritz Hollings, who was the leading Democrat in the Senate Committee on Commerce, Science, and Transportation, and who had helped shape the Telecommunications Act of 1996, which set a new regulatory framework for the industry.

The new Telecommunications Act, while opening up the marketplace and encouraging faster deployment of new technologies, would be disruptive for the many workers at Baby Bells (former AT&T regional operating units that were spun off as separate companies) like US West. Sol Trujillo knew that our next labor negotiations with the Communications Workers of America, as a consequence, would be both different and difficult. So, early in 1998, he convened his top executives to discuss the likely bargaining issues and to review what had happened with recent labor negotiations both inside and outside our industry.

As we did, my grandfather's mantra was in my head — keep learning (keep probing) and remember who you are and where you came from (understand others).

That probing, that learning, led us to take a very different approach. Other companies, when asked to comment about labor union positions or claims, would coldly state that they negotiated at the bargaining table, not in the media. We would change the game by putting ourselves in a position to speak thoughtfully about the issues once the union had gone to the media with its perspective.

But the most dramatic change occurred in understanding that labor unions are first and foremost about representing people. If we were to be successful not just with the negotiation, but most importantly with the growth and future of the company, we needed to speak more directly to the heads and hearts of the people represented by the union. Our mantra was: We negotiate with the union, but love our employees and see them as key to our future.

My career would take many interesting twists and turns and expose me to the worlds of financial services, insurance, health care and food. I would, in the course of that journey, help companies navigate issues associated with corporate restructuring, financial challenges, workplace violence, product recalls, service outages, environmental spills, and responses to 9/11 and Hurricane Katrina. Through it all, being an active learner and striving to understand others would be key.

Not all of this was about playing defense or starting from a point of conflict or crisis. At Cigna, my team and I used our understanding of women and others who transitioned in and out of the workforce to recommend to Congress catch-up provisions in 401(k) programs that allowed people to set aside more money in their retirement plans when they reached the age of 50 to help make up for time outside the workforce, and those provisions were enacted into law in 2001.

At Conagra Foods (which is now known as Conagra Brands), after the company had made some 90 acquisitions in 10 years, we noticed that we had work to do to drive alignment across more than 150 plant sites. One element was not quite understood at first. We did not only have a lot of new and different brands under one roof, we had a much more diverse workforce than we had 10 years prior. Many of our employees spoke Spanish, Vietnamese, Hmong, and Somali, among other languages. So we developed a multilingual plant communication program that not only drove alignment, it improved morale, retention and productivity.

At State Farm, along with our head of marketing Pam El (an African-American female who is now the chief marketing officer for the National Basketball Association), we developed unique programs that connected with diverse audiences — from the "50 Million Pound Challenge" (a health-focused effort in the African-American community) to State Farm's "es Para Mí" (a program focused on helping Latinos through the process of becoming U.S. citizens), and others — and grew State Farm's market share among diverse markets.

All that said, probably the most complex challenge, one of the most rewarding and one that is most emblematic of following my grandfather's sage advice is how at Cargill we transformed our relationships with environmental activists, while better serving our customers' needs and in some small way changing the world for the better.

At Cargill, we decided to change the game by listening to and openly working with a host of stakeholders from farmers to customers, NGOs, and even our harshest critics. It has led to an approach where the company requires specific environmental and labor practices of its farmers and suppliers, and if there was backsliding, the company discontinued the relationship and sought other suppliers.

Where issues arose between various stakeholder groups, we established what we called "learning journeys," whereby Cargill would host a visit to each of the places of concern and help drive a conversation afterward to identify shared beliefs and an agreement about next steps. We would apply this approach beyond the sourcing of soy in Brazil to food security issues in Africa, food safety issues in China, and environmental supply chain issues with palm oil in Southeast Asia.

This shift to corporate activism, where we assumed we do not have all the answers and strove to better understand our critics, not only improved the relationship with environmental groups, it also led to greater transparency that many of our stakeholders appreciated. It led to increased sales with many of our customers like Unilever, Coca-Cola and Mars. And it enhanced Cargill's reputation as it became the first private company to be included in Fortune magazine's list of Change the World companies and led to many other recognitions and awards including PRWeek's Global Campaign of the Year in 2014.

Could all of these successes over the last three decades have happened without my diverse background? Sure. Were they more likely to have happened as a result of my diversity? Absolutely.

And there's plenty of data that indicates this is not just my experience.

Ronald Burt, a sociologist who teaches at the University of Chicago's Booth School of Business, has produced several studies over the years that suggest that people with more diverse sources of experience and information consistently generate better ideas.

Economists Sara Fisher Ellison of MIT and Wallace
Mullin of The George Washington University published a
study two years ago in the Journal of Economics &
Management Strategy that shows "mixed-sex teams" actually
produce more creative solutions than those dominated
exclusively by men or dominated exclusively by women.

And a CEB workforce study suggests that in a more
diverse and inclusive organization: individual discretionary
effort improves by 12 percent; intent to stay improves by 20
percent; and team collaboration and commitment improve
by nearly 50 percent.

As a consequence, through the years I have sought to
hire, develop and promote diverse talent as well. And I am
proud that much of that talent has gone on to make their
own mark on other organizations, serving as CMOs, CCOs
and in other leadership roles, and that PRWeek honored
Burson-Marsteller on my watch with its Diversity
Distinction in PR Award for work we had been doing there.
I also have served on the boards of many organizations
dedicated to greater diversity.

But there is much more to do.

Yes, there has been a lot of change since I became a
chief communications officer in 1996. But is the pace of
change fast enough? There are clearly more Latino, Asian
and African-American CCOs today, yet they represent only
about 6.5 percent of all leadership in the PR community at a
time when these populations account for about 35 percent of
the U.S. population.

Those of us leading agencies and departments need to move beyond pledging support for diversity and inclusion — and just do it. Reduce the cost of candor on the issue of diversity. Don't just hire diverse talent; provide an environment where they can thrive. Set goals and hold key management accountable to deliver the diverse teams that will better meet the needs of clients and customer.

And when it comes to young diverse talent, we need them to be the owners of their career and not the victims. We need them to find mentors, not wait for someone in HR to assign one. And we need them to become masters of their craft. After that it comes back to my grandfather: *Keep learning* and *never forget who you are and where you came from.*

Indeed, turn your birth circumstance and your experience into a competitive advantage. Speak up, provide your point of view, bring the value add of your whole self to your job every day, and provide the unique perspectives that only someone like you can share. Those kinds of insights over time will be valued and rewarded.

My father was one of nine kids in a family that grew up in Spanish Harlem in New York City. I was the oldest of the next generation. The consequence of my birth is that I received a lot of attention from my grandfather. At times, that came with pressure to set an example (like the thought that I needed to graduate from college), but it was mostly a blessing. When he died, he left me his wedding band. I wear one ring on my left hand that my wife gave me. I wear another on my right hand that was my grandfather's and is a constant reminder to never stop learning and to never forget where I came from.

Brenden Lee

*Brenden Lee is on the communications team at Twitter.
Previously he was in the communications and public affairs
department at the National Football League. Mr. Lee received
a Bachelor of Arts in communications studies at West Chester
University of Pennsylvania, and a Master of Science in public
relations from Syracuse University. He volunteers his time to
Manhattan Sports Business Academy and the Liberty
Humane Society.*

I don't think I realized growing up that I liked to write.
But I was always writing, and it came very naturally to me.
Writing is something that has carried me through my entire
life. Even if I'm not writing for a specific project or purpose,
there are a lot of times when I'll just sit and write and put
thoughts down on paper to get them out. It's something I
still really enjoy doing.

I grew up a huge sports fan, and going to high school
and early college I wanted a career in sports. I studied
undergrad at West Chester University of Pennsylvania and

initially was a sports management and accounting major. I had a buddy in my freshman or sophomore year, a roommate who one day said, "I'm going out to try out for the school radio station." And I said, "Oh, wow. I'll tag along with you."

I was immediately drawn to radio and communications. I switched my major to communications, and while I thought I wanted to go the TV or radio route, I didn't want to end up working for some tiny radio or TV station in the middle of nowhere, like many kids do when they first start out. So I looked into different options. I got a PR internship with the Philadelphia Soul of the Arena Football League, and ended up loving communications and public relations. I've been doing PR ever since.

After college, I worked for a year at the Philadelphia Eagles and then landed a job at the National Football League.

The NFL was great in terms of the incredible projects I got to work on, events that most people never get near — like the Super Bowl and the Pro Bowl — and traveling internationally. But my experience at the NFL was very buttoned up, very corporate — very traditional compared to where I am now.

I started working at Twitter in October 2016. Twitter has a very entrepreneurial atmosphere. The culture is young, creative and constantly changing. I sit on the communications team, leading sports communications for the platform. We have a sports partnerships group that works with professional teams, college teams, players, anything you can think of in sports. And they sign deals with those teams and individuals, and work with them to use the platform more effectively. Any way they use Twitter, they're in contact with us. So basically, any activation in sports that they're working on is what I'm promoting and doing PR around.

Twitter is a very diverse place. The company is passionate about making sure that there is diversity not only of people but of thought, of different experience levels and backgrounds. It's been great.

Earlier in my career, when I worked in organizations that were less diverse, I didn't necessarily feel an explicit or outward bias. But I think there is always group-think to an extent when you're in the room with folks who all have the same background and you're the only minority. It's tough to get people to see your perspective on things.

For instance, during my time with the Eagles, I was working with players who are much more diverse than the business community. The players on the team were mostly African-American, and there was often a disconnect between how the players think about things compared to how the NFL as an organization thinks about things. Having a bit of both perspectives gave me a unique look at the business.

I don't think I've been faced with any sort of implicit discrimination during my career. But I think there are always thoughts that have crossed my mind about opportunities I may have missed; or I wondered, "Am I not moving up because of certain things?" But I don't think there is any particular experience that I can point to.

It's great to see that the PR industry is becoming more diverse, not only minority and ethnic diversity but in making sure there are different perspectives from young and old, and from different cultures. When I studied at the S.I. Newhouse School of Public Communications at Syracuse University, there were so many people from overseas. It was great to see that as well.

At Twitter, diversity is something that is top of mind for Jack Dorsey, our CEO, all the way down to HR and communications. Everybody cares about diversity and makes sure it's not just a check mark in a box, but it's actually a part of the culture. We have employee resource groups — Blackbirds, TwitterAsians, TwitterMoms, TwitterAlas, TwitterWomen, TwitterOpen — basically, any group that you can think of where people feel included, feel like a part of the community. That's definitely part of our culture.

It's refreshing to work in an organization where everybody feels included, and if they don't, there's an openness to make changes happen.

As far as attracting more diverse students into the field, one of the tough things is that there's an ambiguity about what PR is. When people think of communications, they naturally gravitate toward TV and radio. That's where they flock to. In PR and comms, we can probably do a better job promoting what we do, how we do it and how we have a role in shaping the messaging of companies.

But we also have to talk about PR people having a seat at the table, and especially, how important it is for minorities to be included at that table. The boardrooms need to hear the perspectives of diverse professionals.

I have had some mentors, most of them having been white men. I think what's definitely lacking in our industry are older men and women of color, people you can go to and speak about what you've been through. I think they are so few and far between that there's a feeling that they're too busy or too high up to approach. That's been a challenge for me — just building the confidence to reach out to a CCO and say, "Hey, I'd love to pick your brain about something ..." It's almost that I don't want to bother them, or I feel like I'm not worthy of their time.

In the same way that I've looked to mentors throughout my career, sometimes a student will reach out to me for advice. Advising them is one of the things I love doing, whether I am giving them 15-to-20 minutes on the phone or grabbing coffee with them. I remember, especially on the sports side of things, that it's very tough to get in the door. A lot of folks are busy. They don't have time or they never respond to you. I like to pay it forward because I remember what it felt like to reach out to somebody and not get a response. And so I always try to make time for responding as best I can. Especially if they're alums of Syracuse and Newhouse or West Chester University; I try to make sure I get back to them and let them know that there's a sounding board for them. I'm here to listen or help or give advice.

One piece of advice I've given is, "You don't get what you don't ask for." You've got to be assertive and ask for different things you want, whether it's a new opportunity or the chance to work on a project or to let people know what you're interested in. People are busy, so if they don't know what you're interested in, they can't help you. Or if you have a creative idea you'd like to try, tell people about it. Those types of things, I've found, make a big difference. If you're never going to say anything, you're never going to get anything.

When I was trying to break into the profession, there seemed to be a lot of opportunities that were of the "minority fellowship" variety. I rejected those opportunities because I didn't want to be known as the minority candidate in the office. I wanted to be seen as a qualified individual. Organizations need to find a way to unearth those candidates without labeling them to check off that box.

I'll say this: I've heard a lot of times in my career from friends and colleagues, whether they were joking or not, "You're the whitest black person I know." That has always frustrated me because why does being an educated African-American mean that you're synonymous with being white? Breaking down attitudes like that will go a long way in helping the comms and PR profession, and society in general.

I've heard that line so much. You know, most of the time you just know folks are joking. But even to those people I'll say, "You know, my grandmother went to college, my great grandmother also went to college. Both my parents went to college and both have degrees. My mother is a successful engineer, and my father has had a long career in pharmaceutical marketing. And I went to grad school."

Those attitudes need to change. And a lot of people don't even realize that's what they're saying to me. I've got friends who have stopped saying that because they understand how I feel. Having others understand that perspective will go a long way.

At Twitter, we recently went through an unconscious bias training program and spoke about things like this. Our leadership wants to be sure that what our colleagues are saying and how they're saying it is delivered in a way that contributes to a welcoming culture. And the funny thing is the organizations that routinely go through these trainings are the ones that probably don't need it as much as other organizations that do. There are companies that only do diversity training so they can check a box.

I think, generally, white people have an uneasiness about saying the wrong thing, so they may decide not to say anything at all. But that's not good either. So obviously, communication can get better on both sides.

Sometimes these conversations can get heated, especially online. For example, my wife is white, and she'll see a minority say something about white people on

Facebook and say how unfair it is for her to be grouped in with those white people. And black people don't feel it's fair to be automatically grouped together for the same reason.

But these conversations need to be had in order for us to make progress. Open communication is so important as our industry continues to make strides in the right direction.

Pallavi Kumar

Pallavi Kumar is a full-time professor in American University's School of Communication and the director of the Public Communication division. Prior to teaching full time, Ms. Kumar served as a vice president in FleishmanHillard's social marketing practice in Washington, D.C., a vice president in Ketchum's health care practice in New York, and as an associate director of international public relations at Wyeth Pharmaceuticals in Philadelphia. Ms. Kumar received a Bachelor of Arts in public communication and public affairs from American University and a master's in corporate communications/public relations from Georgetown University.

I was very entrepreneurial as a kid. In sixth grade I became an Avon representative — the youngest sales rep in Western Pennsylvania. I started selling Avon cosmetics in school to girls who had just started wearing makeup. I had lipstick samples I would set up in the morning in homeroom. Everybody was excited to try my samples. I did pretty well because preteen girls loved to experiment with cosmetics. It was a great experience for me because it helped me understand audience targeting and customer demand, which, of course, are critical in PR.

I came to American University in 1990. I was going to work on Capitol Hill like every other political science major. Once I started taking some poli sci classes, though, I realized they were not my passion. I then happened to attend a Career Center panel and heard from a recent alum in the field. When I learned about what PR entailed — strategy, creativity and writing — I realized it was everything I like to do and it was what I was good at. So I decided to double major, and it was the best decision I made.

My parents didn't understand what public relations was. I don't even think to this day my mother quite understands it. As an Indian-American, that was not a career you get exposed to. Most of the kids I grew up with in our Indian community became doctors, lawyers or engineers. My sister went into business. Those were careers everybody could understand. But PR?

My dad is Indian, but grew up in Uganda. In 1972, the year that I was born, Idi Amin decided to expel all Asians from the country. My dad was one of the many whose whole family was forced to leave. We came to the United States as refugees.

My dad actually didn't meet me until I was almost a year old because I was in India with my mom and sister when the expulsion took place. It took that long for us to come here from India. It was very complicated.

One of the reasons we were able to come to the U.S. was because we had a family connection in Western Pennsylvania. There was a big Indian community in Pittsburgh thanks to the H1B1 visas, and the demand for scientists, engineers and doctors. And since Carnegie Mellon was there along with the University of Pittsburgh and Westinghouse, Pittsburgh became a thriving Indian community. We were lucky to have two temples, which really were the lifeline for the community. It was important to have those cultural epicenters as I was growing up.

It's always been a challenge to be in a field where no one looks like you.

When I started working and got to a major agency in New York, there were two other South Asians there, which I actually felt was a lot! Even today I don't feel like there are many South Asians working in PR.

One day there was a lunch conference sponsored by the agency. There were only three minorities in the room, and strangely, the agency put the three of us together at the same table. The client was showing a video clip featuring a person of Indian descent. When the tape was over, the client started making fun of the guy in the video in reference to his ethnicity. Everyone in the room thought it was funny. But the three of us were shocked and appalled that this was being tolerated by the people in the room.

That was the tipping point for me. I was tired of being a minority in an agency where the client, somehow, was always right. Within a week, I put my resume up on a networking website.

Though, to its credit, the agency had hired an outside firm to do some diversity training. This was in 2000, when diversity training was not really common. One afternoon, the diversity training firm came up for training and asked our group to write down the perceptions we had of various minority groups. Then they asked each of us to share what we wrote down. When the trainer asked a high-level executive to share his thoughts, he panicked, as did the others. They were like, "We can't share this! No, we don't want to share." I could clearly see the panic in their faces. The trainers were like, "No, you have to. That's part of the exercise." But the trainers relented, and to this day I have always wondered what they wrote down. I don't think anyone was trying to be malicious, but for me it really illustrated how much of a divide there is in perceptions about minorities.

After the agency, I went to Wyeth, a major pharmaceutical company. And even though I didn't enjoy health care PR, I can't tell you how important it was for me to be with people of color. It was *so* diverse. Two months after I started, for example, there was the Indian holiday, Diwali. I remember walking into a conference room and one of the marketing directors was like, "Hey! Happy Diwali!" I was like, "Oh my god, that's amazing!" It made me realize how important it was to be in a diverse environment.

It was refreshing to not have to explain our customs to people.

It reminds me of this incident at the agency: I had been to a wedding over the weekend and came into work with henna on my hands. As I was talking and using my hands to gesture about something, my boss said, "Eww! Your hands are grossing me out." And I explained, "This is a traditional custom during Indian weddings." But I also apologized for my hands.

I got so used to kind of microaggression that after a while I just didn't think anything was wrong with it anymore. Only years later did I realize how that chipped away at me, having to defend and explain every custom.

As a professor, I often take my classes on field trips to agencies. We went to one large agency, and I guess they were having a diversity dinner later that week. The agency people kept trying to engage with the one African-American student in the group. They seemed interested in talking to him about a job there. He pulled me aside during the tour and said, "Professor Kumar, I would never work in a place like this. There's nobody that looks like me here." And he didn't want to be that sort of poster child, which was how they were making him feel.

Just recently I was sitting at a table with some industry professionals, talking about diversity, and I shared my agency field trip story. One industry representative, a white man, responded with, "Well that's *his* missed opportunity!

He should have just gone there and he should have just showed them. That was a lost opportunity for him."

"That's on him? He's 21. How do you expect a young person to go into an environment where there is no one that looks like him?" I countered.

But that's still the feeling of a lot of people today. They don't understand how hard it is to be a minority, having never experienced it themselves.

I do have hope for the future: Our graduate class last year was 54 percent diverse. Our undergraduate majors were 33 percent diverse. American University has been extremely intentional in recruiting from all backgrounds, no matter a student's ability to pay. Last year, and the year before, they were able to meet 100 percent of financial need. We've had more Pell-grant-eligible students than we've ever had before. So American University has been very dedicated to making sure that the student population is more diverse as well as offering more opportunities to different populations of people. Many students are first generation and from all income levels, which I think is so important. I have many more students from Latin America now than I've had before.

I'm very open with my students about my own experiences because, first of all, I never want my students to feel alone. I'm very open about the fact that I had to work in college, I had to get loans, I was a Pell recipient, that not having a job after graduation was not an option ... those things. I could never afford to take photography in college because the fees were too high. So I understand what this generation of college students struggles with.

I'm very open with them about all of these things because I don't want them to feel like they can't do it. And I try to help them figure out ways to make it happen. Coaching them for job interviews, helping them with salary negotiations, introducing them to my network — that kind of counseling is important because that's what will keep them in the industry. Otherwise they're just going to give up. And there are plenty of my students who have given up — *plenty* — because they can't afford to intern after they graduate. And so many agencies insist on that even after students have done five internships during college. And then agencies wonder why they struggle with diversity. They need to create more pipelines for talent, and they need to guarantee a living wage.

Agencies need to be more deliberate about increasing diversity within our sphere because that is what the world looks like. It's what their target audiences look like. When you look at some of the big disasters that have happened, the Pepsi Kendall Jenner ad just as an example, that may never have happened if you had diverse people in the room. Clients are now recognizing the need to be more diverse, and for their agencies to be more diverse, to more accurately represent their brands. So it's come to a giant crescendo. There are bound to be more disasters, and when you bring people in the room to address them who reflect the rest of the world, that's how agencies will survive.

Denise Hill

Dr. Denise Hill is an assistant professor of strategic communications at Elon University. She has held CCO or senior-level communications positions at such organizations as Delhaize America, Wyndham Worldwide, Novartis, Quest Diagnostics and Cigna. She received a Bachelor of Arts and Master of Arts in communications from Temple University, and a doctorate in mass communication from the University of North Carolina at Chapel Hill.

I'm biracial; I have a white German mother and a black American father. Because of where I grew up, I spent more time with my German family members than I did with my black relatives. As a result, I learned more about my German heritage and German culture than I learned about my father's side of the family. Yet being of German stock is not what you see when you look at me. Learning about my black heritage is something I wanted to do and did on my own.

Despite the U.S. Census now having the option to check more than one race, we still operate primarily within a black/white racial binary system. In the United States, your race is often determined based on how you look. For example, I read an article by a professor who identifies as biracial, and she refers to herself as a "white-presenting biracial" because she looks white. So what does it mean to "look" a race? It usually includes skin color, facial features, hair texture and sometimes voice. I once had someone say to me, "You don't sound black." *What?!*

In corporate America, I'm a black female. That's how I'm labeled, and I have no issues with that. I'm treated as a black woman and my experiences have been based on that designation. However, being biracial has helped me navigate within a corporate structure. This is because I am able to interact easily and effectively with a very broad range of people at all levels of the organization. My ease often makes them more comfortable than they otherwise would have been. While other African-Americans may have this same ease depending on their experiences, mine relates to my mixed-race background.

In my personal life, I've always had black and white friends, and feel equally comfortable with both. I don't think that's the case for everyone. A 2016 University of Massachusetts Medical School study found that white Americans are less likely to have friends of another race than non-white Americans. Similar results were found in a 2013 Reuters poll. So when people are at work, they probably have these same preferences.

When it comes to making hiring decisions, they may gravitate toward someone who looks like they do because that's what they've always done and that's who they're comfortable with. Maybe I do the same, but with a different outcome. Since I've spent my whole life with diverse groups of people, I make sure I surround myself with a diverse group at work.

If you look at some of the senior-level PR positions at corporations and major agencies, and you don't see diversity in the organization's leadership, it begs the question: Why not? Where are the senior-level minorities? Where are the minorities who are ready to move to a senior level? What's preventing them from getting there?

There are minorities who have been ready to advance to a senior level but haven't been able to do so. At the same time, there are people who are not minorities who are able to rise up the ranks. So what's the difference?

I realized I wanted to work in communications when during my senior year in high school I got a job at a radio station as a news announcer. It was an automated Top-40 station that broadcast news at the top of the hour. The news came in over an AP ticker, and my job was to edit it and read it on the air. From then on, I decided that I wanted to become a television news announcer.

I went to Temple University, which at the time had a top-rated radio, TV and film school. But when I started taking those courses, they didn't interest me as much as I thought they would. Luckily I got two internships, one in an agency and one in a PR department, and I said, "Wow, I really like this!" I decided I wanted to work in public relations, so I took a number of PR courses.

I got a job at an agency in Philadelphia. I was primarily doing administrative work, which is what you did if you couldn't get in as an entry-level account executive. In the PR department, the only other minority was a graphic designer.

Then I took a job at an insurance company, working in the corporate communications department as a PR coordinator. I had a great boss who was very supportive while being hands off. It was a perfect learning environment for me.

I really had a passion for the industry and a passion for learning as much about it as possible. I just enjoyed what I was doing so much. Even as a very junior-level person, I became interested in the idea of how to use communications to make a contribution to society.

There was one other minority person besides me — an administrative assistant. It was not a big deal, and I wasn't reminded on a day-to-day basis of the fact that I was one of two minorities in this communications department and one of a few minorities in the company. I was more concerned with producing quality results.

I then went back to the agency world, including a position at a Foote Cone Belding agency, and then to a small, woman-owned agency where I stayed for four years. There were about 50 people, and I was the only minority.

From there I went to a change management consulting firm where I had the opportunity to develop an additional set of skills that allowed me to get my next communications job. I got a call from a recruiter who was looking for a director of human resources communications for Cigna. I had all the qualifications for the position. The Cigna corporate communications department was set up similarly to an agency, and all the Cigna communications people had an internal client. When I joined Cigna, it was a Fortune 50 multi-line insurance company. It later sold some of its businesses and concentrated on health insurance. I was responsible for all HR-related internal communications for the entire company. I also managed all external communications for anything that had to do with Cigna as an employer.

I was at Cigna for about 10 years. I started as a director and received a number of promotions, eventually to vice president.

The wonderful thing about Cigna is that the executive vice president of human resources was very enlightened and very committed to diversity in the organization, not just in numbers, but in making sure that people throughout the organization had opportunities to grow and develop.

Once I became a vice president, I was the only minority female vice president in the company.

There is this adage: An African-American female has to work twice as hard to get to the same place as somebody else. When I was on the corporate side, and even looking at the public relations industry in general, I would see people get promotions or I would hear about people being called by recruiters for senior-level jobs, and I wondered, why didn't I get called for that job?

I would call a friend who is also a black female public relations executive with extensive experience and ask her if she was called about the job. The answer was "no," and we both wondered how many minorities were on the candidate slates for these senior-level positions at very visible, well-known companies.

We were qualified for those positions and sometimes more qualified than those who got the jobs. We used to laugh about it, knowing that it really wasn't funny. I've seen people get senior-level communications jobs with no communications experience. Can I say for sure those situations were related to bias? No. There are a number of factors that go into hiring. However, some people may have biases they are unaware of, hence the term implicit bias. This implicit bias may contribute to them not giving as many opportunities to minorities as they would a non-minority.

At Cigna, I didn't go to work every day thinking about the fact that I was the only female minority vice president. I enjoyed my job, and I went to work every day thinking about developing and implementing outstanding communications programs. However, when you work for a large organization and you look around and you're the "only one," you know it.

When I was chief communications officer at Delhaize America, I always ensured we had a diverse candidate slate for positions in my department. The slate of candidates was a genuinely broadened pool, not just a slate with one minority candidate so we could check off a box. We interviewed minorities and non-minorities and hired the most qualified. That's how I always maintained a diverse communications department.

I also made sure that everyone on my team was recognized for their work, and I gave them opportunities to grow and develop. Plus, I was their champion throughout the organization.

I recall an instance where a manager in the organization appeared to be favoring a team member who was not a minority. There may have been reasons for that which had nothing to do with race, or it may have been that this white manager was more comfortable with this white communications director.

So I stepped in and made sure that this didn't happen. I made sure that all the people on my team were viewed for the work and the work product that they produced.

I think part of the reason minorities don't move up is that they don't have people inside the organizations who are going to help them move up, to recognize them, and help them acquire the skills to get to the next level. They don't have a network of people above them in the organization that is going to sponsor them, as many non-minorities do.

When I was at Cigna, I had champions inside the company who were committed to my career growth and professional development. Part of the other reason I was able to reach the top communications positions is because I was always very clear about my career goals. For example, when I aspired to become a CCO, I explored the skills I needed to develop and then went about acquiring those skills. When I decided I wanted to get international experience, I developed a plan to do so.

Of course, I've had some jobs that were not rewarding, primarily because there were people at those jobs who were not supportive. I've had setbacks; I sometimes needed to change direction. But there is more than one way to reach a goal. Also, I never lost sight of what I was trying to accomplish.

Everyone has obstacles; I believe minorities have a greater number of them. I was well aware of those obstacles and took them into account in my career planning. Maybe that made me even more driven and determined to achieve my goals.

As an educator, I try to encourage minority students to explore the public relations field. I tell them that the work is rewarding, and there are a variety of PR jobs in different industries. They can align those industries and job options with their interests.

A couple of years ago, I presented at a Public Relations Student Society of America (PRSSA) event on campus. The two sponsoring Chapters invited students from other

Chapters at colleges in the Southeast. The topic was diversity, and the event attracted minority students who might not otherwise have attended, including students from historically black colleges and universities.

After the presentation, the minority panelists had a line of students waiting to talk to us. Minority students need to see that there are minority professors in the same way entry-level practitioners need to see minorities who've become leaders in the field.

I think the universities should have initiatives to ensure they have a diverse faculty. After all, if you look at university communication schools, how many PR faculty are minorities?

At every corporate or agency job I've had, I've always been the only one. For instance, when I was at Wyndham and had a seat at the table, I was the only minority in the room. At Cigna and Delhaize America, I was the only black female vice president. At one of the agencies, I was the only minority employee. When I was at Novartis, there were only two minority female vice presidents in the entire company — I was a vice president of communications and the other was a vice president of sales.

So that "only" aspect of it is a *thing*. When people interact with you as an "only," you can't help but observe that being an "only" makes you very noticeable.

However, there's another way of looking at the many times I was the "only." I also was the "first." If there's a first, there can be a second and a third until we don't need to count.

But the "only" aspect may be one of the reasons we have a retention issue. Also, having to be twice as good to get to the same place as a non-minority can be tiring. I always said, "Fine, bring it on."

But every now and then, it was exhausting. I didn't leave work every day and say, "Oh, my gosh, I'm so exhausted because I had to be twice as good today." However, it's just exhausting watching other people getting ahead when you know you're just as or more qualified.

Regarding diversity, there has been a lot of talk and not a lot of action. But action can and needs to happen. I have worked at organizations where some of the CEOs said, "You know, this is going to happen. This is going to be a diverse candidate slate. I need you to make sure that you look at minorities before you come back and tell me that the best candidate is somebody else." And if the CEO hadn't said that, it could be that a minority would have never been interviewed for the position. We need to give everyone a chance to be selected. And that begs the question: How many CCO positions have been filled by minorities in the past five years? We also need to ensure that minority practitioners have champions and mentors, and those mentors do not necessarily need to be minorities. And everyone needs to be conscious of the fact that bias may be a factor in every corporate decision, whether that bias is outright or implicit.

Another important fact to consider is that PR students don't see people who look like them in textbooks. Most PR textbooks present PR as being developed by a few white agency men. That's not true. It was practiced by minorities as far back as the early 20th century. Public relations pioneers were black, white, male and female. I hope I can help more minorities understand that they have a strong heritage in this industry.

In addition to a lack of diversity in textbooks, PR students see few if any black PR faculty. When they get to work, they see few if any black PR professionals at all levels of the organization, and they have few if any mentors and champions. That needs to change.

When you show up in the room, you don't just show up as a PR person. You automatically get labeled and judged as a black female PR person versus someone else who doesn't have any labels or judgments. They just show up as a PR person.

So let's stop this "few if any" and "only one" and level the playing field for the next generation.

John Onoda

John Onoda is a senior corporate counselor for Gagen McDonald, a strategy execution consulting firm. Mr. Onoda has held chief communications positions with some of the world's leading corporate brands, among them the Charles Schwab Corporation, Visa USA, General Motors and Levi Strauss & Co. Mr. Onoda holds a Bachelor of Arts in communications from the University of Michigan, a Juris Doctorate from Indiana University, and a master's degree from Northwestern University's Medill School of Journalism.

I started off as a newspaper reporter. And then got into PR in 1981 — 37 years ago. Being a minority was just a factor to deal with, among many other factors.

But I'd say I've had a good, fast-moving career.

In the early parts of my corporate career, I was very often the youngest person in the room, and the only minority in the room. When I became senior management in the middle part of my career, heading up communications at General Motors, Charles Schwab and Visa USA, I think I was the only Asian senior manager at any of those companies; maybe except for General Motors. Imagine going into a large management meeting with the CEO, chief financial officer and dozens of others, all expecting some tall, blonde Robert-Redford-looking guy to be the head of communications for such iconic American brands like Levi Strauss and GM, and instead it would be this Asian guy! It was evident in group photos where I was always the one non-white person in there.

When you're a minority or you're an "other" in these situations, you can't let that intimidate you. You can't let that make you think that you're in any way second class or inferior to anyone else.

There's a lot of bonding, with some business mixed in, that's a major part of working a corporate culture. I just have no interest in that sort of corporate socializing and male bonding. I was from a middle-class Japanese-American family growing up. I didn't have a country club background. I don't play tennis. I don't golf. I don't drink. Like many Asians, I'd turn beet red after one sip of hard alcohol. So I just never went there. And in the marketing, PR and advertising space, especially decades ago, that was the major avenue for getting things done that I just didn't do.

I think there were missed opportunities, missed relationships, missed conversations, the small talk people have. Plus, I know very little about sports or sports teams — baseball, football, basketball. I don't follow any of that. So I miss out on the normal chitchat, even just sitting around before a meeting or during coffee breaks. I mean, I'm a nice guy and I'm certainly happy to listen and nod my head, but I don't really contribute to those conversations.

Has this held me back? I don't know. I've had a good career. I worked for the largest company in America at its time. I probably could've done even more, let's put it that way, if I had all those mainstream attributes.

On the other hand, if I'm not spending all my time on sports or spending my weekend on the golf course hanging out with the guys, I'm doing other things. I'm reading. I'm networking. I'm interested in the arts. I'm interested in writing, reading books. I'm a news junkie. So I would spend my time doing those things that I really enjoy.

I don't believe that there's just one path. In fact, there are multiple paths. And the key to managing your career is finding your own path and being true to yourself, finding your own strengths and bringing them into play.

It's hard to tell how much bias ever played into some situations. You get into these dogfights, both personal and political, when you work in any large organization. Sometimes there are personal attacks, but do your differences ever factor into it? You're never going to know. Would it happen to you if you were a white mainstream male? Quite possibly it still would.

I think some are quick to attribute every nasty personal attack and every slight to racism or sexism or homophobia. The fact is, there are just a lot of jerks and nasty people in all walks of life, including the corporate corridors. They could just be nasty people, with nasty behaviors. So it's a waste of time to try to figure that out. Why would I want to pursue whether or not someone is doing it because of my race? I know they were bad to me, and I'm going to have to deal with it in my own way. And so, the way I'm sort of mentally built, I just never went there. I find that a waste of time.

I guess if you live long enough, you see a lot of things you cherish get built up, get torn down, or at least changed by time. So we're in a period where there's no trust in institutions and very little trust in leaders, in politics, religion, government or business. It seems that social media is almost designed for attack. Lies goes around the world, while the truth is still tying its shoelaces. That's just going to unravel society as we know it unless we figure out ways to correct the downward spiral we're in. I don't know where we'll bottom out. I would never have imagined that it could be this bad.

It's not anyone's specific responsibility to fix that, but we are the communications people. We're standing next to all these lightning rod figures, helping to craft these messages and trying to sort through the social media. The PR people are at the forefront. So whether we like it or not, if there's anyone in a position to have a perspective on this and has the skill set to address it, it's us! We can't look around and wait for someone else to raise their hand.

The Page Center predicted that there would be a need for a center focused specifically on integrity in public communications, and holy cow, here we are in the midst of a meltdown in public communications. Integrity and trust are at the core of all great communications. So we may not have solutions, but I do think we are responsible and need to take the lead in showing responsibility.

I think the PR industry has done a pretty awful job around diversity. I know that for decades there have been well-intentioned people and efforts. I've been involved in some, going back 20–25 years in terms of funding a diversity outreach effort. I created minority scholarships for graduates when I was at General Motors. Many people have done these sorts of things, too.

When you look at the situation around diversity in all professions, including communications, senior executives can make a pretty good case that they've been doing an OK job presenting diverse perspectives. And yet, if we had real change in communications and marketing, a different portrayal of what's going on in America would have emerged sooner. Maybe the institutions that have degraded so much might've had earlier pressure, or at least earlier warning, that they needed to do some self-correction. We're seeing this play out in the #MeToo and in the Black Lives Matter movements. We see it play out in the political upheaval. The non-mainstream audiences and non-mainstream stories and perspectives have been going on for decades, in worsening situations, yet somehow the news media, communications and marketing professions didn't get it or didn't reflect it.

I know that a lot of diverse professionals feel like they don't belong. I've had a number of conversations with young professionals and students, especially those who have made this clear to me. They feel like they're facing a lot of adversity and want their situations quickly resolved. I wonder how much of it is the fact that they're minorities, and how much of it is that they're young people. I look at the millennial behavior — like wanting quicker professional rewards and recognition or they're going to move on — that is going on in all professions and in all companies. This sense of dissatisfaction is quite apparent, certainly in the Bay Area, where people are job hopping from Facebook to Google to LinkedIn to Uber like hot potatoes. The way they express different forms of dissatisfaction may reflect a generational factor or an institutional lack of sensitivity. I don't know how to weigh them.

In the Bay Area, we're so diverse, we're so multicultural, you might expect communications and marketing functions to have that same rich mixture and to try to project it, but I don't think that's what we do. It's partly because we're client-focused.

Mentors have been hugely important in my career, so I've tried to repay them by putting a lot of my energy into mentoring people. It's very gratifying. I have worked with a lot of minorities and women especially, as my way to try to correct historical imbalances.

I never had any corporate mentors. I had Al Geduldig, who had a distinguished corporate career in the energy and insurance industries and who then formed an agency with Don Ferguson, who himself is the role model for many people. Al was in New York and I was on the West Coast. I was inspired by his style and his approach to consulting. Otherwise, I had to sort of invent myself because there were no minority role models for me. You can't wait for role models. You can't wait for the mentors. You gotta just go.

I remember my first Page meeting 24 years ago. It was a white, sort of New York-centric country club. There was a breakout session going on and a long table with like twenty-four CCOs, all white men. Marilyn Laurie, CCO of AT&T, was at the head, like a lion tamer, leading the discussion. I just thought it was the greatest thing to see a woman like her do that. I'd never seen anything like it. I became one of her biggest fans.

Big agencies today are scaling back like crazy. There's all this consolidation. I don't have high hopes that in this business environment they'll make significant gains in minority hiring and advancement, despite the best of intentions; but we'll see.

I know the public and private sectors are well-intentioned as they look for minority hires; and they truly are making an effort. But the change we're seeing is like watching water freeze.

I've always told the big agencies that if they ever got their internal makeup sort of proportionate to America — X-percent Hispanic, X-percent women, X-percent Asians and African-Americans — they could go to clients and say "We are America!" I think it would be hard for big consumer-facing brands to pass on the opportunity to work with such a firm, if only to find out whether it would deliver fresh insights and executions.

It's never happened. Maybe it's just one of my pipe dreams.

Mike Paul

Mike Paul is a public relations executive specializing in crisis management, reputation management, corporate communications and litigation-support. He is currently president of Reputation Doctor LLC. Mr. Paul received a Bachelor of Arts in political science and public policy from SUNY Cortland and a Master of Public Administration in international management from Columbia University's School of International and Public Affairs.

It was my first day of this highly selective management training program at a very large New York agency. I arrived to the office building early that morning, around 8:15. Outside the front door, I saw a group of young black women standing around socializing and smoking cigarettes. I recognized a few of them as administrative assistants of one of the largest PR agencies in the world. All of a sudden, as I approached the front door, they burst into an applause, shouting, "We heard you were coming, Mike," "Welcome to the agency, Mike!"

They looked so proud that I was coming to join the firm. To be polite, I shot them back a smile as I entered the doorway. But a part of me couldn't stop wondering why they were applauding me.

Could it possibly be because it was so rare to see a black man working there?

In fact, there were only three other professionals of color on staff. And the rest of the African-Americans were all admins. Once again, I'd be the only black guy in the room.

But I had spent my whole life training for this moment.

I was a little black boy of mixed heritage in Brooklyn when my family moved to Huntington, Long Island — a middle class, mostly white, suburban town. We were the first black family on the block in our neighborhood. When other black families moved in after us, some white families down the street decided to leave for a "better" town. I remember them saying, "This neighborhood's going downhill!" Huntington, Long Island has always been a town most white families desired to live in to raise a family.

In our entire community of several hundred white families, there were only four minority families. It would be decades before this section of Huntington became a more diverse community.

I was one of very few African-Americans in the school system. So I grew up mainly around white people. As one of only a few black kids, I faced prejudice, racism and inequality every day.

My father, a Caribbean-American, was an executive for 33 years at Citibank. My father is from Trinidad and Tobago. His heritage includes English, Irish, African, Chinese and East Indian roots. He had worked his way up with just a high school diploma. My mother was a nurse's aide and then a dialysis technician at local hospitals and nursing homes. My mother's half Jewish and half black. We were raised to love and accept all people from around the world because we were a family of global heritage. We are the world.

My parents divorced when I was a freshman at college.

In 1990, I graduated from SUNY Cortland with my Bachelor of Arts in political science, after spending several years modeling and acting in New York City and Hollywood. I then went to Columbia University for my Master of Public Administration in international management. I was a Patricia Roberts Harris Fellow and a Woodrow Wilson Fellow at Columbia University during my graduate school years.

Sadly, in public relations, few of us are of color. Especially those of us with global experience in many sectors of society and working at the highest level, counseling top clients as executives.

My upbringing in an all-white community and my education made my life experience much different from most other African-Americans coming into the workforce, as I would later discover in my first weeks in PR.

The management training program exposed us to all the PR specialties — corporate, healthcare, sports, entertainment, financial, investor relations, nonprofit organizations, government relations and public affairs. And when I rotated to the crisis group, I knew it was for me. I had a passion to learn from the best crisis managers. Most of them worked for the firm around the world.

I was told by senior executives and clients, "Mike, you have a natural talent in crisis management."

That's the area I've been in ever since.

Since I'd already worked for elected officials who experienced crises themselves in New York and Washington, D.C., I was well prepared to handle crises of all types. In fact, I consider top crisis management counselors the brain surgeons of the PR profession. We have superior training, more responsibility, take on more risks, fix major problems and make more money than others in PR for a reason: we add more value.

After a year and a half at the agency, I was recruited by another large firm. I was named vice president and senior counselor and I had my own division to run. If you look back at some of the major corporate crises of the late 1990s and early 2000s, I was involved in counseling many of them: from telecom to finance, from healthcare to government, from celebrities to corporate executives. That period was a heyday for all types of crises in every sector of society.

After working for two of the world's largest PR agencies, I set out to create my own agency called MGP &

Associates PR. I was pretty young, just about 30 years old. It is with MGP that the nickname Reputation Doctor would eventually become a powerful registered trademark. The nickname came from an early client at one of my birthday parties. The firm's work saved his reputation and his company. He was the CEO of a major, global corporation. He gave me a birthday card which had the Superman logo on the cover. He crossed it out with a black felt-tip pen and inside wrote that name is already taken. You're my Reputation Doctor. It stuck and was quickly used in TV commentator interviews I had around the world. Since then, I've been counseling some of the world's top clients, and if I'm not counseling them, I'm on TV commenting about them. I sold the firm at the end of 2013 after more than 19 years of service. I then started Reputation Doctor LLC in 2014. Reputation Doctor LLC has built a truly global crisis PR and reputation management practice, with senior consultants working in every sector of society.

In all this time, since I started in this business, I've typically been one of few people of color in the room. It's the story of my life. I've had great training to handle this, growing up in a mostly white world.

But despite being black, I've been able to succeed in this business. I've found, when potential clients are deeply in crisis, and need to get the best crisis PR counseling out there, they look past the color of my skin and rely on my reputation of being among the best crisis public relations counselors in the world. I am very proud of that and it was no easy feat. It took focused, hard work, excellent training, superior solutions and the ability to recruit and grow excellent teams to get there.

Look, I've been in this business since the early '90s. And despite all the efforts to improve diversity, there's not been much improvement ... *whatsoever*. Yes, there are a *few* more mid-level and entry-level people of color per corporation or agency. However, there are still only a few executives of color running P&L divisions and still no Black CEOs running a top 20 global firm. With the amount of change that's really necessary to bring the best practices approach to diversity and inclusion, I would consider the situation a crisis. I believe the next generation of corporate and agency leaders are needed to bring long-term change. Sadly, diversity and inclusion (from board to intern) which mirrors the population worldwide, won't happen in my lifetime. It will be the task of the next generation of leaders to stamp out racism, prejudice, selfishness, unethical and immoral behaviors, as well as white privilege.

There are now about a half dozen corporate clients who hold their advertising and PR firms accountable if their staffs don't mirror the markets they operate in. They include corporations like General Mills, Verizon, HP, USAA and several others. New accountability is now starting a tipping point for some corporations. So be warned, eventually, if you don't have a truly diverse staff, you will be fired by the client.

Some people think diversity is a new issue is for PR firms and corporations. But diversity has been a major issue from some corporations for many decades. Mostly with spin and cover-your-butt strategies versus authentic change from top to bottom.

I found evidence going back to 1955 with a memo that was called the "Negro Program.' It consisted of giving a scholarship of $500 to a student going to one of the historically black colleges. And this was the *entirety* of their diversity program: starting a scholarship program for college kids, but not truly seeking diversity within agencies and corporations, especially at the most senior executive and board levels beyond sprinkles.

That stuff is still going on today.

In fact, just a few years ago, I received a phone call from the CEO of a top PR firm. "Hey, Mike, I just thought of something great, and I wanted you to know about it right away," he said. "We're going to give a thousand-dollar scholarship to one of the HBCUs!" A thousand dollars! They thought a thousand dollars was going to solve the whole diversity problem. I told him that won't even pay for a meal plan for one semester. It was pitiful.

I even talked to some of the kids who received those scholarships. Many of them don't even work in the profession anymore. They felt abandoned. They believed the rhetoric. And few people even followed up with them after they received the check. It was all about the person or organization which wrote the laughably small check. Sadly donations like this are not about the students. It was spin. A four-letter word for a reason.

When you build a diversity program, it has to get the buy-in from all stakeholders, from interns to board members, and every position in between. That's the best-practices approach. It can't just be an HR thing. Diversity and inclusion must include every single level within the organization, especially the most senior levels, where executives of color never make up the percentage of the populations in which they serve. Can you imagine a corporation or agency with senior executives making up 15 to 20 percent of all senior executive positions? Can you imagine CEOs of color leading 50 percent of the top 20 PR firms in the world?

Companies should know diversity is very good for business. A recent McKinsey & Company study shows that organizations who invest in D&I and do it *really well*, make one third more money!

So now that we have empirical proof of ROI, why aren't more companies doing it? We don't like to think the answer is related to prejudice and racism, but you decide.

HP is one company that has done great work in D&I. They are seeking to mirror the communities in which they operate. They admitted publicly they had a bias in the way they were hiring people. They owned it and are working to change their hiring practices. Then they made a series of commercials about it. One of them shows different African-American men and women — all professionals and with good resumes — coming in for interviews. At the end of each interview, the interviewer tells the candidate, "We'll be in touch."

And of course, they never do. In the last frame of the commercials, it says: Qualified minorities are three times more likely to get rejected from a job as white people with the same qualifications.

I hear stories like this all the time. If you are an executive of color, this is not new news. But it may be new news to white folks. It is true, but we don't want to believe it. Well, it is high time to believe it. Even better, get off the sidelines and be part of long-term change, especially if you are white. As Rev. Dr. Martin Luther King, Jr. said, "In the end, we will remember not the words of our enemies, but the silence of our friends."

Armando Azarloza

Armando Azarloza is a national multicultural marketing executive specializing in marketing, advertising, public relations and public affairs. Currently he is president at Axis Agency in Los Angeles. Mr. Azarloza earned a Bachelor of Arts in political science and government from the University of California, Los Angeles.

I came into public relations through politics.

I come from a very political family. My parents are from Cuba, and my father was very involved in the anti-Castro movement in the 1960s. He was actually jailed in the '60s as a political prisoner. So when my family left Cuba for the United States, my father remained involved in the whole anti-Castro movement. He taught us from an early age to have an opinion, how to address those opinions with other people, how to debate issues, how to build consensus and how to be a strong advocate. I used to follow my father when he went to rallies and protests, and watched him write columns for newspapers. So my love of writing, my love of communications — as well as for politics — were really inspired by my father.

I cut my teeth on identifying issues we could use in campaigns within the voter community, advocating for the candidates and the campaigns that I was working on.

I started working on political campaigns at 16 or 17 years old, starting out as a volunteer for California races, then eventually running a couple of congressional campaigns myself. My interest from a communications perspective relative to politics is not on the legislative side or on the political side, but on the communications — the marketing and messaging — side. So I come at it from that perspective.

In the '80s I had the privilege of working for Nancy Reagan as part of her advance team. I traveled with her during the last two years of the Reagan administration. And as part of the advance team, I was responsible for putting together events, working with local political parties and with law enforcement to secure and prepare events for the first lady such as programs with the Just Say No Foundation.

After that I ran the campaign for Buck McKeon, a local mayor in Southern California. He was running for an open congressional seat in LA. It was a difficult campaign. Five other Republicans were running. But we won. I was his press secretary for a number of years, up until 2000, and worked mostly on defense and education. He ultimately became the chairman of the Armed Services Committee. I worked with him on a lot of defense, aerospace and national-security-related issues as well as managing the communications and political strategy.

One of the things I learned very quickly during these two experiences was the need to identify the specific messaging that spoke to specific communities. I got pretty good at understanding the audiences, and became aware that the microtargeting of messaging, the segmentation of a particular audience was critical. We would know exactly who we were talking to, at what time we were talking to them, in order to deliver not only the right message but also the right message through the right channel, and when it would have the most impact.

After I left government I came back to LA and in 1998 started working for a public affairs/corporate communications firm, Bozell Sawyer Miller. I took the lessons I learned in political campaigns and applied them to corporate campaigns. It was a great match for me.

When I went to the agency side I discovered that there was a lack of diversity in communications and marketing. There was an interest to communicate more directly with Hispanic audiences that I saw as an opportunity for myself. So back in 2001 or so I started working almost full-time on Hispanic marketing campaigns. I was working with Fortune 500 companies that were interested in having conversations with Hispanic consumers. I counseled them on how to engage in meaningful communication with Hispanics, which would lead to increased awareness and sales among Hispanic consumers.

That ultimately led to creating Axis, the company dedicated to serving the Hispanic community.

Obviously, growing up Latino was a big advantage in my ability to communicate with this audience. But more than that, it was my understanding of the values, heritage, tradition and culture that are key to engaging with this audience. I try to be an advocate for our community, to represent the interests of Latinos with corporate America. I try to get corporate America to dedicate the resources to activate programs that are meaningful for our community.

The public relations industry has a long, long way to go in terms of ensuring that we have a diverse workforce. What happens is new recruits come in and they get lost, and then they decide to leave because they don't see anybody in the higher ranks who looks like them, or thinks like them, or speaks like them.

I also am deeply committed to mentorship and sponsorship. I've been leading diversity efforts within Interpublic (the large holding company that now owns Axis). I've been trying to bring young people of color into the industry. But even more important than that, I try to mentor and sponsor people as they go through the company ranks. I think there's nothing more important than taking a young person when they come into the company and providing them with the tools and resources to guide that person's career through the company, and putting them on the path to success.

When I advise young people of color, I say to network as much as you possibly can. There are really good networking communities out there that really do provide good opportunities. You can introduce yourself to folks who ultimately you might be able to work with. You can get information about organizations that are hiring.

I'm a very firm believer in having somebody who's a good writer, who's articulate. I always tell young people, "Spend your time learning the craft of writing. If you can write, you can communicate. If you can communicate, you'll be a good communications counselor."

There are not enough people of color at the higher ranks of organizations. We're still dominated by Caucasians. I could see how this could turn a young person off. They don't see a path to move up the ranks. But when they see somebody like me, they may think there's hope that that could be them one day. If they don't see a Hispanic, if they don't see an African-American, if they don't see women at the top, that could certainly impact whether they want to continue with the company. We need people who speak different languages. We're better practitioners if we represent what the rest of America looks like today.

A lot of companies still haven't quite figured out that diversity is not just an HR function. It's a business function. And once you get them into your organization, your job is not done. You've got to work with them to help them climb up the ranks and get them into management.

When I look back on my career, I've been very lucky. I've had really good people who have helped and mentored me, moved me along the process. People have sponsored me through different opportunities. Those things don't happen through happenstance. Fortunately, I've worked in positions in those places where I could get that sponsorship.

We need to spend more time training, mentoring and sponsoring young people of color as they come into our organizations in order to achieve workforces and management teams that reflect more accurately the country today.

Brandi Boatner

Brandi Boatner's current role is social and influencer communications lead, Global Markets, IBM. She also serves as the brand communications manager for the company's senior vice president and chief marketing officer. Ms. Boatner serves as the current co-chair of the social media committee of the national PRSA Technology Section, and is an advisory council member for the LAGRANT Foundation. Ms. Boatner received a Bachelor of Arts in public relations, advertising and applied communications from Loyola University, New Orleans, and a Master of Communication, Public Relations and International Marketing from Hawaii Pacific University.

You could call me a "child of PR."

I remember being in high school and teachers saying, "Oh, Brandi talks a lot. She's a really good communicator." I was a good writer at a very young age, but actually, I really didn't like writing.

Prior to attending Loyola University, I entered Marquette University as a pre-med physics major because I love sciences and I love physics, not biology, not chemistry, but physics. But after about a year or so of doing experiments alone in the physics lab, I realized quickly that for someone who likes to talk a lot, this is not for me. So I switched majors and schools into PR and went to Loyola University, New Orleans. When I got there I felt like this was a wonderful fit, like when Cinderella puts on the glass slipper, and I knew I wanted a career in PR.

While I was at Loyola, I joined the Public Relations Student Society of America (PRSSA) and also had a part-time job. I got to work on really cool PR projects and got to travel, too. I would not be where I am today had it not been for PRSSA.

After I got my Bachelor of Arts in PR at Loyola, I went to Hawaii Pacific University (HPU) and got my master's in PR, and also was elected president of the PRSSA Chapter. After becoming president of the Chapter, I decided to run for a national office on the National Committee. At HPU, I had done a master's thesis, which I called the "digital butterfly effect." It was about the advent of social media and what effect it would have on PR. I mean, this was 2010, before Snapchat or Instagram had come into prominence. Facebook was everything at that time. To prove my thesis, I didn't use communications theory. I used a math theory. My professors were surely confused about this: "What are you doing? What are you talking about?" After a lot of blood, sweat and tears, I successfully defended my thesis and got my degree.

Then one of the professionals in my network said, "Why not share it with all the people you know in PR? Let them see what you're talking about with social media." People would read it and say, "You know, you should send this to so-and-so at Johnson & Johnson," or "You should send it to somebody at GE." Finally it got shopped around at IBM, right around the time my parents took me off the family payroll.

So I took my master's and headed for New York, leaving Hawaii, trading one island for another. Determined to get a job, I started talking to some companies and talking to my network. I had already built up a strong network of great people I knew from PRSSA Chapters all over the country.

When my thesis arrived at IBM they contacted me and I did a phone interview. Then I went to the headquarters in Armonk and did six back-to-back one-hour interviews in person. I was super nervous. They called me back — six months later — and offered me a job that actually didn't start until the following January. Yes, it took a very long time. A PR professional I knew gave me some of the best advice I ever got. He said, "Brandi, it's not all about you. Companies have their own timelines. No one is trying to fit into your timeline. That's not how business works. You don't just interview on Tuesday and on Wednesday there's an offer."

My "digital butterfly effect" thesis on social media was part of the reason I got hired. I had a unique skill set understanding social and digital before the PR industry was looking at the analytics around social.

But when I first got to IBM, nobody seemed to want to talk about social media. "Twitter? OK, little girl, well, go sit over there. We'll call your name when we're ready." I was young and eager and talking about a thing that not everybody had wrapped their heads around yet. Getting people to embrace social media was a challenge.

It was also a challenge being in a work environment with so many more men than women. My intern coordinator cautioned, "Never wear open-toed shoes. When you are in an office environment around a lot of men, you need to dress how you would dress if you were having Sunday brunch with your grandpa." As certain as I was that my grandpa would have been completely cool about open-toed shoes, I do not wear open-toed shoes to this day.

Internships and mentorships have been very important to me in my development in the PR profession. During college, I had two amazing internships, one at Edelman in Washington, D.C., and another at Walt Disney Studios. The PR legend Betsy Plank herself was one of my mentors. While I was looking for a job, Betsy would call me every week. She was like a part of my family. She'd ask, "Who have you been talking to? Have you talked to this person? What does this person say?" Betsy believed in me. Students sometimes need kind words and reassurance. They need to hear, "I see the potential in you. You can do this." I know how badly I needed to hear this while I was waiting to get that first job with IBM.

When I started working at IBM, they gave me a connections coach, someone to help me navigate my first 90 days. She showed me a lot of the processes, introduced me to a lot of people and showed me a lot of different technologies. After those 90 days, they encouraged me to seek out a different mentor to kind of help me with my career. But I liked my coach so much I asked if she would stay on as my mentor. And she remains my mentor to this day, eight years later!

Being a person of color at IBM has been both good and bad. The good part was I knew I wasn't alone. During my first year at IBM, I joined the Black Employee Network of New York business resource group where I eventually became the chair of the organization, serving for four years. The IBM Black Employee Network of New York had about 600 members or so — amazing people. Having that network within IBM and having people to go to with various questions has been amazing. I'm so grateful for it. It's such a huge part of my career being in the Black Employee Network at IBM. But sometimes at meetings I'd look around and say, oh well, I'm the only black female in the room, or I'm the only young person in the room. I don't get upset or depressed — I just say, well, we have to do better. That's one of the reasons I was chosen as one of the founding members of the Diversity Council within IBM to help us be better in terms of diversity and inclusion for the marketing and communications function. Some people remember IBM as the white-guy-with-the-briefcase-who-lives-in-Connecticut company." I say to them, "Do I look like a white man with a briefcase?"

So if we were to look at data that shows us what career fields are the most popular, what is data telling us about why kids don't choose a career in PR? What is the data telling us about our exposure problem? Let's use that data to try and turn the numbers around. I'm sure we can get data somewhere, perhaps from the Department of Education, and find out where they are going. Why aren't they choosing PR? Is it an issue of exposure? Do they not know what PR is?

I've gone out to high schools at underserved communities as a black female talking about PR. I start off by asking, "Do you know what PR is?" And what do you think their first response is? "Oh, you plan parties. You promote celebrities and rappers and athletes."

I tell diverse students who want a career in PR that the opportunities are endless. Everyone needs a communicator. Every organization, nonprofit, corporate, agency, you name it, needs communications. It's the foundation of any enterprise to have good communications.

The key question I ask them is, do you have the drive and ambition to take it, because no one is giving it to you. Jobs are not falling out of the sky.

But all in all, it's been a wonderful, wonderful career so far. I work with some of the smartest people on the planet on some of the very coolest things on the planet. It's only been eight years, but I know I've made the right decision. And I continue to learn and tell students coming into the profession, the ability to learn is their greatest competitive advantage.

Helen Shelton

*Helen Shelton is a consumer, lifestyle and multicultural
marketing communications strategist specializing in the arts
and culture, health, fashion, spirits, entertainment and luxury
goods. t. She is currently senior partner at Finn Partners, and
previously was executive vice president, Multicultural &
Image Marketing Group, at Ruder Finn. Ms. Shelton received
a Bachelor of Arts in art history from Dartmouth College and
a Master of Science in communications from Boston
University.*

My mother always tells me, "When you have a seat at
the table, bring more than your appetite." You don't always
have to say something, you don't always have to have the
answer, but when you do say something, when you do
contribute, make sure that it is something that is going to
make a difference and that reflects well on you.

And yes, you're going to run into people who are going
to be difficult. You're going to run into people that may be
racist. But if you have it within you, with your girded armor,

to prevail, you can. Because you're not alone and this is something that you want to do, and you can't let anything or anyone deter you from doing that.

This is a tough business. You can't be Little Bo Peep and operate in PR in New York or anywhere else. So gird yourself every day with your own arsenal and your own armor, whether that's your education, your expertise, your making a difference.

Over the years, this is an issue that has come to the forefront. Major agencies and corporations have taken on the importance of diversity and inclusion and are really moving forward to make a change. And I'm very happy to be part of an agency that has made it part of the founding pillars of the firm.

But I can tell you that when I started out, diversity was really not something that was thought about. Even I didn't think about it. Certainly, in my experience to this day, I'm very often the only senior black person in the room. When I was at Ruder Finn, I was the first-ever executive female vice president of a department. That means black, white, whatever, I was the youngest, and of course the only black person to hold that title. But the issue of race really never was an issue there for me. I just made it my business, in my own way; I was able to ensure that the audiences we addressed in our campaigns were diverse. If we did press trips and things of that nature, I was making sure that it was integrated. But I've also been a strategic counselor for clients when they look at things from a non-monolithic perspective.

Diversity has opened up people's minds. It's not mandated that you have to be a minority or a person of color or of a different background to understand the importance of having diverse perspectives at the table. Even if there are situations where there may not be a person of color in the room to help make decisions, I am very hopeful that because this issue is at the forefront, people will think about the issue from a diverse person's perspective. Whenever I can, or whatever platform I may have — whether it's speaking on a panel or teaching a class or talking to people in PR or being a part of affinity groups that advances this issue — we constantly have to be articulate, proactive and assertive about making sure this issue is at the forefront, and that these perspectives are taken into consideration. Even though the needle is moving, it's not always being done.

Diversity is a core pillar of PRSA New York, where I have served on the board of directors as vice president of marketing for two years. This year we launched an initiative to encourage agencies to share their diversity data with one another so that we all know what the playing field looks like. Those agencies who were comfortable sharing that data, including Finn Partners, were recognized for that effort, and we were among three agencies to receive the inaugural Diversity Data Honor Roll award. We've been able to show consistently that in the seven years that we've been in business, we've increased our diversity because it's the right thing to do for our clients, for the industry and where we work.

More and more companies are mandating diverse representation on their account teams. And increasingly, request for proposals (RFPs) are requiring that information. Clients are mandating this as well. I'm happy to see that it is not just a trend. It's something that will continue for many years to come.

It's a business that's driven by billing hours, and sometimes the diversity piece, the multicultural piece of the RFP, is not the lion's share of the assignment. I have seen this in my lifetime; and when it's not the "lion's share," they will bring out the "multicultural person." But then when it comes time to doing the assignment and having the hours assigned to that person, they don't get it. It behooves clients to hold agencies responsible for that.

There's no substitution for having a real working diverse team, not just the people who show up for the presentation. You can see it in the results for the client. Unfortunately, you often have people who are in charge of the RFP and they don't even get it. And I see that very often. I've worked in the spirits sector for a good part of my career. It's one of those sectors of PR where urban, ethnic minorities drive sales. These are people who are the influencers. They impact how spirits marketers market.

When these RFPs go out and they don't always include an agency that has a diverse staff, it's frustrating.

Part of my job at Finn, as head of the Diversity and Inclusion team, is to make sure that people know that diversity is a pillar of our firm. It's a differentiating factor for us, but it's also something that, thankfully, Peter Finn has mandated. We have senior management who are responsible for driving diversity on down with their own teams across our entire network. Certainly we're not the only agency that does this. But I'd like to see more people stepping up to the plate, creating an environment that is inclusive, making sure that the diverse people hired are not shifted off to the side or left out.

Before coming to New York, I worked for the City of Chicago. I was appointed by Commissioner Lois Weisberg, the commissioner for Chicago's Cultural Affairs Department. God rest her soul, she was one of my mentors. Under her leadership, the City of Chicago mandated that cultural affairs would have the same operational budget as the city's municipal agencies such as fire, sanitation and safety. Culture remains an integral part of the infrastructure of Chicago.

I got to work on many signature initiatives in the Chicago cultural landscape like the Taste of Chicago, the Sister Cities International Conference and public programming at the Chicago Cultural Center.

I also worked for the largest health and human services agency organization in the state of Illinois. I was responsible for a lot of public affairs work, especially in the areas of substance abuse and neonatal care. There are still parts of

Chicago, particularly the West side of Chicago, where the neonatal death rate for infant mortality is higher than in some Eastern-bloc nations.

Retention is a big deal. It can only be addressed by creating inclusive environments and by putting programs in place to enable people to identify a mentor and enhance their skills.

Case in point: I met this young woman who was at an agency, and she told me that at least once a week she would escape into the ladies room because she had been reduced to tears. The environment was too tough for her. If you look at her you see someone who is very poised, beautiful to look at, but equally beautiful inside, with a lot to contribute. Frankly, I think we've all been there. It was an imperative for me to provide her with some wisdom and guidance, and mostly to let her know that she was not alone.

On the plus side, there's a lot more opportunity today than there was when I was getting out of school. The nature of our industry is now so diversified and integrated, there are infinite numbers of opportunities to get into the field.

In college I had been a double major in art history and government. It was the early '90s, when people were either going to become bankers on Wall Street or lawyers or traders. I took the LSAT, did well on it and was planning on law school. But I realized that it wasn't what I really wanted to do.

Instead I opted to go to Boston University and got my master's in communications — and won a full academic scholarship from RKO General, which helped launch my career trajectory into the arts and entertainment. At the time, RKO General owned RKO Pictures and WRKS-FM radio where I interned as part of the RKO General Scholars program.

I tell students to get the best foundation that they can in order to be able to operate in a functional capacity. You've got to delve a little bit deeper. You have to have some substance to you. You can't say to a prospective employer, "I think I want to go into PR because I like people."

Even though there are a lot more opportunities than when I began my career, you have to have the same, if not more so, competitive edge and level of professionalism and commitment. And you have to have a deep, deep understanding and respect for the power of strategy.

I happen to be a fan of liberal arts. For undergraduate I went to Dartmouth College and I believe that foundation helped me to this day. It was an enhancement for me to go on and get a master's degree in communications. But I would say that a solid liberal arts foundation could benefit you in ways an undergraduate degree in PR might not.

When I went to Dartmouth there was, what, 8 percent African-Americans? I was happy to be up there in the wilds of New Hampshire. After all, I was raised to be hardy and confident. I was just as good as anybody else. I was sitting next to Nelson Rockefeller Jr., and here I was coming out of Harlem. My Daddy's money was just as good as anybody else's, and the love of reading and learning I got from my mother propelled me forward! If you have the wherewithal and the sheer grit to be able to perform in a rigorous, nearly all-white environment like, say, a Dartmouth (including snow that lasts through spring), I say, "go for it!"

I've handled a great variety of clients in my career — consumer, entertainment and health care. And since my passion has always been the arts, I've tried to use this to drive the strategy. After all, culture and arts are what link people together.

I've worked on campaigns that helped drive awareness of diseases among minority communities. And having that responsibility, that huge responsibility, is a heavy burden to carry. But it's one that I am proud to carry. I am literally the architect of how we communicate to people of color about things like hypertension, sickle cell disease, diabetes and obesity. I've been able to use my background in the arts and create messaging based on my understanding of the black community. I've been fortunate to lead some really stellar campaigns.

One of my best campaigns was called "Believe in Healthy BP." This was a blood pressure awareness campaign on behalf of our client Novartis. We got our client to sponsor a national tour for gospel singer Yolanda Adams. We also used an interactive blood vessel exhibit from the client. We went around the country offering free screenings for people at various community centers, megachurches and schools. We promoted the tour with radio public service announcements using leading cardiologists to talk about the importance of maintaining healthy blood pressure. We ended up getting the Multicultural Campaign Award from PRWeek.

I've done lots of similar campaigns over the years that have managed to raise awareness for health issues and at the same time generate sales for the client. Working in the public interest, helping the black community and at the same time helping the client — it's the best of both worlds.

At this point, yes, I'm battle weary, but I prevail and get out there every day to do the work I must do in our industry. I've got the scars to prove it, but I also have reaped tremendous rewards and satisfaction. And I've managed to soar in this career because I have the foundation that I have, I have the experiences that I had, and I've had people in my life who encouraged me and who believed in me.

Oscar Suris

*Oscar Suris is an experienced head of corporate
communications with a specialization in banking, automotive
manufacturing and retail. His most recent position was as head
of corporate communications for Wells Fargo & Company
where he served for nearly nine years. Prior to that, he was a
director of corporate communications at Ford Motor
Company. Mr. Suris received a Bachelor of Science in finance
from the University of Florida. He also worked a decade in the
news business, including five years as a staff reporter at The
Wall Street Journal.*

I was nine months old when my mom, who was just 20,
and my dad, who was barely 21, decided to bring me to the
U.S. from Cuba. We first settled in New York, and then
moved to Miami. If not for their decision to take me out of
Cuba, who knows what my life would have turned out to be?
Of course, I'm very grateful to them.

When I was growing up, I took to journalism early on.
For my high school paper, I was not only the editor-in-chief,

but its sports editor and features editor. Even before that, in middle school, I became editor of the yearbook.

By the time I was ready for college, I had my sights set on the University of Florida, which even then had a wonderful reputation for its journalism school. I was fortunate enough to be able to go there, and the first of my siblings to go to college.

And that was when a really wonderful thing happened. As a freshman I won the Florida Publishing Company scholarship. It came with a little bit of money, but more importantly, it included a paid internship that summer at The Florida Times Union in Jacksonville. I was getting published bylines and could not have been happier. Having that internship so early in my college career — the internship is normally given to juniors — I figured I was already ahead of the game. With all the sacrifices my parents made to put me through college, why not try to learn something I couldn't easily pick up from the streets.

But then I decided to change my major from journalism to finance. I always loved business. I was always inspired by business success stories. They were so representative of the American experience and the opportunities we have here. I just felt like it let me make the most of this college thing. So I got a degree in finance. It turned out over time to be really, really helpful to my career. It positioned me well for a job in business journalism, which was a really fast-growing area at the time. It was the mid-1980s, there was a lot of interest in the stock market, and metro daily newspapers were adding

Monday business sections. And so I just wanted to be part of chronicling these great stories, and writing about entrepreneurs and business trends.

Those interests carried me through a career in journalism, starting at the Miami News straight out of college. But one day the News just closed its doors. Fortunately another one soon opened. I became a business news reporter for the Orlando Sentinel. It would be there, in Orlando, where I would ultimately meet my wife. So if not for the Miami News going out of business, I may not have ever met her.

I think that there is opportunity in everything that happens if you choose to find it.

A lot of people don't like to make changes during the course of their careers. Tough things do happen, but it's really in those hardest, darkest moments that there is an opportunity to learn, grow and let go, which is sometimes just as important as moving on.

In 1992, within three months of meeting my wife, I had an interview lined up with The Wall Street Journal. That meant moving to Detroit. We both agreed that if she was going to follow me, she'd have a ring on her finger. So we got engaged within three months of meeting each other.

I had the opportunity to cover the automotive business. It was a wonderful four years in Detroit. My son ended up being born in the suburb of Royal Oak. Then I transferred to the Atlanta Bureau for a while and covered the U.S. Hispanic market, which was a lot of fun.

And then I had the opportunity to join the publisher's office of the Miami Herald as an executive assistant. No longer was I part of the newsroom; I was now part of a leadership team, working alongside sales, marketing, operations, HR, legal and finance. As an "insider" now, I got to see how the gears worked in concert to make a business run. When you are an insider, you are actually part of making something happen every day. You're suddenly going from writing about how people make sausage to actually being part of the sausage-making process. The publisher of the Miami Herald, Dave Lawrence, had been publisher of the Detroit Free Press, editor of The Charlotte Observer, wonderful Florida Gator in his own right, and also a man who's devoted his post-professional career to early childhood development causes in the state of Florida. I was his executive assistant, which meant my job was not part of the newsroom, it was part of the publisher's office, and it was my first opportunity. And I loved it. I thought it was fascinating, energizing and challenging.

When I left the Journal, a gentleman up the road in Fort Lauderdale said to me, "If you ever want to work for a real company, call me." He was head of communications for a publicly traded company called Republic Industries, which would later on become Auto Nation. It was started by Wayne Huizenga, who also founded Blockbuster Video, Waste Management and many other companies. He had the "chutzpah" to attempt to do something no one else had really ever done in business before: to buy many car dealerships, and in less than five years build the country's largest automotive retailer.

So I had covered the auto industry for The Wall Street Journal, plus had a degree in business, plus I clearly knew journalism. So I thought maybe I ought to try out this PR thing. Where else are they going to find somebody like me? So this is how I started my career in PR.

What I like about PR is that I help people tell their stories. I help people make business decisions. I help people express things in words and pictures and sounds. I help bring different perspectives together. I anticipate problems, and I anticipate opportunities. And in doing all those things, I end up influencing a lot of people and situations and have an impact on the world. It's the quiet work that often goes on behind the scenes that makes an undeniable difference.

Corporate America is a tough club to break into. No matter what your ethnicity, color or orientation, I think that's why the conversation about inclusion and diversity is so important. We are all striving to have workplaces where some degree of meritocracy can be really enjoyed; where people can be judged by their contributions, their talents and their smarts.

The fact that I was a Cuban-American immigrant trying to go to a four-year college from a very modest background, it certainly didn't hurt to get that first scholarship that led to my first job in journalism. Some people have an advantage because they went to Harvard. Some people have an advantage because they are from a great, well-established family. My children, who are all young adults now, have benefits and advantages I would have killed for at their age. I had different advantages. Over the course of my career I have been the first Hispanic in many work situations. I have been a factor in the diversity equation in a lot of workplace settings.

I'm very cognizant of being Cuban-born, but I really don't look very Cuban, and I don't have much of an accent. Even in my own household, my brother was significantly darker than I. So I've been confused for all kinds of ethnicities. I don't think of myself so much as a person of color or as a person of specific ethnicity. I see myself as an immigrant. My diversity challenges are totally different from people whose color is more of an issue for them. And I have a lot of respect for that.

And yet I've been very fortunate to be bicultural. It's been a tremendous advantage for me. I am very comfortable in Los Angeles or Miami, or any "barrio" where español is being spoken or "cafecitos" are being sipped. I can toggle between those worlds with ease. And that's been a tremendous advantage in the corporate world. I've been able to mix in well, set people at ease, and have been able to relate to all types of individuals.

For the PR industry specifically, the good news is we're having a conversation about diversity. It's wonderful that organizations like PRSA and many other pillars of our profession are doing their best to keep the conversation alive. It's a necessary conversation to be having, and without it, I don't think progress can be made.

But what's tough about an ongoing dialogue is that sometimes talk can sound cheap. Every job opening needs to be looked at as a moment of truth, an opportunity to have a diverse slate of candidates. Every job opening needs to be an opportunity to challenge one's self, to seed talent and potential in different forms. Every promotional decision is another opportunity to do the same. That's ultimately where actual progress is being made — by sponsoring, mentoring and having faith in others.

I've long believed that every hiring decision is a leap of faith. It doesn't matter how many interviews you conduct or how much due diligence you put in or how many references you rely on. At the end of the day there is a gut call you're making on an individual, diverse or otherwise. And you're saying, "You know what? I'm going to go with this person because somehow I think it's going to work." And sometimes that decision will work out fabulously well; sometimes maybe not so much. But there's no getting around that.

I think the profession's heart is in the right place. I think communications and marketing professionals, perhaps more so than anyone, understand how our country is becoming more brown, more yellow and more diverse. That's just America. Our profession gets that. We've become champions for encouraging other businesses to lean into diversity, and over time, build teams and organizations that are representative of the America and world that we now serve. But it's a journey. It's going to occur over a long period of time.

I think we have to celebrate progress when it happens. But we also have to continue demanding a lot of ourselves, and make sure we keep the conversation at the forefront.

Here are pieces of advice I like to give young people considering entering the profession:

First, you are 100 percent responsible for your career. You'll still need the help of others, you absolutely will. But at the end of the day, you're still responsible for your career, and there is tremendous power in owning that. Also, own the story you build about yourself.

Every now and then you can find places that are very nurturing and very committed to professional development, and that's wonderful. I've experienced that on occasion in my career. But sometimes that's just not there. And that's why you have to remember that you're the one who's ultimately responsible for how rich a career you create.

Second, don't underestimate yourself. Plenty of people limit themselves by constructing their own ceilings. Look at every day as an opportunity to test that ceiling, and grow beyond that.

When I took on my first PR role, I discovered that there are so many other ways I can bring value to people and make a difference in the world. It can be gratifying and rewarding. Whether it's for a major corporation or a nonprofit with a passionate cause or an agency that's in a position to provide counsel to others, you can make a difference in the world by being of service to others. You'll have the opportunity to do it in so many ways, you can't even imagine!

The PR profession doesn't give itself enough credit sometimes for the difference it's making every day in our society just by virtue of all the many ways in which we help guide people to become better communicators, make better decisions, and have better outcomes.

Look, in a perfect world most companies would be more active with diversity programs. A place you're working at could be resource-constrained. Or the operating culture doesn't have a vision to act on that. What's important is not to let that be an excuse for your own lack of success, however you would define success for yourself.

When I went back to Cuba, I saw what could happen to a country without freedom of speech. So I'm incredibly grateful to have that freedom here. Another thing that's really fantastic in the U.S. is that there's always an opportunity to reinvent yourself. All successful careers include setbacks and periods of adversity. It's just inevitable. And that's probably something we don't talk about honestly enough. But you've got to be prepared for those moments and expect them in life and also in your career. I mean, even Steve Jobs was fired by Apple.

One of the best pieces of advice I've ever gotten is that listening is an active activity. It involves engagement. It's not just a passive activity, although I think a lot of people mistake it for that because you're not using your mouth. But actually, it's through the act of listening that some of the greatest work gets done — listening and observing. Also, recognize the difference between a mentor and a sponsor. A mentor is someone who has an interest in teaching you and coaching you. A sponsor is all of that, plus they are willing to stake their own credibility on yours. They are the ones who are going to say, "Hey, you really should hire so-and-so ... you really should interview so-and-so ... I want to promote so-and-so." That's a sponsor.

If I could give my younger self some advice it would be this: Worry less. It's not productive, although I think people in our profession are professional worriers. We are so often trying to think about how things can go wrong. But I think worrying less is something that's good for all of us.

Rebecca Carriero

Rebecca Carriero is a communications strategist for Bloomberg Philanthropies. She previously worked for Goldman Sachs, The Financial Times and the Parsons School of Design. Ms. Carriero received a Bachelor of Arts from The New School and a Master of Arts in corporate communications from CUNY Baruch.

The public relations profession has a unique opportunity to shape narratives and present new sources of information that give voice and credibility to those traditionally excluded. Working in media relations specifically has allowed me to develop a greater understanding of and appreciation for how news stories shape our perceptions.

For example, news outlets have acknowledged a need to quote more women in fields like technology, government, science and corporate leadership. In a 2018 column, The New York Times op-ed contributor, David Brooks, said, "[Journalists] are allowing sexism to help dictate their sources — and are perpetuating the problem. The people who get quoted today, after all, are more likely to be invited onto a panel tomorrow and offered a sweet new job next year."

Like our journalism colleagues who realize the need for diverse representation among sources and experts to challenge and change socially accepted notions, public relations professionals must be aware of how the people their companies serve are portrayed and communicated with.

My background in public relations, working for a Spanish-language bookstore, a major international newspaper, a bank and now a global philanthropic organization, has made me conscious of how image-makers construct visuals or narratives. In philanthropy, there is a tendency to depend on images or narratives that pull at the heartstrings. You see it all the time — an image of a poor child or a downtrodden city meant to evoke sympathy and funding. While the intention may be noble, these images reinforce stereotypes, victimhood or simply rob the subject photographed or quoted of dignity. Thankfully, there is growing understanding in some spaces that images or communications materials should uplift the communities they represent. There has been a notable shift *away* from relying on this type of imagery or narrative framing. I have noticed concerted efforts to promote charity as a way to unlock human potential in my personal and professional environments.

Public relations requires a conscientious approach to everything from selecting interview sources, convening panels, thinking through "photo-ops," creating the imagery for a public event and so much more. A diverse team with varying experience and background increases the chances that there will be a conversation and steps are taken to reflect a wider range of perspectives that help avoid unintended landmines around cultural representation.

Companies that are comprised of homogenous groups, whether by race, ethnicity, gender or class, do not represent the world we currently live in. Communications campaigns that only reflect the ideas of one group will lack the authenticity, empathy or intelligence required in a globalized business world. If we only learned one thing from our journalism colleagues, it should be that when limited voices are reflected, we risk missing major changes and shifts in public sentiment.

In addition to creating diverse teams, public relations practitioners — especially those from underrepresented groups — must have the courage to speak up when a population is not being represented fairly. As much as you may not want the responsibility, you must have the conversation about why using an image or presenting a group in a certain way is harmful to your organization's position and to the group or community being served. We also should make intentional efforts to diversify the sources and experts we pitch, or who are at the table during these discussions in the first place.

I recently had an experience that highlighted the value of diverse teams. While discussing a publicity event in South Africa, one critic pointed out that some of the imagery was too reminiscent of "The Lion King" and did not demonstrate a respect of the modern country. Another person's point of view was that the imagery was paying homage to the country's folklore. This was an informative discussion.

While the event organizers were likely not acting with malice, intention doesn't always matter. What's more important is understanding how an audience receives or responds to the message. How do you have that conversation? You bring people with different backgrounds to the table. And you have to have a trusting and open enough space to have those critical conversations, and if needed, the courage to change course.

Neil Foote

Neil Foote is the president/CEO of Foote Communications LLC, a full-service integrated marketing and communications consulting firm. Mr. Foote is also a principal lecturer at the Mayborn School of Journalism, University of North Texas. Previously, he was a public relations director/consultant for the Tom Joyner Foundation. Mr. Foote received a Bachelor of Arts in government from Wesleyan University, a Master of Science in Journalism from Northwestern University and a Master of Business Administration in marketing management from The Southern Methodist University – Cox School of Business.

When I bring up the fact that agencies have got to be accountable to their clients about their diversity, I hear, "Neil, you know, you're such a bleeding heart! Don't you understand how business works?"

Well, of course I understand how business works! Business works better with a diverse workforce. This isn't rocket science.

I have a hybrid background. I started out my career as a newspaper reporter for the Miami Herald and then for The Washington Post. I eventually started up an integrated marketing and PR firm in Dallas — Foote Communications.

Four or five years ago, I was working on a project with Richelle Payne, the then president of the National Black Public Relations Society (NBPRS). She encouraged me to join the board at that time, and so I did. I became a very active member of the organization on the board level, and then moved up the ladder to become president about 2 1/2 years ago.

The mission of NBPRS aligns with my own passion to build inclusive diversity in all ranks of the public relations industry. I'm no stranger to the challenges and opportunities of this industry, but we've been working on this for years, and *still* trying to figure out how to become a more diverse field.

In the four, five years that I've been deeply involved with NBPRS, I'm finding that there is an incremental gain — nothing significant — in the number of diverse employees in the field. A couple of years ago I participated in a Diversity Summit organized by the PR Council that was hosted at Ogilvy PR. We had some two dozen industry executives including NBPRS, ColorComm and the Hispanic PR Association. But we also had executives from the major agencies in the room. You know what they said? That they're *still* struggling to find talent. Why? Because they couldn't hold on to them once they got them in the door.

This is not good talent management. We can't keep using the same excuses that we can't find the talent, or that we can't hold on to them. I hear people say, "Oh, well, that's just the way it is." Well, it doesn't have to be that way.

It's a several-pronged problem. First, we need to get diverse students in the front door. We have to convince them that PR is an exciting and intellectually stimulating industry to work for. Granted, there's been some improvement finding great talent, but we just have to work that much harder — and be much more creative.

The second issue is retention. After five to seven years, the employees tend to get frustrated because they haven't been promoted or assigned to bigger accounts. So they relocate to another industry; they relaunch their own careers.

After 12 to 15 years, the few who are still in the business seem to hit a glass ceiling. Either they have to hang in there with little hope of moving up, or they decide to leave. Many decide to move to other industries or launch their own PR firms.

So what do we need to do to keep this experienced group of diverse professionals in the industry? Well, that's the big question. From a basic perspective, let's make sure these individuals get access to the experience that will prepare them to succeed. Perhaps that includes training to acquire key technical skills, or greater opportunities for client management so they can rise through the ranks to begin to lead accounts, go out on new business pitches, and begin to work with major clients at those companies.

If there are opportunities to get to the executive level, how do those mid-career professionals get the backing, the understanding, the skill set, experience and the right mentorship? Let's face it, the godfathers and the godmothers in these companies — typically the most senior executives — aren't tapping diverse future talent on the shoulder and giving them the opportunity to rise though the ranks.

The studies we've seen — and what's suggested in conversations with the ones who've transitioned out of the agency world — is that they feel they never seem to get access to the major accounts or major projects. When they get inside the front door, despite their best efforts to succeed, they never get enough critical feedback to get promotions like their non-diverse counterparts.

So these diverse executives think that they have the right skill set, get somewhat limited experience in getting the right kind of exposure they need, work as hard or harder than others, and then when it comes to trying to use that experience to get a promotion, they still get passed over. What the heck?

What we know is that there's been some strategic hires in the last several years. There are folks that, interestingly, have been hired from the media business, from the journalism side, from Bloomberg and The Wall Street Journal and the The Washington Post.

Another good friend of mine who spent years as a newspaper reporter for The Wall Street Journal was hired about a year ago by Edelman to be one of their senior executives for content, working with clients. So, yes, some progress, but not enough.

I wish I had more anecdotes about those individuals who have been showcased because they came in the business and then stayed there. Of course, Judith Harrison at Weber Shandwick, Trisch Smith at Edelman, Sandra Simms-Williams and Donna Pedro at Oglivy, are wonderful examples of how their hard work and perseverance has had a huge impact on their companies — and the industry. These individuals likely feel there are great opportunities within those agencies.

You need good champions within the company itself. You need good people in the company who understand good talent when they see it. If we're investing in hiring good people and great talent, that's kind of the key. Every hire is so strategic that you're making a big investment. So you've got to make sure that this person you're hiring really has a future at the company. If you believe that, then you need to figure out how to make these employees successful.

I'm sure there are cases where individuals come in without all the skills that you need. If you have good leadership at the company, there'll be a strategic effort to get the employees to acquire the skills they need. What's critical for young professionals to succeed is that they have to know their immediate bosses will get them exposure to the leadership.

I saw this in the newspaper industry, and I think it's the same case in PR: Where there is diverse senior leadership, there is potentially more diverse talent being hired, recruited and promoted at the company.

I remain hopeful that this will become a more frequent occurrence at agencies across the country. One of my strong beliefs is that if you have diverse individuals in the room, it helps broaden the conversations. Companies should make sure it's just not the same old boy network continuing to make decisions for the company. If they only work with a small network of people, if they hire people from certain schools and certain backgrounds, they may never get exposed to different perspectives.

If my customer base is comprised of Hispanics and African-Americans and there is no one in the room who understands how to talk with them, then that's not helpful to my business. Good business requires diverse employees — now more than ever. That leads to more diverse thinking, and that leads to more creative product development. Seems like a very simple business equation.

Diverse students tend to start off at a competitive disadvantage immediately out of the gate. They don't have the resources to spend their summers working at big city agencies and renting apartments in places like New York or Chicago. So instead of graduating with three or four agency internships under their belts, they'll have three to four

summers working at a fast-food restaurant or coffee shop —
just to help pay their school tuition and living expenses.
Even before they get started in their professional careers,
the diverse kids have to struggle to catch up. They don't get
the advantages of having the real-world experience of an
agency, and also miss out on the chance to make
connections and begin building their professional networks.

BPRS is solid as an organization. We're building in
New York, Chicago, Dallas, Houston, Detroit, Atlanta, Los
Angeles, Philadelphia, and Washington, D.C. It's a
volunteer organization, but we're all passionate about this
cause in cities throughout the country. We need to keep
NBPRS and its mission alive if we are going to live up to the
promise of increasing diversity in this industry. We're in the
midst of our 20th year and looking forward to the next 20
years. We're looking forward to working with our industry
friends — and eagerly seeking new partners to help us lead
the change.

Micheline Tang

Micheline Tang is a strategic communications, media relations, crisis management and marketing professional currently serving as director of communications at King & Spalding, a global law firm. Previously, she was a managing director and co-head of the Litigation Support practice at Kekst and Company. Ms. Tang received a Bachelor of Arts in international studies from Johns Hopkins University and a Juris Doctor from Boston University School of Law.

As a corporate attorney, I always had a belief that there was something I would enjoy doing more, but I didn't know what it was. One day as I was discussing it with my sister, she asked me, "What do you want to do?"

I said, "I want C. J. Cregg's job from "The West Wing." I want to do it for companies." After all, I still had law school loans.

After graduating from Johns Hopkins University, I worked as a litigation paralegal at Brown & Wood, which has since merged into Sidley Austin. Knowing I planned to attend law school, I moved to Taiwan to work and study Chinese. I was in Taiwan less than a year when the law governing foreign workers changed, so I returned to the U.S. and began serving as a legal assistant supervisor at Brown & Wood.

Three years after graduating from college, I started law school where I knew I would learn how to analyze complex legal issues and how to write a compelling argument. I also thought law school would be an excellent credential to have since I wasn't sure what I wanted to do.

Having worked at law firms in the U.S. and Taiwan, I suspected that being a lawyer for the next 60 years wasn't what I wanted to do, but I knew it was the right education for me. After working as a corporate lawyer in New York City for six years, I learned that I enjoyed explaining what I was working on more than I did documenting it. I started to network to figure out what I wanted to do next.

As a lawyer, I knew about S.E.C. (Securities & Exchange Commission) filings and earnings calls. To better understand investor relations (public companies' communications to investors), I joined NIRI (National Investor Relations Institute) and started attending their events. IR professionals typically have strong finance backgrounds, so I signed up for the CFA (Chartered Financial Analyst) exam, thinking, "I don't have to pass it, I just have to prove to people I'm not afraid of numbers." Luckily, I never had to take the test.

As I was networking with contacts at large public relations firms like Hill & Knowlton and Burson-Marsteller, Kekst, a boutique strategic communications firm, kept coming up. After hearing about them for the third time, I finally got the name of someone to call.

I reached out to the person, made my pitch and was told that while they were not looking, I should come in and talk to the hiring partner. After interviewing with 11 people, I was cleared to meet the founder, Gershon Kekst. I interviewed with Gershon and stayed at the firm for 11 years.

Gershon had a wisdom and gravitas that few others have. He was a good mentor to numerous people at the firm. If you were feeling off your game, for a rational or irrational reason, he would somehow know, and a new, interesting assignment would appear for you to tackle.

Just listening to him on phone calls was an education. I once heard him give a reference for a woman he described as smart, strategic and thoughtful. Not only did she understand the issues, she was capable of executing tactics. I remember thinking, "That's what I want somebody to say about me."

During my time at Kekst, I had an opportunity to work on everything — crises, investor surprises, activist investor defense and everyday corporate communications issues for everybody from public companies to private schools. There was a lot of traveling, working on vacations and even trips on three different corporate jets.

I got married later than many people, and had my first child at 40. In taking stock, I knew I needed a change to keep learning and being challenged, and to maybe have a schedule that got me home in time to read a bedtime story.

In the decade I was away from law firms, these institutions grew their non-lawyer side of the house. There were now professionalized marketing, branding and design positions there. I went to speak to a number of firms, and after working briefly at a litigation boutique, I landed at King & Spalding, where I have been for over four years.

My work in-house has supplemented my Kekst experience. While at Kekst, I focused on sophisticated high-profile crises and paid less attention to branding, marketing and events. Working in-house, I realized how critical internal communications was to articulating the strategy and driving desired behavior. I also have learned to build a team, collaborate with other departments and scale processes.

Communications within law firms is a quickly evolving area as law firms become more sophisticated about messaging and content creation. It is a good source of opportunities for young people looking for a way into the field. Unlike an agency like Kekst, you don't have a lot of peers internally, so I joined the Legal Marketing Association (LMA), which is the trade organization for the marketing "staff side" of law firms, to connect with people who are similarly situated. I have had the opportunity to speak about the value of internal communications at LMA's national conference and on a webinar for them. Connecting with others outside of work is critically important for one's career to meet others in your industry and to see what it is you still have to learn.

I think, for me, gender has had a bigger impact on my career than being Asian-American. Being the only woman in the room, I suspect, changes behavior in a way that being the only person of color might not. Of course, it's impossible to know what happens in rooms when you are not there.

In terms of mentoring, there have been many influential people in my life who have provided me with insight, advice and counsel. Except for my dad, none of them looked like me. I think it's natural for people to mentor and develop a close relationship with people who remind them of a younger version of themselves. When you don't have exact role models, you have to piece it together from multiple sources.

Diversity is important because people with different experiences — whether it's gender, ethnicity, socio-economic level, country of origin — provide a richer perspective from which to evaluate a situation, and offer suggestions and counsel. The wisdom of crowds only works if members of the crowd have different opinions and points of view. Differences are an advantage.

Ultimately, whether at a law firm or any company, it is hard to know why you were not selected to be a member of the team, because you can't know if someone lacks faith in your abilities or if they just don't want to work with you. Having spoken to other women, women of color, and men too, I think everyone is looking for where they fit in. In the end, we all want to work with colleagues or bosses who respect us, value our experience and give us opportunities to evolve. Whether you are diverse or not, that is always going to take effort.

People have often asked me if I miss being a lawyer. Nope. Working at a law firm now, I can see how hard it is, and I definitely didn't have the passion necessary to succeed at it. But the issues around how to better tell a story still fascinate me, which is why I know I am in the right field. For as much as I have seen and learned, I am excited to see and learn more.

Andy Checo

Andy Checo, currently associate vice president at Havas FORMULATIN, has over 15 years of public relations and marketing communications experience. Specializing in the U.S. Hispanic market, Mr. Checo's experience comes from both the agency side, having worked at RL Public Relations, Edelman, The Vidal Partnership, Interpublic Group's ICC Lowe and Arcos Communications, and from publicly listed and privately held companies including MundoFox, Maximus Inc. and Healthfirst. Mr. Checo holds a Bachelor of Arts in public relations/international studies from Mount Saint Mary College, and attended Middlebury College's Spanish Language School Master of Arts Program.

I am Dominican. I was born there, but was raised in New York. I came to the U.S. when I was 9 years old, back in 1989. I'm from a rural part of the Dominican Republic outside the town of Mao, a part of the country where you don't see many tourists. There you don't really get to experience the diversity of broader Latin American cultures like you do here, or perhaps in the capital city of Santo Domingo.

When I moved to the U.S. I became aware right away of how similar Latinos are because we all speak the same language. But then we're also all so different because there are distinct nuances to the culture, the language, the food and even the music.

Being from the Caribbean, we're known for talking extremely fast and being outgoing, unlike being from Central America or Mexico where people tend to be a little bit more reserved, and their tone of voice is calmer. It is not until you get here, to the U.S., that you see how the rest of the Hispanic world behaves.

I was raised in the Bronx. My high school had over 3,000 kids. I lived in a neighborhood where my parents were able to be a part of the community without having to learn English. A lot of my high school peers did not have the chance to get out and experience something beyond the neighborhood. I was lucky enough to have that chance. As part of being in that school — Theodore Roosevelt High School, right across the fence from Fordham University — I had the chance to take courses at the University while still in high school. That totally opened up my world.

I was always well-connected with the administrators at my high school and so was always placed in key programs. One day an opportunity came to attend a summer camp, Keewaydin, in Vermont. It was a scholarship offered to inner-city kids, and I was lucky enough to have been selected. That experience took me out of my environment at a young age and exposed me to different non-Hispanic cultures. There were kids and counselors from all over the world and around the U.S. Camp made me a more independent and well-rounded person by the time I was ready to move on to college.

I attended Mount Saint Mary College in Newburgh, New York, where I graduated with a Bachelor of Arts in communications. Somehow I gravitated toward communications, but I wasn't 100 percent sure about it at first. I probably would have changed my career were it not for the fact that I found out I could work in the Hispanic market and contribute to something bigger, something that I had a connection to.

My first job was a bit more marketing than PR. It was in New York City (Wall Street) on the client side in health care. My first day was Sept. 4, 2001. It was in a consulting firm, based out of Virginia, called Maximus. What they did was manage the New York City Medicaid and Medicare programs. Being a public program, they had to go out and market to and educate multicultural audiences, with Hispanics being the larger focus of the efforts. The program had to target audiences in five different languages that included Spanish, Russian, Haitian Creole, Chinese and English. I was in charge of producing collateral, educating the New York City residents who had to switch from Medicaid to a managed care health plan.

I was in health care for the first three years of my career. Then I had the opportunity to move from in-house to an agency in a PR role. In 2003, a friend connected me to The Vidal Partnership (TVP), which was the largest independent Hispanic integrated agency. They were mainly known for advertising, but the agency offering included promotions, digital and PR.

At TVP my role was mostly PR-focused, and 100 percent Hispanic. I was working on leading programs for major brands like Home Depot, Sprint and Johnny Walker.

In the 15-plus years that I've worked, I would say 10 to 12 of those years have been entirely Hispanic work, and about three of those I would call multicultural.

I have always been passionate about the Hispanic market. I see the value of what I do. Regardless of the brand I'm working with, there is an educational component to the community.

For example, I currently work with TurboTax. The work I do with them is targeted toward the Hispanic market and it goes beyond product familiarization and awareness. I am educating the consumer about the U.S. tax system, something that they may not be familiar with, especially if they are recent arrivals. As a practitioner serving the Hispanic consumer, language is very important. You have to be a good writer in both languages. You have to be able to communicate your story angle to all kinds of media. The great thing about marketing and communications is that your skills are very transferable.

Relationship building is very different when working within this market. You tend to chitchat more with reporters about topics unrelated to your pitch. Most of the time, when you call a general market reporter, you have to get straight to the point.

There is a lot of diversity in the types of Hispanics living in the U.S. You have Hispanics who have been here for multiple generations. I feel that with my parent's generation, when you talk about language, once you come here they want you to learn English because it is a way to be part of the society, but most importantly, a ticket to success. Today, the second generation of Hispanics that are here want their kids to actually learn Spanish! They want to connect to that part of their heritage now more than ever. We are now proud to say we are Latinos and our language is a part of who we are.

There has been a change in the mentality. Those who were raised here back in the '60s were discouraged and shunned if they spoke Spanish. Now we teach our kids to speak Spanish so they get to have more opportunities, as we realized that knowing two languages opens up more doors.

Language has always been a debate. When it comes to what we do (PR), there's always the dilemma of whether you communicate using Spanish or English. But we have learned that while language is important, the context is what really dictates its use. As a Latino, I'm connected to my culture and my roots, but the communication does not have to be in Spanish for me to relate to it.

There are some 57 million Latinos in the U.S. now. When you think about that number, it might be a small percentage of the U.S. population — 18 percent. But when you think about 57 million people, which is more than most Latin American countries, we are a powerhouse. In fact, we're the second-largest Latino country in the world behind Mexico.

At my first job, my bosses were Latinas, so I was lucky enough to be working in an office where I was able to have people who understood my background. I went from there to work at a Hispanic agency where 95 percent of the staff was Latino. So I had a whole different experience than most Latino professionals in the industry. They might go into an agency or in-house to a culture that does not reflect the diversity in their lives. They might feel out of place. I feel that I was fortunate to have working environments where I had leaders I could relate to.

Once my career became a little established and I worked in general market agencies, I did notice a difference. I worked at Edelman for a short period of time. The Latino program was pretty large; we were about twenty-something at Edelman in the New York office, so we did have that community of people who could relate to each other's background. However, we were part of an office that had a few hundred employees, so I felt like a fish out of water.

Once you go into an environment like that, there are very few Hispanics or people of color in higher-level positions. It's a challenge for them attracting multicultural talent for those higher-level positions. What I've seen is that there comes a time in a Latino PR practitioner's career path when they get out of the industry. They freelance. Or they come to the conclusion this industry's not for them. For some, this is due to roadblocks on progression within established organizations.

I think that diverse professionals are underrepresented in the communications industry. Within the last year I have seen a little bit more of a push to bring awareness to diversity. I hear talk about diversity, but not that much action about making changes.

There are a lot of organizations that make a commitment toward diversity. They may sponsor something that would position them as supportive of diversity, but don't go the extra step of taking action toward improving the future of the industry.

By talking about it, hopefully we'll get some traction and start seeing some changes within the industry. I believe it all starts with educating the younger generation. It starts in school, maybe at the high school level or even younger. By the time you are in college it's a bit late. We should start familiarizing young kids with our industry early on.

Our industry is underrepresented when it comes to diversity at top-level positions. That will have to change. I am an advocate of mentorship programs. I had a mentor growing up. We can do much better to foster young professionals and see them through so they have a better chance to claim those senior-level positions tomorrow.

Back in high school, I had the opportunity to be part of the New York City Mentoring Program. Once a week I would go in Bear Stearns and meet my mentor every Wednesday, whom I would shadow for two hours. I would get on the No. 4 train and go down to 45th Street and Park Avenue, walk into the Bear Stearns offices and learn what he did and how people behaved in a corporate environment. It was a big deal.

I have been in environments where my allies were non-Hispanic professionals, high-ranking in their industries, and I didn't have Hispanic role models. I also have had the chance to work with non-Hispanic individuals who believed in me. That's made all the difference.

You don't have to be Latino to do Hispanic PR. You just have to know the market, the nuances. If you are a Spanish-language speaker, that is a huge plus, but you don't have to be. It is more about finding good people who have a genuine interest in our industry and work hard every day to advance our community.

As a board member of the Hispanic Public Relations Association (HPRA), I am supportive of nurturing the next generation of Latino professionals. HPRA aims to raise awareness of the work being done by industry leaders.

When you look at our trade publications, there's no one publication that covers the Hispanic side of PR, so we must be advocates of shining a spotlight on our achievements, because otherwise nobody will really know about the great work that's being done. And if it's not us doing it, it won't get done, and the rest of the industry will never know who we are, what we do, how much we've achieved and what a difference we made.

Lisa Osborne Ross

Lisa Osborne Ross is president of Edelman in Washington, D.C. Previously she served as the managing director of APCO Worldwide, also in Washington, D.C. Ms. Ross received a Bachelor of Arts in journalism from Marquette University.

My first job was with the Pittsburgh Press, but I never took it. This was right after I graduated from college and my father's cancer had become terminal. He encouraged me to take the job, and I went up to Pittsburgh to look for housing. But I felt a tug to come home. I had a great conversation with the editor and explained the circumstances. I told him, "I just don't think I can do this." And he said, "Don't start your career compromised. You'll have to do enough of that later." It was great advice. And so I came home to spend that summer caring for my father with my mother. He passed that September.

After my father's death, I spent a few months traveling with my mother before eventually taking a job with the Tobacco Institute (TI). I had always been interested in policy, having majored in journalism and minored in political science. As a 22-year-old, this was an extraordinary opportunity to apply that educational background. I was walking into a job in one of the most volatile, controversial industries of the time. The industry was at a fork in the road, and split internally, with one group of people saying, "We have a legal product that people enjoy and that creates lots of jobs," and then another group saying, "All that's true, but there are some problems with our products and in order for us to continue to market and sell them, we're going to have to make some corrections."

To be able to be on the side of the team that said, sure, we can market the product, but we have to do things differently, was a wonderful learning experience. And the most important things that I've learned about issues management and public policy I learned in that job.

The best thing, however, about working at the Tobacco Institute was meeting my husband of now close to 30 years.

At the time, smoking restrictions in public places were starting to be legislated, but the real issue of the day was deadly fires attributed to cigarette smoking. Because of the forward and progressive thinking of the people that I reported to, I had the opportunity to make a material difference that I dare say saved lives and shed light on the issues around fire safety.

When I started at TI, it was not uncommon to drive to work, listen to the news and hear on the radio or on TV, or read in the paper: "Family of five killed by cigarettes," or

"Non-English-speaking family killed by cigarettes." The industry realized it had a real problem and addressed it head on. We recognized that the nation, and particularly vulnerable populations, needed to be better educated about fire safety. And so the industry committed a tremendous amount of research and money into the issue of international fire safety. And then they chose me, a young black woman, to be the face of an industry that was old, white and male.

I spent 18 months traveling the country, communicating our commitment as an industry to fire safety. I met with metro chiefs, I met with fire safety experts, I met with volunteer fire departments — every group of fire safety practitioners that you can think of — and I would say, one, "We realize that our product is contributing to a problem, and for that we are sorry,"; and two, "The real issue is fire safety, and toward that end we are cooperating to help educate the community about fire safety — not just with cigarettes, but across the board."

It was extraordinarily satisfying. I was able to help solve a problem, I saw outcomes, and I was able to tell a story that wasn't being told. And it hit me when maybe seven years later I was driving and listening to the radio and heard the announcer say, "Family of two injured by careless smoking."

That was the first formative experience of my career, and it showed me the extent of my ability to have an impact. I have spent a good part of my career since then focused not only on having an impact through great client work, but on promoting the idea of equity in expression — the ability to have a voice and to be yourself in the workplace no matter what you look like or where you come from. I learned that others weren't going to fight that battle for me, but it was a mantle that I could and should take on for others that followed.

I was working at an agency after the Clinton administration and the person I reported to had become a dear, dear, friend of mine. We worked together for almost 15 years. We raised our children together; even buried our parents together. He was a white man with white men all around him, and without even consciously knowing it, he protected and advanced and helped some of these other men. And I eventually realized that he had never — and would never — help advance my career. I became stuck. It was challenging, particularly because we were friends.

At the same time, others in the company, recognizing my talent, began to wonder why they weren't using me at the global level. Why wasn't I leading an office? Why wasn't I doing all the things they could have me do? It was great to be recognized and I was really excited about the opportunity to do more. And serendipitously that's when APCO called and offered me the managing director position. It was the first time I was actually able to lead an office. I took the opportunity, but before I left I was sure to speak my truth to ensure that others that looked like me wouldn't get lost.

I was never able to really put into words what it felt like to be of color or black in the workplace until a young man I worked with compared his agency experiences. Of one he said, "I don't have to walk around and explain my blackness, I could just be." I think for many of us, we feel pressure or a personal need to educate, explain, coach or excuse our beautiful blackness. So I think that the ability to "just be" is essential to success. But if you have to walk around and be the black girl on the team, or the brown girl, or the gay guy, or the Republican, or whatever is different from their norm, you end up carrying two — or even three — jobs, where others just have one.

I would say to those who are trying to nurture and grow talent, be intentional about it. It doesn't just happen. So identify your talent, grow that talent and put that talent in a good place. And for others I would say, I don't care what color you are, if you work for me, I expect you to be very, very good, but I also expect you to be yourself. Be good and be yourself. That's it.

Omar Torres

Omar Torres is currently a public relations and communications lead at Northrop Grumman. Previously Mr. Torres was the director of communications for AECOM and held similar roles at AIG and Booz Allen Hamilton. Mr. Torres received a Bachelor of Arts in political science from the University of California, Berkeley; a Master of International Affairs (MIA) from Columbia University; and is certified in Change Management from the Georgetown University McDonough School of Business.

As a child I would grab our VHS camcorder and start interviewing my brothers. Or sometimes I pretended I was a news reporter and would have my siblings film me in our backyard where I would report on current events and the weather. I spent time interviewing family and friends too. It was difficult to keep me off camera.

At an early age my parents introduced me to Cesar Chavez, Nelson Mandela, Gandhi, Dolores Huerta. I would visit the local library and check out biographies and history books to dig deeper and learn about these figures who were able to change the world. I really loved their compassion for others, their dedication to social justice and their ability to inspire people from all walks of life. To this day, I am still inspired by these figures. They serve as a compass in my life and as a reminder to me of what's right, and to act with integrity.

When I was going to Berkeley as an undergrad, I started working in nonprofits to help underserved kids. The role was heavy in stakeholder management and required face time with school district officials, city employees and county administrators. I even pitched to downtown banks and corporations to explore additional funding sources. I wanted the business community to be part of our coalition and help the children of Oakland.

My first glimpse into PR was as an intern for Governor Gray Davis of California. I was in charge of putting together the morning news clips and faxing them to our field offices. That's basically how my career in PR began.

Once I graduated, I landed a job with U.S. Senator Barbara Boxer on her constituent services team in San Francisco. I had interned for her before, and the director had taken me under his wing. That's when I discovered the importance of mentors.

You see, my mentor was my boss. He did everything to share his experience and knowledge with me so that I could be successful. He invested in my development and went above and beyond to help pave my path. Aside from being an amazing mentor, he became a good friend and to this day remains a trusted confidant and someone I regularly go to for advice.

Feeling empowered, the role helped me strike up a relationship with the press secretary. I had a hunch that it would be in her best interest if our office gave her a heads up on any sensitive case coming across my desk that could be newsworthy or generate press.

It was a real eye-opening experience to work directly with constituents from all walks of life or with community groups having trouble with the federal government. Sometimes a news headline about the work I was involved in would make the paper or show up in the evening news. I took my job very seriously and understood the power of media and perception, how it could help and sometimes hinder efforts.

At 23 years old, it was really fascinating to be a staffer for an elected official. I was working with over 100 federal agencies to help veterans, families, nonprofit organizations and businesses of all sizes navigate through our federal government. This job helped me learn to read people, to be more compassionate, and the importance of building relationships and consensus with stakeholders.

After the Senate, I went to Columbia University for graduate school. At the same time, I interned at a PR agency in Manhattan. That was my first glimpse of PR and communications in the private sector, and my introduction to Wall Street. I was writing all sorts of newsletters, employee communications and white papers for an array of clients in various industries. Even my Portuguese came in handy during calls with a Brazilian energy client.

One of the most exciting opportunities I had as an intern was to help put on Mexico Day at the New York Stock Exchange (NYSE). Over a dozen CEOs from 15 NYSE-listed Mexican companies came for a day of interviews and media roundtables with financial publications and TV networks. It was my first time inside the mythical building and it felt so surreal. I ushered the CEOs and their handlers to the right reporters. And being a native Spanish speaker helped things run smoothly and allowed me to communicate with the visiting guests.

I found it very similar supporting C-level executives and elected officials such as Senator Boxer and Governor Davis. The common elements among these individuals was their enormous responsibility and how much they had on their plate. They relied heavily on PR and communications to achieve their goals and get their message across.

While at Columbia University I was pretty sure my dream job was to be a diplomat or spokesperson for the U.S. State Department or the United Nations. I spoke Spanish and Portuguese and had studied abroad in Spain and Brazil. Plus, the thought of travel and being part of the international stage really appealed to me. I was eager to kick off my career and start making an impact, but reality hit, as detours do in life.

The detour landed me with Booz Allen Hamilton, a consulting firm that serves defense, intelligence and commercial clients. I first heard about them through friends who had recently completed internships with them and had great experiences. I saw consulting as the perfect "hybrid" career — working for a company with a strong corporate culture but whose clients are government agencies. It sounded perfect. I had government and nonprofit work under my belt and now I was going to be on the other side helping them with communications planning, stakeholder engagement and media relations.

I had actually been trying to join Booz Allen for months and was in touch with three or four employees who were all sharing my resume with recruiters and managers.

When I finally joined Booz Allen, I began to thrive from the very first day. I was in and out of the Pentagon writing communications plans for the U.S. Army and working with their public affairs teams from various commands and functions to strengthen messaging, congressional relations, print and digital content, and media relations. Jumping back and forth from a government environment to a corporate one every day made me flexible and adaptive, it really kept me on my toes.

Aside from the client work, it was easy to thrive in a corporate culture that encouraged me to bring my whole self to work. The culture valued strength in diversity, so it was very easy to be openly gay and share my experience as a Mexican-American with others. I had an army of mentors, joined five employee resource groups and participated in many community sponsorship and recruitment efforts. Professionally, Booz Allen's culture enabled me to explore additional skill sets such as crisis communications, change communications and communications strategy.

I strongly believe it's important to bring your whole self to work, to build your personal brand and showcase your commitment to your projects, work and customers. In my case, I wanted my personal brand to be synonymous with "getting things done" and being the person my colleagues first think of whenever a big project, challenge or crisis was on the horizon. While I executed assignments and communications plans, on the flip side I was heavily involved in our LGBT and Latino employee resource groups (ERG). I wanted our LGBT employees to have an army of allies, and I wanted our Latino resource group to build cultural awareness. So I began to invite employees I knew, employees I spoke to on conference calls and employees I met in the office — anyone I could speak to was a target to join the ERGs. The first question was always, "Do I have to be LGBT or Latino to join the group?" The answer: Of course not. The point of the groups was to celebrate our diversity and capitalize on what we had in common as employees. Through this process, we learned that we shared government customers as well as professional and educational backgrounds, and this was a force multiplier for our business. It strengthened our own professional networks while simultaneously raising cultural awareness and educating employees about LGBT issues.

I am proud to be gay and Mexican-American, and felt it was my duty to share my cultural heritage and LGBT identity. I found that this opened professional opportunities and I also was able to build a network of mentors and friends.

I left Booz Allen and moved to New York City to join American International Group, Inc., otherwise known as AIG, the insurance giant. AIG and the insurance world was very new to me, so the learning curve was steep. From my standpoint, it was exciting to dive into a new industry. The financial environment is a different animal; it's a different frame of mind. I was supporting both internal and external communications, working on special initiatives and helping launch new products globally. What kept things really interesting for me at AIG was the global footprint: we had calls at all hours on different projects and with various offices around the world. That was a new thing for me. I loved the global aspect of the work and enjoyed building relationships with our PR folks leading communications in the Middle East, Asia, Europe and Latin America.

After AIG, I joined AECOM, a multinational engineering firm that does design, construction, consulting and management services for clients around the world. We were building everything from stadiums to skyscrapers to manufacturing and energy facilities all over the world. The PR work was enjoyable, I got my first stab at helping pitch stories to The New York Times and worked with industry trade publications.

After several years on the East Coast, I moved west and am now working for Northrop Grumman. Words cannot express the interesting and exciting work we do to advance technology and human discovery. I am definitely loving the work, learning new skills and beginning to plug myself into some of the diversity and employee resource groups.

Over my career, I've worked in several industries — insurance, construction, defense, government, nonprofit — in multiple functions, internal, external, with PR agencies and creative agencies, and I've managed both small and large teams. I got to a point where I know what hard work feels like and when someone is passionate about their work. I tend to gravitate toward those people who believe in what they're doing and want everyone to be just as excited as they are. I enjoy their energy and professionalism, and I enjoy learning from them.

Vanessa Wakeman

Vanessa Wakeman is founder and CEO of The Wakeman Agency. She is a trusted adviser to nonprofit organizations providing public relations, event management, fundraising, and thought leadership. She received a Bachelor of Arts in English from Hunter College and attended The City College of New York and Columbia University for her graduate studies.

I know this sounds crazy, but the way I got into public relations was by launching my own agency. I started The Wakeman Agency and learned PR on the job. That was 15 years ago, and we've been growing ever since.

We started out as an events agency. Our very first client was a nonprofit organization that had hired a freelancer to do PR, and the person sort of disappeared a few weeks before the event. The organization's director was desperate and pleaded with me to help. I knew in theory what public relations was, but didn't have any idea how to "do" PR, so I did some research.

Well, we ended up actually getting some good placements for their event. It made me wonder if other organizations would be interested in receiving event and PR support from one company. After speaking with a few organizations and getting positive feedback for that idea, we began to include public relations in our service offerings.

I had no knowledge of how a PR agency was traditionally run. I was definitely figuring it out as I went along.

Nonetheless, I started the company and opened a physical office in 2003. Although I had no contacts in PR or events, and had no clients, I went out there, beat the pavement and told people what I was trying to do. One organization took a chance on us — and here we are.

I had previously been a technologist on Wall Street, and while that was lucrative, it wasn't work that I loved or wanted to do forever.

Here I was, a woman of color, working at a big financial firm — Morgan Stanley — where I had great access and benefits and bonuses. That was a source of pride for my family, particularly my grandmother. Here was her black granddaughter working in circles that were beyond reach for her during her career, and having opportunities for advancement and mobility.

So my grandmother and some of the other elders in my family were very uncomfortable with me leaving what they thought was a successful career. They didn't understand how I could give up a "sure thing" where I was doing well and getting promoted, to go and start a business of my own. I was disappointed they weren't more supportive initially, but I realized it was based on their experiences. For them, once you got a really great job, you stayed there until retirement.

When I first started the agency, I found that a lot of the organizations we were approaching, particularly in certain geographic areas, were not open to working with us. It was very challenging to convince people that we could offer something of value. I remember there was one conversation that I had where the prospect said, "This all sounds great, but we have an agency already, and we aren't going to change." I said, "Do you love the work that they are doing?" And she said, "It's OK."

How could I win, I thought, if people are not willing to change agencies when they aren't happy? It was a leap of faith, but I was determined we could succeed. There were a lot of conversations asking people to give us a shot. However, after we had those first early wins, it became less difficult to have those conversations.

During this period, there were a number of times when I strongly considered not making it known that I was the owner of the agency. I often wondered what would happen if, while I was out on a sales call, I represented myself as working for the company versus being the owner. Would the conversations have gone differently?

I remember reading a story about a white woman who owned a PR company in Chicago who invented a male partner because she didn't feel that people were taking her seriously. I identified with that. I even thought of not putting CEO on my business card. Maybe if they didn't know that I was the CEO, the conversation would be more favorable. But I stayed true to who I was. I felt proud of what we were doing, particularly for the nonprofit sector that made up our client base.

I think in those earlier years I experienced a little bit of "imposter syndrome." After all, public relations is not a field that I studied in college, or had any experience in prior to starting the agency. In the early stages of building the business, I often wondered, "Are we doing this right?" Most of the practices and procedures were built around what I thought made sense.

This entrepreneurial journey in an industry in which I had no prior experience was definitely challenging. There were some experiences that made me feel that people didn't want to work with us because I was a woman of color. I'm wiser and more confident now and know that my race, and the lens through which I see the world, offers a unique set of advantages to our clients.

I also want my team to be diverse. Having someone be able to see a situation from a different perspective really excites me. As a leader, my goal is to always give our clients what they didn't know they wanted. By creating a team of people with different backgrounds and experiences, we are able to consistently do that.

Diversity provides tremendous value to our clients because the world is so diverse, and so are these organizations' target audiences and stakeholders. There are so many benefits to having differences of opinion, thought and insight. All that diversity of thought plays a role in everything we do, even the way someone crafts a story pitch.

Right now, there's actually an opportunity to go beyond the idea of diversity and inclusion, to equity. What does equity look like? It's great to have diversity, but if the diversity is not allowing people to fully share who they are and what they have to offer, then we really haven't moved the needle. Equity is top of mind for me as I think about the young people I mentor and the future generations of leaders. Equity really is the only way that we can solve the retention issue for good.

It seems that there are many more conversations happening now about diversity, and many more organizations saying they are focused on creating more opportunities for diverse talent. But there is still a lot to be done. An agency executive said at a conference last year, "If women want to be heard, they need to speak more loudly." That's so ridiculous and it speaks to the issues that women and people of color face. If I don't have the opportunity to be heard, this is likely not a work environment where I will thrive.

If I have an idea and nobody responds to it, but then a man says the exact same thing two minutes later and he's getting high-fived, the light bulb goes off for me that this is not an organization that is going to value what I offer.

This is not just a PR industry problem. This is an American problem. In theory, we all know what needs to happen, right? We say we want more women in leadership roles, we want more people of color in these roles. That sounds fantastic. And even the CEO can have an agenda that says, "I want to have this many diverse recruits, this many new hires." But if we don't have a plan to really engage people, nothing changes. Companies should be measuring how effective they are in ensuring that people are heard and able to contribute, not just boosting the number of diverse people they bring on.

If professionals know that they will be celebrated for showing up as their authentic selves and be valued by an organization that sees what makes them different as an asset, that's the organization where everyone will want to work.

At The Wakeman Agency, we try to attract great talent and are constantly experimenting with ways to build the team that best reflects our core values while also serving the needs of our clients. It's inclusive, it's equal and it's ever changing.

Rosemary Mercedes

Ms. Mercedes currently serves as chief communications officer for Univision Communications, and had previously served as its senior vice president, corporate communications. She has been with Univision for 12 years. Earlier in her career, Ms. Mercedes was senior account manager at Halogen Communications, a PR firm in Edinburgh, Scotland. Ms. Mercedes received a Master of Arts in corporate and public communications from Seton Hall University.

Growing up in New Jersey, I looked at my Latino friends, neighbors, and classmates — people from Ecuador, Colombia and Cuba — and I was struck with how people from all these different countries, thousands of miles apart, were unified by language. And even though Mexicans insisted they were different from Dominicans, who were different from Puerto Ricans, who were different from Venezuelans, it was plain to see we were unified by language. It was our big connector. And that observation — how

Latinos were so unified here in the U.S. — would years later become a defining theme in my professional life.

My own family immigrated here from the Dominican Republic. And a few years later, I was born in the U.S. and raised in Jersey City. And though I was born an American citizen, I have always related to and empathized with the plight of immigrants navigating a new culture.

I'm the first member of my family to graduate from college. I went to Seton Hall University where I was given a daunting list of possible majors to choose from. But how does anyone that age know what to pick? I had limited exposure to career options outside of the traditional paths — teacher, nurse, doctor, lawyer — jobs that are easy to explain. My immigrant family could easily get their head around those. But *public relations*? Not so much. "You want to do *what*?" my mother asked. "And someone is going to pay you to do *that* for a living?"

Well, I did in fact choose PR as my major. And I absolutely fell in love with it from day one! Fortunately, they've got a terrific undergraduate communications program at Seton Hall that exposed me to not only the fundamentals, but also created opportunities to touch real-life communications work. I was so into it, I even joined the Public Relations Student Society of America (PRSSA). In my senior year, I interned for the Catholic Church at the Archdiocese of Newark. It was a busy media relations office responding to a steady flow of inquiries from reporters at English- and Spanish-language press outlets looking for the

Church's position on issues. The experience was great preparation for my eventual career. And my bilingual skills, while not a job requirement, came in *very* handy.

My next job was in the PR department for Seton Hall. I worked full time for the university supporting several deans and schools on media relations, communications and editorial projects. I also spent my nights going to classes for a master's degree. I'll tell you, it was one of the best decisions I have ever made. The master's really helped me early on get a more expansive view of the profession. And I believe it helped form an even stronger foundation for the career I would soon begin.

It was 12 years ago when I arrived at Univision, the leading media company serving Hispanic America, which also includes the nation's first Spanish-language TV network that grew out of a local San Antonio station in the '60s. Back then people asked, "Why do you need a Spanish-language TV station?" All previous waves of immigrants — the Irish, the Italians — they all assimilated. You didn't need to have an Irish channel or an Italian channel. When we put up the first all-Spanish station in Texas, some thought we were crazy. But for the newly arrived Latinos, our station became an important and trusted ally.

Today, people are retaining culture instead of shedding their family's heritage. It's an *and* not an *or*. You can be 100 percent Venezuelan, Colombian, Dominican, or from wherever your family's roots originate, and still be 100 percent American. And technology — everything from ease of travel, mobile phones and television — has facilitated that.

When I was born, my newly arrived parents felt the need to help prepare me for a life of assimilation. They named me "Rosemary," not "Rosa Maria," because they came from a generation that associated success in the U.S. with assimilation. In contrast, this new generation doesn't subscribe to the idea of abandoning their Hispanic identity to assimilate. I named my own daughters Elena and Amelia in the spirit of celebrating our dual cultures.

Never in my biggest dreams did I believe that as an "immigrant" kid in Jersey City, struggling to learn English, I would one day lead communications for one of the most trusted and respected brands for Latinos, and at such a pivotal moment in history.

We are in a time when public relations, on behalf of our community, has never been more critical. Today, not only have the ways we distribute and consume news changed and multiplied, but the very definition of news is being challenged. There is a seemingly constant drumbeat of "fake news" being injected into the social and political narrative. That means that our jobs as PR professionals are more important than ever. We are champions of truth. In the case of the Hispanic community, that means not just promoting our truth, but defending it from lies and stereotypes, and making sure a full spectrum of stories are getting told.

The funny thing is, when I started looking for a job after college, a career in PR that would help me evangelize diversity never occurred to me. Sure, my first language was Spanish. I am Afro-Latina and everything about my upbringing was steeped in pride in my heritage, pride in my language and pride in my culture. I just didn't know that I could combine my passions. But as I began my career, I became all too aware of the lack of communication directed at my community.

So, little by little, project by project, I brought that insight and pitched my own ideas to include more diverse perspectives. I can still see the confusion on the face of former bosses, colleagues and partners: "You want to do this in Spanish? Why?" And it wasn't until they saw the results that they understood the strategic value. I quickly recognized this was the "added value" I brought to nearly every job.

Every other employer since has recognized the value of my professional and bicultural abilities, and none more so than Univision. I feel very fortunate to be the chief communications officer for Univision. Occupying this seat, at this company, at this moment, is a responsibility I embrace with a deep and unwavering commitment.

I am proud of the role Univision plays as a beacon of advocacy for our audiences, even in the face of risk. There aren't too many companies willing to break contractual agreements and take a public battle with a presidential candidate running for office — all to take a stand and defend their consumers. And the mission to empower Hispanic Americans continues. Today we are empowering and informing our audiences on a wide range of key issues such as the developments related to the fate of the U.S. DACA (Deferred Action for Childhood Arrivals) program and immigrant family separations as well as the upcoming 2020 Census and much more.

Being in this seat also means working with top-tier business editors and journalists to evolve from filing a "quota of Hispanic stories" to thinking about the contributions and impact of Hispanic consumers and Hispanic media in the totality of the landscape.

As I reflect on my purpose-driven career, I recognize how important mentorship has been along the way. And I don't mean formal arrangements in the, "Hey, will you be my mentor?" kind of way. I've always taken the view that you learn from everything, good and bad. One of the bosses I learned the most from early on in my career was someone who, in my view, just wasn't effective. So I learned from this person all the things I didn't want to be. At the same time, I saw people who were great role models. So some of my most important mentors probably have no idea of the vital role they played in shaping my career path.

I, myself, try to be a mentor to young people. While I don't have formal mentor-mentee arrangements, I gladly accept opportunities to talk to students and young professionals. The upcoming generation needs to see examples of people of color, or those not in the majority, doing jobs that they may want to do someday. They need to see people like themselves in leadership roles.

But while attracting diverse students is one thing, retention is quite another. You go to conferences at certain levels and it's all women. Then as you navigate and participate in more senior circles with agency principals and other heads of communications, the gender and racial diversity is lacking.

So what's happening to the women in the pipeline? What is happening to Latinos and other minorities? Why aren't they running the show and becoming the leaders of their companies? It's amazing how far we have come, and how far we haven't.

Women need to see other women in similar positions, they need to see how others juggle work and families. What I often hear from young women is, "How do you *do* it?" It's why I made the decision to be less discreet about how I juggle my career and family obligations. I let people know when I am taking a conference call at the supermarket or under the hair dryer at the hair salon. They need to know that *that's* how it's done.

So as far as retention, young people need to see themselves represented in the field. We need to go out to schools more and earlier, create opportunities to engage with the professional sector. But the reality is, whether you're talking about Hispanics, Asians, African-Americans or LGBT professionals, it's not unique to communications.

There's a dearth of diverse talent in corporate America. When you see these moments in time when brands do things that don't resonate, or they fall flat, it reminds us about the scarcity of empowered, diverse voices in boardrooms and the C-suite.

How do you create a workforce environment, where the workplace is inclusive? It's much more than, "Okay, I checked the box, I hired a person of color, I hired a diverse candidate." It's how do you make sure that everyone feels included? How do you harness the power of rich and dissimilar backgrounds and experiences to grow your business and break through?

When you have a breadth of different minds focusing on a problem, you're able to see around blind spots and strategize through things that maybe a more homogeneous group wouldn't be able to see. Diversity is not just a nice thing to do. It's not just a box to check. Diversity drives growth. In an increasingly global and connected economy, diversity is a competitive advantage.

In the case of public relations, which ultimately is about storytelling, diversity means everyone is able to take part in the conversation. And when everyone has a voice, as that young girl from New Jersey once noted, even people from different countries and cultures can be unified.

Veronica Potes

*Veronica Potes is currently director of integrated marketing at
the USA and SYFY TV networks. She is also the president of
the National Hispanic Public Relations Association (HPRA).
Ms. Potes received a double Bachelor of Arts in
communications and psychology from the University of
Southern California.*

As a Hispanic woman, I have the advantage of being
100 percent American and 100 percent Latina. That's a
value that's often overlooked in the corporate world. Hiring
Latino talent not only opens the organization to diverse
languages and perspectives, it also provides a direct line of
sight into the nation's fastest-growing ethnic market.

I remember when I first started in the industry I was
trying to be a little more of what I thought corporate
America wanted to see. I would wear more muted-color
clothes, and did my makeup a certain way. I felt that if I
played the part I thought others *wanted* to see, along with
my experience, I would eventually get a seat at the table.

What happened is that I started to feel less like me, and that didn't sit right. I began soul-searching — how do I embrace corporate culture but also express my individuality that makes me so unique? That was the secret sauce I had to find.

It's important to note that there *is* a corporate etiquette that must be followed. But when I started to undermine my individuality with the thought that being more muted would get me further in my career, I thought, "Who is this woman? This isn't me."

It hasn't been easy regaining my individuality and owning my differences and passions. I've heard people make remarks about me that shouldn't have been made. I've been called names. I've been told I am emotionally immature. It's hurtful, but I always make sure that I use these incidents as educational opportunities for myself and others.

Latinas are a triple threat. We are bilingual; sometimes trilingual. We look at things through a different lens than others. "Ambicultural" perspectives provide market insights that others can't.

I wanted to be able to express myself in a way that was in sync with how I grew up but also played to the corporate culture that I recognize is so important. There has to be a happy medium. My point of view, as a Latina and marketer, is valuable, and I wanted to have a voice. Throughout my career, there have been times when I have been the only woman in the boardroom, not to mention the only Latina. But it's then that my opinion is *most* critical to be voiced.

At USC (University of Southern California), I was formally trained in communications, but was not introduced to the world of multicultural PR. In 2006, I was lucky enough to be connected to the largest network of Latino communicators, the Hispanic Public Relations Association (HPRA), and saw the bountiful opportunities that laid within.

I first dipped my toe into the world of multicultural public relations, marketing and advertising at an agency in California. My job was focused on Hispanic PR, and it was then that I saw a dedicated need for it. But at the time, Hispanic was considered "niche," so budgets were small, if even allocated. A few years later, and due to the connections I made through HPRA, I was hired by a large agency and moved to New York specifically to work in their multicultural group. They were looking for passionate communicators who had the language and cultural competencies, and I fit the bill.

After a few years on the agency side, I was hired at Univision, again via connections I made at HPRA. I led corporate communications strategy for the Univision Television Group (62 stations) and Univision Radio (69 stations) across the nation, as well as worked within the integrated marketing division spearheading consumer campaigns for some of the largest brands in the U.S. A former supervisor then recruited me to work at NBCUniversal, first for E! and Esquire, and now for USA and SYFY TV networks.

As I grew into my career, I saw that my point of view was increasingly valued. I've been in meetings sometimes where ideas were brought up, and I'd say, "Well, that's not going to really fly for the Hispanic community. We need to consider X scenario."

Latinos are becoming an overwhelming force in our nation, and we need to make sure content, especially across the media industry, reflects that. It's so empowering for Latinas to see themselves represented on-air. Take Mariana Atencio, a reporter on MSNBC, for example. While a Latina, she does not cover only Latino affairs. Seeing her on television is empowering for younger Hispanic journalists. But even more important, it solidifies the idea that being Hispanic does not mean you only have to work *in* the Hispanic market. Even within NBCU's cable networks, you see shows like "Queen of the South" on USA and "Total Bellas" on E! showing such strong multicultural groups of people, especially women. We are moving in the right direction.

I personally owe a lot to HPRA. The organization opened the right doors for me to move to New York and is the reason why I was able to connect with mentors and land positions at top agencies and media companies. The connections I've built are not only professional mentors, but I've created lifelong friends that share the same passions I do.

Ten or 15 years ago, we were in a communications industry where you either did Hispanic PR or mainstream PR. Those days are gone. As Latino communicators, we have to make sure that what we communicate reflects the story we want to tell. While language does matter, we have to appreciate the evolution of our community. As we continue aging, we become more bilingual and we become more "ambicultural."

As I grew and continue to grow in my career, I saw that my rich cultural upbringing set me apart. Being bilingual opened a lot of doors for me early on — I was able to read Spanish, speak Spanish, *conversate* in Spanish. In addition to language, I can toggle between two cultures, and am able to craft messages that resonate with both. This is such an advantage in marketing because, as *one* Latina, I am able to engage with *two* different communities.

Finally, some years ago at a conference I came across the recipe to my secret sauce: Play the game, win the game and only then can you change the game. When I first started, I couldn't make people listen to what I had to say. Nor could I change their preconceived notions about my culture or background. However, what I could do was show them how capable I was at my job and how my different upbringing, perspective, energy and style only added to the rich output of our collective product, not diminish the final result.

As my mentors changed the game for me, I try to pay it forward every chance I get. Paving new avenues for the future generation of Latino leaders is critical to the overall well-being of our nation, especially within the realm of communications and marketing.

Play it. Win it. Change It.

Felicia Blow

Felicia Blow is the associate vice president for development and campaign director for the $150 million comprehensive campaign at Hampton University. She has a Bachelor of Arts in mass media arts from Hampton University, a Master of Arts in marketing from Strayer University, and is pursuing a doctorate at Old Dominion University in higher education leadership. She has served twice on the National Board of PRSA.

Ever notice how people float into your life at the time they're supposed to and then they float back out? This is something I reflect on a lot at this stage of my life.

You see, I grew up in a rural, very country, area. No one in my family had ever gone to college. But there were people around who noticed something in me, and steered my trajectory toward college. So after staying home for a bit, in 1986, I went to Hampton University.

Right after college, I was recruited by Caterpillar, working out of its world headquarters in Peoria, Illinois. I had no idea that I would be doing PR for a heavy equipment manufacturer — one of the most non-sexy things I could imagine.

I was actually lucky to be in PR. My college friends who were looking for jobs in TV or journalism weren't able to find jobs easily, and they sure didn't pay as much as my gig with Cat. This was during the recession, and it was tough for them.

After I left Caterpillar, I moved back east and began work at a waste management and environmental services organization — another business I never thought I'd get into. I had expected I would work in an agency, jet setting, or working on magazines. But here I was working with what I like to say are real "salt of the earth" people. I was working on real initiatives and real activities that affected everyday life. I think I was at the beginning of the movement where PR was becoming a critical aspect of corporate life. It was at that time that PR leaders were writing editorials about how PR professionals needed to have a seat in the C-suite, they needed to have the ear of the leader, and they needed to report directly to the CEO. We've gotten past that now.

I stayed at the Southeastern Public Service Authority for a long time. I loved having an impact on something much bigger than me. I was working on initiatives like environmental protection and educating young people about it; doing the right thing.

Then, in 2008, I went to Cox Communications as director of public affairs. In addition to doing straight PR, I managed an effort to make broadband available to low-income communities. At that time there were underserved populations that didn't have access to the internet. They couldn't afford it. It became known as the digital divide. Today you could call it the "rural divide" as a lot of areas in rural America now don't have access to the internet and the many opportunities it can open up. In my role, I helped position the company to be a thought leader, and to make sure we were perceived as ahead of the curve.

I also was able to build the Cox Charities Virginia program from the ground up. The Cox Charities initiative put me in the thick of philanthropy. It was really fulfilling and interesting.

When I left Cox, I became vice president and foundation director at Paul D. Camp Community College, a community college in Virginia. That, too, got me back into my mission-based approach to things.

From there I became vice president of institutional advancement and executive director of the foundation for Tidewater Community College. I was in charge of fundraising, which is a discipline that uses many of the same skills as PR.

Now I'm back at Hampton, my alma mater. It's great to be back. I now have "street cred" here, as I am an alumna, and my daughter also attends. Hampton is a truly international brand, and being at such a prestigious HBCU, every day I'm excited to tell our more than 150-year story — and how we are doing things to change the world.

Looking back at my career, I can see that in every position I've had, I've tried to develop programs that help society in some way. I did that with my former environmental engagement activities, broadband access opportunities and definitely with access to education — especially at the community college level.

I absolutely have had some challenges in my career, but I picked myself up and kept on going. And I've learned from all those experiences. I've gotten used to being the only person of color in the room. I don't let it bother me. It's akin to being the only woman in the room.

For instance, at Caterpillar, I was one of a limited number of black professional women in the company at that time. It was like this at most places where I've worked. At Southeastern Public Service Authority I was the only black leader on the executive team. And at the Virginia Community College system, I was the first and only African-American vice president of institutional advancement of all 23 community colleges in Virginia.

I didn't want to get used to being the only woman of color in the room. But I had to. So I'm glad there's now a focus on bringing more diversity into the industry. To that end, I have served as a volunteer who has supported and led a multitude of diversity engagement initiatives at PRSA, and I have performed this role at other organizations. I think about diversity as having a seat at the table and then having the wherewithal to put forth thoughts that others hadn't had.

You see, in my judgment, folks choose to be around other people who look and act the way they do. And if you are not reminded of this practice, you can continue to do that and think that's OK. It's now my job as a leader to remind those with whom I engage that this is not OK.

That's why we have all these diversity initiatives. You need talented students. Organizations can't continue to overlook whole swaths of people. Also, there is a wide variety of demographics with money to spend, and in that regard, they also can't continue to be overlooked — that is, you want to improve your market share.

But here's the thing: There's resistance to this point of view. We, as PRSA leaders, have to work to build relationships with different organizations. We have to be proactive. And even if we don't get the outcome we think you ought to get, we need to keep at it.

I think we can get to that color-blind state by going about it the same way we do PR for our clients: Identify the stakeholders, build plans, work the plan, measure success. It's not a one-off. It's an ongoing and consistent effort. It's not led by volunteers who change every year. It's something that's ingrained into the fabric of the organization.

For example, in academic environments, if PR faculty embrace the philosophy and goal of increasing diversity, the impact will be great. After all, how do students typically get engaged around any kind of field of study? It's the faculty. So what are we doing to better support and engage diverse faculty? I can tell you from firsthand knowledge that advisers and faculty members are overwhelmed with the day-to-day things they have to do, so we need to do more to help them. I believe that can be a game-changing area that will help the industry.

Lorenz Esguerra

Lorenz Esguerra serves concurrently as the executive vice president and general manager of Weber Shandwick Minneapolis, and of Creation: Open Minds. Mr. Esguerra received a Master of Business Administration from the Anderson School at UCLA.

I started my career in digital marketing at Blast Radius, now part of WPP, and most recently was with integrated advertising agency, Colle McVoy, which also had PR as one of their offerings. I was the head of business development there.

I have a Master of Business Administration from UCLA Anderson School, so marketing and communications was basically my major. Back then I was thinking of becoming a CMO or a CCO of a Fortune 500 company, or heading up an advertising or PR agency when I "grew up."

I had a few mentors along the way. As I progressed there were key people I tapped into, what I call my personal board of directors.

Right now *I'm* the one mentoring people. It's one of my favorite things to do. In other words, I like helping young professionals who want to move ahead.

A few of them have been really doing well in advertising and marketing. They are in various locations and companies — Google, General Mills, Target, a few advertising agencies around the country, etc. I continuously reach out to them, and I'm always available when they need advice.

Here at Weber Shandwick, I'm general manager of the Minneapolis office. A typical day would include meeting clients, managing staff, resolving any issues regarding project assignments. No two days are the same.

But it all boils down to three key goals: client satisfaction, a healthy culture and a growing business.

Being Filipino, there's always been this "difference" about me that I needed to manage through. I'm conscious of this difference whenever I communicate with other people. I do have a bit of an accent, so sometimes people do not completely understand what I say.

There are times when I sense people who first meet me have preconceived notions about how I conduct myself, how I speak, how I look.

But over the years I've grown, and have gotten more confident about what I can bring to the table. I think people have been a little bit more conscious and sensitive about working with people of color and people of diverse backgrounds.

Nowadays, it seems, people tend to be more interested in hearing what I say. They tend to be more accepting of my value. So I think the awareness about diversity and inclusion has helped a lot. In this sector especially, there is a great need for more diversity, but there also needs to be a better grasp of what inclusion means.

We provide services to companies that require great ideas and innovative solutions. Now, a diverse team ups the ante of how these innovative solutions are brought to life in ways that are culturally relevant and authentic.

There was one Request for Proposal, for instance, where a key requirement was that 50 percent of the team needed to be women and 25 percent of the team needed to be people of color. When a client mandates that you include people of color, then people become more aware of and interested in people who can bring to the table differences in culture and approach as well as sensitivity.

As far as improving diversity in the field, there are a couple of things that come to mind. One is outreach. It's really important for agencies, when they're looking to hire new talent, to make sure they reach way out into the community. They need to stop being so insular with how they create a slate of candidates to interview.

I think agencies should be more conscious about bringing in diverse perspectives and making sure that their work reflects racial diversity. It's evident when agencies don't have diverse people on staff to guide them in messaging and imagery.

Agencies should celebrate diversity both in the work they do for clients and in programs that they do internally for employees. In fact, diversity and inclusion also should be one of the key values of advertising firms.

Speaking up was definitely important for me as I got into my career, to make sure I learned how to express myself. I can't blame anyone for not understanding what I'm saying or where I'm coming from if I don't really express myself.

I'd advise young people coming into the field to learn how to speak up. You won't be heard unless you speak up. Learn how to communicate and share who you are with people because that's the only way for people to be able to listen to you and really know what you bring to the table.

I think the most important thing that's ever happened to me as a person of color is becoming a general manager of a major public relations company like Weber Shandwick. I'm not necessarily what you would call the norm. I'm really proud of that. I had to compete against dozens of people for this job. They easily could have chosen a white guy or lady, but they trusted me, and so far it's been working well.

Strengthen your network. Get to know people. I think that's important. Having people to call, having people to guide your career or provide you access to opportunities would really be very important in terms of getting your career in the right place at all times.

I love what I'm doing. I love the fact that I'm touching the lives of a lot of people. That's really important to me.

Charlene Wheeless

Charlene Wheeless is principal vice president, Global Corporate Affairs, at Bechtel Corporation. Previously she was vice president, communications, site executive at Raytheon Intelligence and Information Systems. Ms. Wheeless received a Bachelor of Arts in journalism/public relations from New Mexico State University, a Master of Arts in public communication from The American University and a Master of Business Administration from Keller Graduate School of Management.

There comes a point in your career when it's no longer about you. It's about who you can help. And if we've experienced inequities or harassment — and most female executives have — how dare us not use our experiences to help bring up other people?

Fortunately, and unfortunately, I've been in situations where I have been the only black female professional in the room. Most times, I'm still the only one.

When I was younger, I didn't pay that much attention to it. But now I no longer wear it as a badge, like, "I'm the one who made it." It no longer feels like an accomplishment. It feels more like a reflection on how slowly it's taking the industry to recognize the importance of diverse voices, diverse people, diverse faces.

I took my first journalism class when I started college at 17. It was the first true writing class that I had taken. It tapped into a very natural curiosity that I had — I am curious about anything and everything — and journalism afforded me the time to be able to dig deep on a lot of topics. It just felt right, like, "Wow, this is what I was meant to do!"

My major combined both journalism and public relations. I will say, I focused more on journalism because back then, in the '80s, PR was still thought of as party and event planning. It was the old, "Oh, you're good with people, you should go into PR!"

I didn't really switch over to real PR until I graduated and started my career. Although my focus was on journalism, and I loved it, I didn't want a career in broadcast journalism (too cutthroat) and I didn't want to be a reporter; I just wanted to write. My first job out of college was an internal PR role. And that's when I knew, "Okay, this is what I am really meant to do."

I did my undergraduate work at New Mexico State University and Texas Tech, but graduated from New Mexico State. After five or six years of working, I decided to also attend graduate school. I went to The American University for a Master of Arts in public communication. After that, I went to the Keller Graduate School of Management for a Master of Business Administration, with an emphasis in marketing.

This degree has been helpful and valuable as it relates to my career growth. Today, if a communications professional asked me if they should get a master's degree in PR or business administration, I would say get *both*, but get the business administration degree first.

One of the reasons I found this to be valuable is that it taught me that PR and communications happen within the context of a business. If you're going to be in corporate communications, you have to understand how business works, how your company makes money, and that communications is a means to an end, not the end itself.

There weren't a lot of communications professionals pursuing a Master of Business Administration back then. I was asked more than once why I was getting it, since I'm in PR. Most assumed it was because I was planning on changing careers. I would answer that getting it will help me be a better strategic communications professional.

I have never once regretted the blood, sweat and sometimes tears of earning a Master of Business Administration. I loved it.

My first job was for IBM in Maryland, in their internal communications department. I was mostly writing for company publications. One thing I learned very quickly about being in communications is that it gives you the opportunity to engage in many aspects of the company. When you're in communications, you're with this business unit one day, you're talking to the chairman the next day, you're talking to HR another day, and you just get to move around the whole company.

I spent a year at IBM and decided, with all the wisdom of a 22-year-old, that I couldn't work there my whole career the way most IBMers did. I remember the days when everybody had on a blue suit; everybody looked exactly the same, and I thought, "Well, that's not me."

I left and went to a smaller company, a family-owned petroleum company, as their manager of communications, responsible for all company communications. It was a one-person department and a lot of learning as you go. I thought it was great. I really enjoyed it.

I knew absolutely nothing about the oil and petroleum industry. But it didn't really matter. A great thing about communications is that our skills are transferable to pretty much any industry. In communications you are able to learn a lot about different companies and industries.

After a year at that job I started to get a little bored, so I quit, without another job lined up. When you're 23, you don't really have any sense of needing to have a job right away so you can pay your bills. I pretty much figured, "How hard can it be to find another job?"

Shortly thereafter I worked with an association, and that was by design. Someone had told me that if you work in an association you will be overworked and underpaid. But you will learn a lot and be able to determine where and if you want to specialize.

The association I went to was the Automotive Dismantlers and Recyclers Association. It was an association for junkyard dealers. There, I ran all of its communications and exhibitions. And I learned a lot about communications, and how different audiences have different needs.

After two years, I was offered a communications role at another large corporation: DynCorp. From that moment on I've always worked at large companies.

DynCorp was a great place to work. While I was there the company transformed itself from a management and operations government contractor company into an information technology firm. I worked for the company for about four years and led the rebranding effort. I later left and went to a competitor, but a year later I came back as the director of communications. And then, about four or so years later, they named me vice president of communications.

I was the first vice president of communications for the company, the first female vice president, and the first minority corporate vice president at DynCorp. That was pretty exciting, and I felt like I had accomplished a lot in my career at that point.

After the rebranding, DynCorp executive management decided to sell the company. While I felt confident I was going to have a job with the company after the sale, I just didn't know if it was going to be a job I wanted.

I was offered a job by another company. This company hired me to rebrand it so that it could be sold at a premium. And that's what we did. I worked for that company for two years to the day.

Around that time, I was beginning to think that I needed a break. I had two small children that I wanted to spend time with so I decided to take a year off and hang out with my girls.

Well, that lasted for about four months.

I was offered the opportunity to become vice president for communications at the Intelligence and Information Systems unit of Raytheon Company, a very large and successful government defense contractor. I was at Raytheon for about five years. (I think that I have a five-year attention span!)

I received a call from a recruiter who asked if I'd be interested in working for this company, a very large, privately held company in the engineering, procurement and construction (EPC) industry. This was — and in some cases still is — an industry not known for hiring women or minorities. But I'd never heard of them before. How can a company with $40 billion in revenue have such a low profile? I was intrigued.

I started learning about the company and meeting with people. Every one of the executives had such a passion for the work, it was palpable. They would just light up talking about the company.

It made me wonder: "How can this company be so great if nobody has ever heard of them?"

I started doing my own due diligence, which was tough since they were privately held. What few things I was able to find told a story that was the exact *opposite* of what their people were telling me. While the employees said that this was the best EPC company in the world, the media articles I found questioned its ethics, business practices and technical skills.

People inside the company just weren't affected by the negative publicity. But, of course, in our world, perception is reality. I thought this would be a great opportunity to study the gap and help change the public's perception of the company.

At the outset I tried to bring a little bit of reality into the company, and urged people to pay attention to our reputation. As a privately held company, reputation is the biggest currency we have. I transformed the role of communications from just getting the information out, to managing the company's reputation.

One of my daughters has a degree in PR, and she asked, "Did you map out every step along the way?"

"No," I said, "I took what sounded attractive to me at the time, and it all just built upon itself."

She's now working at an agency in Washington, D.C. And she's loving it. But she's finding that many people are disrespectful of women, and particularly, young women. She's called me a number of times about so-and-so who was being condescending to her; or about people saying she couldn't possibly have a good idea because she's so young; or about how younger men who don't have a lot of experience will treat women of the same age as though they are less important.

The difference today is young women will say something about it. They don't just swallow it and move on. They'll risk being told that they're being insubordinate. They have less tolerance for the inequities, and I'm proud that they do.

As for diversity, I think that companies have to look at this systemically: If talent is equally distributed, then in any given company, why is it that in five or ten years, their best of the best are all men, and often, all white men?

The typical company rhetoric is, "Well, we put most of the efforts to attract more minorities and more women into the workplace. We've done this, we've done that." Companies have to examine what's the path to success in their organization. Does it favor men versus women? Is it fair for everyone?

And when looking at the hiring and the promotion process, how are companies taking bias out of the process? In our company, we no longer conduct one-on-one interviews. They are now panel interviews. Everyone weighs in as to whether the candidate is the right fit.

In PR, we have to be willing to shake things up. We have to be willing to take risks. Historically, management has been willing to take a risk on a man who may not have all the qualifications, but who had enough to get by. With women, on the other hand, you often feel that you must have all the same qualifications, and then some.

We have to be willing to put women and minorities in stretch positions. Give them the tools they need to be successful. We'd like to say everybody's on an even playing field. But let's face it, everyone *isn't* on an even playing field.

And whether we'd like to admit it or not, people bring their biases to work. They can't check them at the door. People are human.

When people are first coming into an organization, regardless of gender or race, they should be given a mentor or a sponsor — a champion. Otherwise, you don't know how to maneuver your way through an organization. Most people who ultimately become successful have had people who've advocated for them behind the scenes. They're the ones extolling their virtues when they are not in the room. Champions make it part of their responsibility to get the most out of and for every individual.

When I started out in this business, I didn't see a single person who looked like me! There were no role models for people like me.

Today, people looking at potential companies ask what the leadership teams look like. Are there people who are like them? And if they don't see someone who looks like them, then maybe that's not where they want to be. Sometimes companies who do have people of color or gender diversity are hesitant to talk about it. They are concerned about exploiting the situation."

And I completely understand that. No one wants to be exploited. At the same time, we have to find that balance so that when people see someone who looks like them, they are not the only one.

And I think that in my role working for an engineering and construction company, I get such a kick out of when I go someplace where I represent the company, I am the last person that someone expects to see. They're expecting to see some old guy in his steel-toed boots and his hard hat. If the company wants to hold me up as an example of their workforce, and if that helps to get more women and minorities into this industry, then I'm all for it. Let me be part of the solution, not part of the problem.

Whether we want to be or not, we are in the position to be change agents. And if you go to some company that is uncomfortable with women or minorities, and you throw your hands up and say, "Forget it. I'm going somewhere else!" then nothing ever changes. If you leave, everything goes right back to where it was before. No progress is being made.

Although I believe we should stay to fight another day as the saying goes, I don't believe anyone should ever stay in a situation that causes them to question their capabilities. That is a very unhealthy environment. I always encourage people to fight the good fight and do what they believe in. But if you are in an organization that is so difficult that it makes you question *you*, then it's time to leave. Resilience is important, but not at the expense of you.

Afterword

By Joe Cohen

Joe Cohen is president-elect of the PRSA Foundation and chief communications officer at AXIS Capital, a global specialty insurance and reinsurance company. He was senior vice president and head of communications at KIND Healthy Snacks and was a senior vice president within the Corporate Communications and Consumer Marketing Practices at MWW (now MWWPR). Mr. Cohen graduated with a Bachelor of Arts in broadcast journalism from the S.I. Newhouse School of Public Communications at Syracuse University. He is a past National Chair of PRSA and a vocal advocate for diversity and inclusion within communications.

At some point in our lives, many of us have experienced what it feels like to be an outsider.

As a Caucasian male, I've often benefited from being surrounded in the workplace by colleagues and managers who look like me and share a similar background. I've never come close to encountering the challenges and obstacles that have been so bravely and candidly shared by the individuals who appear in this book. But I do know what it feels like to be an outsider, to not fit in.

I grew up in a suburban Jewish community in Northern New Jersey, and while I shared the same cultural background as many of my neighbors, I stood apart as the child of a divorced couple. At the time, divorce wasn't as common as it is today. My brother and I, who were 1 and 5 years old at the time of the divorce, were labeled by some as kids who came from a broken home.

As the years passed, the neighborhood became more diverse and most of my closest friends were kids who didn't look like me, and I often found that I had more in common with kids who were black, Indian, Korean and Chinese. I was fortunate to have had these friendships, and they helped shape my worldview. I also like to think that the learning worked both ways. There were many nights during my childhood when my mom would host Shabbat dinner for these same friends.

My perspective further expanded when my parents remarried. My dad's second wife was Moroccan and came from a big, gregarious and welcoming family. I was exposed to Moroccan-American culture and became an older brother to two sisters who grew up to be proudly half-Moroccan. On my mom's side, I have stepsisters who are lesbian. My brother's wife is African. I'm fortunate that my wife and I are raising our son in a family where diversity is embraced and celebrated.

I was a teenager during the 1990s and was drawn to the hip hop movement. Everything about hip hop appealed to me — the raw, powerful social messages delivered by the artists, the beats and rhythms in the music, the genre's roots in soul, jazz and funk. Without consciously realizing it, I was broadening my thinking and gaining an understanding of a completely different culture. This extended into college where I landed an on-air job as the only Caucasian jock at the local hip hop and R&B station in Syracuse.

Like many of the contributors to this book, I didn't intend to go into public relations. I wound up in my first job at MWW by chance, and in the beginning had difficulty adjusting to agency life. I was bored with the administrative work that comes with serving in an entry-level position, and I also had trouble fitting in with my colleagues.

Everything changed when another recent college grad named Reggie joined. Reggie happens to be black and we hit it off immediately. We became close friends and soon worked together on a successful project for a big retail client that helped to put us both on the radar of MWW CEO Michael Kempner. (Michael would become both a mentor and a champion, and he is also a great advocate of D&I within communications.) With Reggie as my friend at work, my overall comfort level and confidence improved, and I began to connect better with my other colleagues as well.

I stayed at MWW for 15 years and rose from entry-level to senior vice president and a senior leader at the agency, but if I had not found a friend in Reggie, I likely would have left the firm before my career accelerated.

The mission of PRSA Foundation is to help improve diversity and inclusion within the profession through scholarships and grants, research and education, and awareness initiatives like this book.

One of the many benefits of increasing diversity within communications is that it enriches our perspective and improves our ability to communicate effectively to a multitude of audiences. This is a key theme of "Diverse Voices."

With this work, we also are hoping to show that our commonalities are greater than our differences. The interviews in this book illustrate the unique challenges faced by multicultural professionals, but they also detail relatable moments that many face during their careers: exciting accomplishments, painful setbacks, mentors and champions who made a difference, moments when a true sense of community is discovered within the workplace.

Creating a sense of belonging is the fabric of any strong community. Within the community that is the communications profession, we all stand to benefit from building a more diverse and inclusive field. And we all stand to lose by allowing our profession's future leaders to be on the outside looking in.